The Career Portfolio
Workbook

The Career Portfolio Workbook

Using the Newest Tool in Your Job-Hunting Arsenal to Impress Employers and Land a Great Job

FRANK SATTERTHWAITE
GARY D'ORSI

McGraw-Hill
New York   Chicago   San Francisco
Lisbon   London   Madrid   Mexico City   Milan
New Delhi   San Juan   Seoul   Singapore
Sydney   Toronto

9 10 11   QDB/QDB   12 11 10

ISBN 978-0-07-140855-4
MHID 0-07-140855-X

McGraw-Hill books are available at special quantity discounts to use as premiums and sales promotions, or for use in corporate training sessions. For more information, please write to the Director of Special Sales, Professional Publishing, McGraw-Hill, Two Penn Plaza, New York, NY 10121-2298. Or contact your local bookstore.

Career P.E.A.K.S.™ is a trademark of Frank Satterthwaite and Gary D'Orsi.

Permission is granted to purchasers of this book free of charge to photocopy the Career P.E.A.K.S. forms in the appendix of this book for personal use.

 This book is printed on recycled, acid-free paper containing a minimum of 50% recycled, de-inked fiber.

Library of Congress Cataloging-in-Publication Data
    The career portfolio workbook : using the newest tool in your job-hunting arsenal to impress employers and land a great job / Frank Satterthwaite and Gary D'Orsi.
        p.   cm.
    ISBN 0-07-140855-X (pbk. : alk. paper)
    1. Employment portfolios.   2. Job hunting.   I. D'Orsi, Gary.   II. Title.
HF5383 .S27   2003
650.14'2—dc21
                                                                2002152912

This book is dedicated
to Frank's wife, Martha Werenfels, and two children, Peter and Toby;
and to Gary's wife, Julie D'Orsi, and two children, Zachary and Amanda,
with deep gratitude
for their immeasurable support, encouragement . . . and patience!

Contents

PART 2
EXAMPLES OF TARGETED PORTFOLIOS

Acknowledgments

The authors would like to thank Dr. John Yena, Dr. Stephen Friedheim, and Celeste Brantolino for their useful comments on our original proposal for this book. We would like to thank Jeffrey Krames and Mary Glenn of McGraw-Hill for making this book happen; Michelle Howry for helping us shape the outline for the final draft; Donya Dickerson for her careful editing; and Janice Race for coordinating the production of this book.

We would also like to thank Deans Louis D'Abrosca and Joe Goldblatt of Johnson & Wales University for supporting our desire to create and continue to develop a career self-management course for the Alan Shawn Feinstein Graduate School. This course became the initial testing ground for many of the ideas in this book. Dr. Martin Sivula has given us many insightful comments and suggestions for the research that has informed our understanding of what makes an effective career portfolio.

We are indebted to Ames Brown for his ideas on digital formats for portfolios and for writing a section of the digital options chapter. Jim Abbott and Ralph Florio made special contributions by providing ideas for key sections of this book.

We also want to thank the clients for whom we are career coaches. Each of you has inspired us to do our very best to help you find effective ways to create portfolios that document and present your many impressive career P.E.A.K.S.

Reflecting on his own career, Frank would like to especially thank Dr. Douglas T. (Tim) Hall, now at Boston University, for providing a fascinating introduction to the study of the field of careers when Frank was a graduate student at Yale. Frank still treasures his notes from that course, though some of the pages, alas, have turned brown and curly along the edges!

This book would not have been at all possible without the support and encouragement the authors received where it counts most—at home. Our wives and kids were always there when we needed them, though we weren't always there when they needed us. With regard to the latter, Frank would like to thank his mother, Emily (a.k.a. "Granny") Satterthwaite, and our kids' world-class caregiver, Claire Custer, for being essential members of our extended family, particularly during the crisis of meeting a book deadline.

Part I

BUILDING, USING, AND MAINTAINING YOUR CAREER PORTFOLIO

1

Introduction: What Is a Career Portfolio?

OVERVIEW

This warm-up chapter is intended to stretch your mind and get you acquainted with the key concepts you will need to put together and then use a *career portfolio* that gets you a high-paying position or your dream job. We will be introducing a lot of ideas that we will explore further throughout the book.

This chapter focuses on what career portfolios are and aren't, who should use them, what they should look like, how they are put together, and how they should be used. By the end of this chapter you will be ready to delve into each of these topics in greater depth. Studying these chapters and taking a careful look at the examples of targeted portfolios in Part 2 of this book will enable you to put together an irresistible portfolio that will lead to employment success.

However, if you are in a big rush and need that portfolio as of yesterday, we suggest that you skip right to Chapter 10.

WHAT IS A CAREER PORTFOLIO?

You first need a clear understanding of exactly what a career portfolio is and isn't. A career portfolio is a collection of documents and other easily portable artifacts that people can use to validate claims they make about themselves.

A career portfolio is not a resume, which simply lists your experiences and accomplishments. Nor is it a cover letter in which you write about yourself and your qualifications for a particular job. Instead, it is a collection of actual documents that support and make tangible the things you want to say about yourself in a cover letter, a resume, or a face-to-face interview. Letters of commendation, performance evaluations, certificates, papers, and pictures of things created or of activities led are all examples of items that might be included in a career portfolio.

The carrying case for a career portfolio typically looks like a leather briefcase that can be zippered shut. The kind of impression you wish to make (along with your budget!) will determine the actual look of the carrying case you use for your portfolio. When you open it, the carrying case reveals a three-ringed binder.

Placing original documents in your portfolio would be a mistake, since if you were to lose your portfolio, you'd lose everything. Instead, use photocopies of originals, a practice which has the added advantage of enabling you to scale the size of the documents you include in your portfolio to the size of your binder. Smaller photographs or memo-pad notes of appreciation can be made bigger, and huge spreadsheets can be reduced in size to fit comfortably in your carrying case.

An alternative to punching three holes directly in the photocopies is to slip each photocopy into the sleeve of a clear plastic page protector with three holes in it.

Whatever system is used for physically storing documents inside the portfolio's carrying case, the important point is this: A career portfolio should contain documents that support the important things you want known about yourself.

In Chapter 2 we will discuss in greater detail the different kinds of items you might want to collect and how you can obtain the ones you don't presently have. As career coaches, the authors frequently find that many of our clients at first feel they don't have any items to use in their career portfolios. But as you read Chapter 2 you will likely discover, as our clients inevitably do, that you really *do* have many portfolio-worthy documents. The key point to know right up front is that career-relevant documents can come from most anywhere, not just from a person's work life. You can, in fact, build an entire career portfolio using only items that come from your school, volunteer, or leisure activities.

WHY SHOULD YOU USE A CAREER PORTFOLIO?

In fields such as art, advertising, architecture, writing, photography, design, and fashion, students and practitioners have been using portfolios as the primary vehicle for marketing themselves for years.

Nowadays, the use of portfolios is spreading to other fields as well. Career-minded people, whether they are students or practitioners, high up in an organization or just starting out, are discovering that a well-thought-out and presented career portfolio is an effective self-marketing tool that enhances their ability to present themselves both clearly and credibly.

If people are already using career portfolios in your field, you'd be wise to have one. And if not many people are using portfolios yet in your organization or field, so much the better for you, if you have one.

Whatever your field or background, a well-targeted portfolio that is properly presented can be a great self-marketing tool for five main reasons:

1. It draws *attention* to the key information you want to convey about yourself.
2. It provides *links* that connect you with an opportunity.
3. It makes the key *intangibles tangible*.
4. It adds to your *credibility*.
5. It builds *confidence*.

■ *Portfolios get attention.* We've all known ever since kindergarten that "show and tell" is more powerful than just tell. The simple act of handing a potential employer a document from your portfolio not only gets that person's undivided attention, it also piques her curiosity.

■ *Portfolios provide links.* Once you have a potential employer's attention, each item that you present in a well-targeted portfolio helps to make the link between what you can do and what the other person is looking for.

■ *Portfolios make key intangibles tangible.* As we will see in future sections, our research indicates that employers and bosses are looking for certain key intangibles that can be brought to life in a portfolio.

■ *Portfolios add to your credibility.* When you present an item from your portfolio, you are not just *saying* you are something, you are *showing* that your claims about yourself have real substance. In this way a portfolio that contains the right items adds to your credibility. Selectively shown items help to answer the question that always lurks when people are meeting for the first time: "Is this person for real?" There is something to that old adage, "Seeing is believing."

■ *Portfolios build confidence.* Even if you show up for a job interview and discover that you have forgotten to bring your portfolio, all is not lost. If you've done your homework and created a great portfolio, you will know exactly what you bring to this opportunity and will be able to articulate why you are the right person for the job with great confidence. You will know that what you say about yourself is true, and the sense that you truly believe what you are saying will come across, with or without your portfolio. But, of course, you will be more effective if you do remember to bring your portfolio with you!

WHO SHOULD USE A CAREER PORTFOLIO?

Anyone who is presently using, or intending to use, a resume should consider using a career portfolio. A career portfolio should *not* be viewed as taking the place of a resume. Instead, it should be viewed as a way of substantiating the information from your resume and cover letter once you have gotten the job interview. In Chapter 5, we will show you how to create a resume that works in tandem with your portfolio. The fundamental point is this: Use resumes to get interviews, and then use portfolios to get jobs.

Among the obvious users of a career portfolio would be the following:

- *Students seeking employment.* Whether you are a student at a two-year community college or a physician completing an advanced residency program, a career portfolio enables you to package what you have learned in a way that is appealing to potential employers.

- *Students seeking admission to college or graduate school.* A properly targeted portfolio can give you a significant advantage if you are competing for admission to a school that interviews its applicants. The items in your portfolio can bring to life and make credible the things you say about yourself in your written application. And the fact that you have gone to the effort of assembling a portfolio to bring to an interview conveys the impression that you are strongly motivated and are well organized to mount your campaign for admission.

- *People preparing for a key job interview in a highly competitive field.* A career portfolio helps you differentiate yourself from your competition. It creates the impression that you are well organized and properly focused—that you've "got your act together," so to speak. It's also the perfect antidote for that common career malady: "pre-job-interview jitters."

- *People who are "between opportunities."* If you were fired from or quit your last job, creating a portfolio is a very constructive thing to do during your downtime. It not only gives you an edge in future job interviews, it also helps you rebuild whatever confidence you may have lost due to the manner of your parting company with your former employer.

- *People who want to re-enter the world of work after time off.* Let's say you've taken time off from your work career to do something else—to travel, to start a family, or maybe just to do nothing in particular for a while. A portfolio helps you present the noncareer accomplishments you've done in a way that makes you a viable job candidate. Assembling a career portfolio also enables you to overcome the fear and hesitation many people feel when they have been away from the world of work for a period of time.

- *People who want to change careers.* If you are looking to do something different in your work life, a career portfolio is a great vehicle for presenting your transferable skills to an employer in a field that is new to you. Going on *informational interviews*, which is part of the process we propose for targeting your portfolio, will also help you identify the new direction you want to go in. We explain how to do informational interviews in Chapter 4.

■ *People going for a promotion, a work reassignment, a raise, or an annual review.* Portfolios are not just tools for getting new jobs in different organizations. A portfolio also helps you make the case for a promotion or work assignment within your present organization. And during an annual review a career portfolio can be useful for demonstrating the value you bring to an organization. In Chapter 7, we explore how portfolios can be used to great effect in these and other career advancement situations, including going for a raise.

■ *Independent consultants looking for business or referrals.* If you are an independent consultant or contractor, a portfolio is an effective way of demonstrating what you can do for clients. Advertising professionals have always used portfolios to showcase their talents.

In Part 2, you will find several examples of targeted portfolios.

In addition to individuals, organizations such as schools and corporations can make good use of portfolios. For example:

■ *Portfolios can improve teaching and placement in schools and universities.* Many school systems are beginning to use student portfolios as an assessment tool and as a means of focusing their teaching on outcomes that will prove useful to their students in their future academic and work careers.

Colleges and universities are also beginning to encourage, and in some cases require, their students to create portfolios that will give them an edge in the job market. Placement offices are discovering that students who have well-thought-out portfolios are getting more job offers at higher salary levels than students who only use a resume. In Chapter 7, we will discuss some techniques universities can use to help their students prepare portfolios.

■ *Portfolios can improve staffing and other human resource activities.* Given the fact that change is now a constant in most organizations, those firms that are most adept at reshuffling their employees to capitalize on emerging opportunities can gain a significant competitive advantage. Requiring employees to create and maintain career portfolios can help management identify the right people for internal reassignments. Including the use of portfolios in annual performance reviews enables managers to gain a better understanding of the range of talents of their subordinates. We will also cover this topic in greater depth in Chapter 7.

HOW CAN CREATING A CAREER PORTFOLIO HELP YOU MANAGE YOUR CAREER?

The process of assembling and then targeting your portfolio doesn't just give you a great self-marketing tool, it also serves as a very effective technique for managing your career. The knowledge you gain both about yourself and about potential career paths will enable you to make career decisions that are right for you and increase your feelings of career security. Here's how:

- *Make better career decisions.* As you begin to gather and then assess the documents for your *Master Portfolio* (the collection of every item that could be included in your portfolio), you are likely to notice that your life has certain themes and patterns. The process of identifying the skills and accomplishments that you are most proud of will give you a strong sense of the things you like to do and the situations that seem to bring out the best in you. The process of doing *informational interviews*, which are used to target your portfolio, will also give you a clear idea as to which jobs and fields are most appealing to you and whether or not you have the qualifications to succeed in these areas. Armed with this self-knowledge and marketplace knowledge, you will be in a good position to make career decisions that are right for you.

- *Increase your feelings of career security.* Since few organizations these days can guarantee lifetime employment, your ability to continue to be gainfully employed will depend upon the level of your employability. Having a high level of employability means that you have the qualifications that employers are looking for. Your present employer may let you go, but if that happens, there are likely to be many others who will quickly hire you. The more versatile you are, of course, the more potential directions you can go in, and hence the higher your level of employability.

    In Chapter 8, we will show you how to use our portfolio system to achieve a high level of employability. Job security may be a thing of the past. But career security is quite attainable when you learn how to create and maintain a career portfolio.

WHAT FORMAT SHOULD A PORTFOLIO BE IN?

The format that you use for the portfolio you bring to an interview will influence how well you use your portfolio during that meeting. If your documents are organized in appropriate, easy-to-remember categories, you will be able to easily select the right document at the right moment. During an important interview you do not want to be continually fumbling within your portfolio to find something, as this will disrupt the flow of the discussion and may leave the impression that you are not well organized. This is certainly not the effect you are trying to achieve with your portfolio!

Your Master Portfolio

Prior to going on an interview (or ideally, even before you start looking for a job), you need to collect every item that you feel you *might* be able to use at some future date. We call this collection of potentially usable items your *Master Portfolio*.

When you are at home, leafing through the items in your Master Portfolio, you are reviewing documents at your leisure. You have plenty of time to pause over certain items and consider their value. The important point to remember with your Master Portfolio is that you keep collecting and evaluating potentially useful documents and that you file them in a way that you can retrieve them easily. In Chapter 2, we suggest categories that might prove useful for filing and retrieving items in your master collection. But the system you use for organizing your Master Portfolio is up to you.

With your Master Portfolio you can be as sloppy or as neat as you like. But when you are in an interview you want to come across as being well organized and right on target. For this reason you need a carefully thought-out format for your targeted portfolio, the portfolio that you'll bring to the actual interview.

Your Targeted, "Can-Do Portfolio"

We call the career portfolio that candidates bring to meetings their *Can-Do Portfolio*, since this particular collection of documents has been selected to give evidence that they *can do* whatever is considered most important in the job under consideration, whether it's a full-time job, a consulting assignment, or the "job" of being a successful student in college or graduate school. A good Can-Do Portfolio enables you to make a convincing case that you are ready, willing, and able to get the job done. In Chapter 3, we will discuss in depth how a career portfolio can be successfully targeted in this fashion. In Part 2 we also give specific examples of Can-Do Portfolios that have been targeted for different uses.

Our experience with clients indicates that a highly effective targeted portfolio can be organized around the following five categories, which can be easily recalled using the acronym, P.E.A.K.S.

THE P.E.A.K.S. CATEGORIES

- Personal Characteristics
- Experience
- Accomplishments
- Knowledge
- Skills

Prior to conducting our research, we thought, as many people do, that what employers are primarily seeking in job candidates is an applicant who has the right combination of *knowledge*, *skills*, and *experience* for the job, along with a history of noteworthy *achievements* in comparable situations. Clearly, these are all very important qualifications in most employers' minds. But there was something missing from this list, and it turns out it's the most important dimension.

When we surveyed people who interview job candidates and asked them to rank the relative importance of a job applicant's knowledge, skills, experience, accomplishments, and personal characteristics that add value, *the majority of the employers surveyed ranked personal characteristics first*. Our research has been quite consistent on this point. Personal characteristics are ranked highest, whether the groups being surveyed are recruiters at a collegiate job fair or employers of physicians completing residency programs.

Which personal characteristics are employers thinking of? Are they looking for workers who are creative, attentive to detail, or people-oriented? The particular personal characteristics considered most important will, it turns out, depend upon the nature of the job, the culture of the organization, and, of course, which person you happen to ask. We will discuss how you can determine which personal characteristics to feature in your portfolio in Chapter 3. But for now, the important thing to know is this: It is very important to include evidence of your personal characteristics that add value in your Can-Do Portfolio.

One of the distinct advantages of having a properly targeted portfolio is you can make key intangibles, such as personal characteristics, quite tangible. Rather than just saying, "People tell me I have a lot of initiative," and leave it at that, with a portfolio you can also show an interviewer an actual document, perhaps a commendation you received, that gives evidence of your initiative.

But a portfolio can only make these important intangibles come alive if you include a personal characteristics section. And so we suggest that you use the P.E.A.K.S. format to organize the items in your targeted portfolio. The rest of this section provides a synopsis of each of the P.E.A.K.S. categories so that you can begin to get a better idea of exactly what we mean by each of these entries.

What Is Included in Each of the P.E.A.K.S. Categories?

*P*ersonal Characteristics That Add Value

Your personality traits or characteristic behavior patterns make you a valued employee or work associate. An example of a document that indicates a desired trait might be a letter commending you on a perfect attendance record, which you could present as evidence that you are highly dependable. Or, you might have a copy of a performance evaluation that refers to a successful project that you initiated. This can be presented as evidence that you are a self-starter.

Particularly useful in this category are letters of appreciation that make explicit reference to your desirable personal qualities. An example might be a letter of appreciation for completing a project that makes reference to your work ethic, commitment, or dedication.

*E*xperience

Included in the experience section are items that document your participation in activities that are similar to the kind of work you would be doing in the job for which you are interviewing. This experience does not have to be from the world of paid work. You may have done something as a volunteer or when you were at school that in an important way is similar to the kind of work you would be called upon to do in the job for which you are interviewing.

An example might be a copy of a marketing plan you created while volunteering for a community service organization. You could show this as a way of indicating that you have had experience creating marketing plans. A letter commending you on the job you did coordinating some event at your school could be presented as an example of your experience as an event planner.

Accomplishments

In this section you would include items that document your ability to do outstanding work. You might have a copy of a letter associated with an award you won or maybe a picture of you receiving an award.

The actual award is not necessary, though a photocopy of an award is certainly an option. Another possibility would be a summary of figures describing a situation before you took charge and a second set of figures that document the results you were able to achieve. (Naturally, you will want to be careful not to release or share any proprietary information owned by the organization you were working for when you achieved these results. To avoid doing this, you might have to blank out certain proprietary information on the printout.) A letter of appreciation that details what you achieved could also be an entry under "Accomplishments."

The items included in this section should highlight your ability to solve problems and to create value.

Knowledge

In this section, you document the useful knowledge you have that would help you to excel in the job for which you are being interviewed. Include evidence of your *special* knowledge that adds value and sets you apart from other candidates.

Certificates and diplomas are, of course, a way of demonstrating your formal mastery of a subject. However, there are many other ways of demonstrating that you have significant knowledge in an area that is important to an interviewer. For example, if you have traveled extensively or lived abroad, and the job for which you are interviewing has a strong international component, you could include a copy of your visa or copies of the pages of a much-stamped passport. If you do so, take time to point to some of the stamps in your passport and describe things you learned about these countries that you think would help you perform well in the international arena.

Skills

While the knowledge category focuses on the things you know, the skills category in your portfolio focuses on your ability to *do* certain things that would be valued by an employer. Obviously you have to know a lot to be proficient at something, but the emphasis here is on your ability to put this knowledge to work so that you can actually do something productive, rather than just talk about it.

Evidence of areas of expertise, like language or computer skills, should be included in this section of your targeted portfolio if these skills are important to have for the job.

In preparing for any job interview, it is important to determine what key skills are needed to be successful at the job you are interviewing for. Again, informational interviews are an excellent source for this kind of information.

Once you know the skills the employer is seeking in a job candidate, you can indicate your proficiency in these skill areas in many different ways. For example, you can present a document that gives evidence of something you accomplished and then use this as a pretext for discussing the kinds of skills you needed to get the job done.

A word of warning: Make sure that the skills you highlight in your portfolio are the ones that you not only are proficient at but also enjoy using. You don't want to get hired to do something you are good at but can't stand doing!

In the next several chapters of this book we explore how you can identify and get documents that verify your desirable P.E.A.K.S.

HOW DO YOU ACTUALLY USE A CAREER PORTFOLIO—AND WHEN?

So far in this chapter we have talked about what a career portfolio is and isn't, who might use one, and what a portfolio might look like. Here we take a quick look at *how* a portfolio can be used in an actual meeting or interview. We will explore this topic in much greater depth in Chapters 6 and 7.

Typically, a career portfolio is not shown in its entirety during an evaluation or an interview. Instead, at appropriate moments during the interview, you *selectively* show particular documents that both validate and bring to life the claims you are making. You must find the right moment to show a particular document, such as responding to an important question during a job interview, as in the following example:

Interviewer:

> *"This position requires a person who has a strong work ethic and the organizational skills necessary to work on multiple projects at the same time. Can you describe a situation where you had to work on several projects at the same time and what you did to achieve success?"*

Job candidate:

> *"Yes, last fall I was charged with creating a business plan for my division. This was a very comprehensive plan that detailed the potential of my division as well as set baseline goals to help the company make large profits. At the same time, I chaired a steering committee set up to recommend changes in the organizational structure of my division. Even though both projects were demanding and time-consuming, I was able to get both tasks competed successfully. In fact, I would like to show you some letters of commendation I received from my company that describe my work ethic and creativity on these projects."*

The candidate would then present two letters of commendation from his or her portfolio. (For an example of a letter of commendation, please turn to Part 2.)

Obviously, the letters of commendation will not cover everything that was involved in these projects. But they do lend credibility to the candidate's claim that he has a strong work ethic, is creative, and can get results while working on more than one project at a time.

The letters of commendation may not, in fact, refer explicitly to the candidate's "organizational skills," but the candidate will have the opportunity to discuss the organizational skills used on these two projects. And, because of the evidence presented, the interviewer is likely to be a willing listener.

Documents in a portfolio are not meant to tell the whole story. A document that is properly selected and presented will pique the interviewer's interest and lend credibility to the statements that the job candidate makes in explaining the context for the document. In the above example, even though the letters of commendation may not refer to these specific traits, the job candidate can talk about how he or she had to set priorities and get the right people going on the right tasks in order to get things done successfully and on time.

One important thing to remember: *You can show portfolio documents from non-work situations.* In the previous example, the job candidate showed documents that came from the world of work. But if this person were a student, he might show documents associated with several projects accomplished at the same time while in school. A person who has taken time off from a work career to raise a family might show documents associated with volunteer projects, such as fund-raising for the PTA or organizing a neighborhood block association party. A picture of the latter event would enable the job candidate to discuss the many activities that had to be organized to have a successful turnout. The point: Use the best stuff you have, which will vary according to your background.

Another key point to know about using a portfolio is that you should never leave your portfolio behind at the conclusion of an interview. In fact, it's not even a good idea to hand your portfolio to the person with whom you are meeting. Once you let go of your portfolio, you lose control of how you present the information in it. We will discuss the particular do's and don'ts for showing your portfolio in future chapters.

The example in this section of how a portfolio might be used occurs in the context of a job interview. There are, of course, many alternative uses for portfolios, including asking for a raise and going through a performance evaluation. We will discuss how you can use a portfolio in these and other situations in greater depth in Chapters 6 and 7.

Before ending this chapter, we will give you a brief overview of the P.E.A.K.S. process of assembling and targeting a career portfolio for effective use.

HOW DO YOU CREATE A PORTFOLIO THAT FEATURES THE RIGHT CAREER P.E.A.K.S?

In Chapters 2 and 3, we will walk you through an easy process for creating a portfolio that features your best P.E.A.K.S. for the situations in which you intend to use your portfolio. The following is a summary of how the process works.

The Four-Step P.E.A.K.S. Portfolio Creation Process

1. Collect all the documents you can get your hands on that demonstrate one or more categories of your career P.E.A.K.S. and that may be appropriate for inclusion in a future, targeted portfolio. This all-inclusive collection of documents is your Master Portfolio.

2. File these Master Portfolio documents any way you want, but keep track of what you have using Career P.E.A.K.S. Master Summary Sheets. All of your documents are listed on these summary sheets, along with ratings of the relative strength of the P.E.A.K.S. that are demonstrated in each document.

3. Analyze a desired job or promotion in terms of the P.E.A.K.S. that candidates should have for this job or promotion. You can use informational interviews and a Job P.E.A.K.S. Worksheet (see the appendix) to assist you with this process.

4. Finally, using your list of the P.E.A.K.S. that employers will find desirable as your guide, select the documents from your Master Portfolio that would be most impressive in your upcoming interview. Since all of the documents in your Master Portfolio are listed and rated on your Career P.E.A.K.S. Master Summary Sheets, finding the right documents to include in your targeted portfolio can be done very quickly.

Still hesitating? If you need a little more inspiration to get started, please take a look at some of the examples we have provided of P.E.A.K.S. portfolios in Part 2. Once you get the hang of it, creating a P.E.A.K.S. portfolio that gets results is very easy to do. So let's get started.

2

Assembling Your Master Portfolio

OVERVIEW

Assembling your Master Portfolio is the stage where you get your hands on as many different types of documents as possible that you will later hone and refine for specific targeted Can-Do Portfolios. But first you need some useful documents to choose from. We call this collection of portfolio-worthy documents your Master Portfolio.

This chapter details the kinds of documents you should be looking for and some strategies you can use to obtain new documents for your Master Portfolio. We'll show you how to assess the value of each item in your collection, a practice that will help later as you create a targeted portfolio. We'll review different techniques for filing these documents, and finally we'll suggest a method you can use to summarize everything you have in your Master Portfolio.

We have created two worksheets that you might find useful for assessing and summarizing the items in your collection. These worksheets are totally optional. The last thing we want to do is discourage you from collecting items for your Master Portfolio because you dread filling out a bunch of forms! You do not have to fill out any forms or create a fancy filing system in order to have a useful Master Portfolio. The worksheets are there for those of you who find them helpful. Whatever you decide to do, the important thing is for you to begin collecting documents that might prove useful for future targeted portfolios.

Get ready for a treasure hunt. One last point. If you are hesitating about getting started because collecting and sizing up all these documents about yourself seems like an awful lot of work, here's something you should know. The process may start slowly, but it builds. One idea leads to another, and before long you almost feel like you are on a real treasure hunt. The items you find are, in fact, personal treasures. Each item demonstrates your outstanding qualities. Assembling a collection of items that reveal your best features can be a huge confidence builder. So get started!

A MASTER PORTFOLIO IS MORE "STORAGE BIN" THAN "PORTFOLIO"

Your Master Portfolio should contain every item you can get your hands on that you feel *might* at some future date be considered for inclusion in a portfolio you would bring to an interview. In point of fact, you will likely end up taking only a small percentage of the items in your Master Portfolio to an interview. But prior to deciding which items to bring to a meeting, you need a collection of items to choose from. And the more items you have to choose from in your Master Portfolio, the better your targeted portfolios are likely to be.

As your collection of portfolio-worthy documents builds, you will likely discover that you have accumulated more items than you could easily carry from place to place. It is true that portfolios are, by definition, meant to be readily *port*able. So in this sense, your Master Portfolio eventually becomes more like a storage bin than a portfolio you can carry around. A more accurate term for it might be "master collection of potentially useful portfolio documents." To save words, we call it your Master Portfolio.

We suggest that you initially place items you wish to include in your Master Portfolio in a box or filing cabinet *at home*. (Keep in mind that when people are terminated, a security guard sometimes appears at the former employee's office to prevent the former employee from taking *any* files home.) You may also decide to scan these items onto a computer disk. If you decide to create a *digital portfolio,* you should, nevertheless, keep hard copies of everything you have scanned. In a face-to-face interview, you most likely will want to present documents that you can actually hold. People tend to put more trust in things they can touch and feel. And, as with all computer files, it's a good idea to have backup hard copies.

Later in this chapter (see "Different Ways of Filing Master Portfolio Documents") we will discuss filing systems you can use to keep track of everything in your Master Portfolio. But your first task is to start collecting items.

WHAT YOU SHOULD BE LOOKING FOR

Ultimately you are hoping to find documents that give evidence of P.E.A.K.S. that would appeal to the particular people to whom you will be showing your portfolio at various times in the future. Remember from Chapter 1 that your P.E.A.K.S. are your personal characteristics that add value, experience, accomplishments, knowledge, and skills.

Unfortunately, you can't really know in advance all of the possible situations where you might wish to use your portfolio. And you can't know for sure which of your P.E.A.K.S. future employers and clients might be most interested in. So you would do well when starting out to cast as wide a net as possible, picking up everything and anything that might be viewed as giving evidence of one or more of your P.E.A.K.S.

Too much ain't enough. Err on the side of collecting too much, rather than too little, for your Master Portfolio. If you get too picky early on, you may reject something that could be quite useful at some unanticipated future date. Just because you have grabbed an item and tossed it into the box storing your Master Portfolio documents doesn't mean you have made a commitment to using it. You can always discard that item later on, if over time it does not seem to add any significant value to your portfolio. So, *if in doubt*, don't *throw it out*, is a good general rule to follow when first assembling a Master Portfolio.

If you can't find a key document, make a note to yourself. As you start to collect items for your portfolio, all sorts of things will occur to you. You will remember things you once had but can't put your hands on right away. Maybe they are in a relative's attic or even in another country. It helps if you can keep a running list of portfolio-worthy items that you can eventually get a hold of but are not in your possession right now.

As a general rule, the more recent the document, the more powerful its effect. We are often asked, "How far back should we go when we are collecting items for our portfolio?" If you have been out of school for, say, ten years, documents relating to school activities and accomplishments will have less impact than similar documents from a recent graduate. That said, an ancient document that suggests you have always had a particular talent or personal characteristic that is highly desirable for the job could be quite powerful. Generally speaking, however, you should be looking hardest for documents that were generated in the past five years.

Focus on kinds of documents that might prove particularly useful. We have found that focusing on documents that fall into one of the following seven categories can help people find items that exemplify particularly desirable P.E.A.K.S.:

1. *Bio stats.* Documents that give basic information about you. An example might be a document showing that you have security clearance.
2. *Targeted task skills.* Evidence of skills you have mastered that enable you to perform specific tasks.
3. *People skills.* Evidence of your ability to work effectively with people: your ability to handle many different types of people with tact and skill, to be an effective "team player," to lead people, and so on.
4. *Learning skills.* Evidence of both your ability to learn and your interest in continuing to learn.
5. *Self-management skills.* Evidence of your ability to organize and manage yourself effectively.

6. *Task accomplishments.* Evidence of specific things you have accomplished in response to a problem or perceived need. These items could range from creative products (such as a paper you wrote or a logo you created) to things you have accomplished in an organization (like finding new sources of revenue or implementing a new computer system).

7. *Community service.* Evidence of volunteer activities that are of service to your community.

In the accompanying table we give some examples of documents that would fit into one or more of the above categories. This is not meant to give you a complete list of all the items that might be included under each category. The goal is to help you brainstorm useful items you might have gotten or might be able to get easily.

Table: Examples of Portfolio Documents

1. Bio Stats
- Resume: on paper, disk, or other format
- Personal history
- Hobbies
- Extracurricular activities
- Passport, work permits, and visa enabling you to travel/work and/or study in countries other than your own
- Foreign travel and languages
- Your e-mail address
- Web site address and home page printout
- Business cards, past and present
- Evidence of good health: for example, a record showing you've accumulated credit for not taking sick days
- Attendance record or letter commending you for excellent attendance record
- Letters of introduction/recommendation from faculty or past employers/bosses
- Professional photo (the kind used in press releases)
- Military service, honors
- Sports affiliations, honors
- Security clearance
- Letters from police showing clean record, if applying for a high-security position
- List of references (make sure you've first asked these people to be your reference)

2. Learning Skills
- Degrees
- Transcripts from schools you have attended and/or reports on academic progress
- GPA (Grade Point Average)
- High grades in individual courses
- Academic awards: dean's list, honors, prizes
- Scholarship award letters
- Certificates
- Licenses you hold
- Experiential learning (self-directed)
- Professional development activities: seminars; workshops; conferences; professional networking; professional organizations
- Letters from faculty noting your accomplishments
- Favorable faculty evaluations
- Examples of academic work: papers, projects, etc.

3. Targeted Task Skills
- Evidence of communications skills: written, oral
- Writing sample with highly favorable handwritten comments; samples of articles you have published
- Still photographs from a video of a presentation you have made

3. Targeted Task Skills (cont.)

- Evidence of competence in more than one language
- Project or work samples that illustrate a task skill, such as the ability to create a marketing plan (black out or delete proprietary information)
- Evidence of computer and other technical skills

4. People Skills

- Leadership activities (at work, in school, or in community)
- Evidence of being appointed to a leadership position and commendations received for your leadership skills
- Evidence you were elected to a position by your peers (captain of a team; student or employee representative)
- Evidence that you are an effective team player: favorable peer and leader evaluations
- Management experience
- Organizational affiliations and positions held
- Letters or articles announcing a promotion or new assignment received
- Evidence of interest in and exposure to more than one culture; proof of foreign travel/study

5. Self-Management Skills

- Personal mission statement
- Your personal and career goals
- Your personal S.W.O.T. Analysis* giving a self-assessment of how best to capitalize on your strengths
- Time management skills
- Personal financial plan: e.g., plan that enabled you to attend school
- Career self-management course documents

5. Self-Management Skills (cont.)

- Professional presence: lectures, presentations, publications
- Networking skills: evidence of professional contacts
- Listed in professional or honorific directories (professional lists, who's who lists)

6. Task Accomplishments

- S.T.A.R.s[+]
- Creative products
- Pictures of something you created or documenting your participation
- Awards for task accomplishment
- Letters you have received relating to your accomplishments
- Letters of appreciation, employer testimonials
- Letters from satisfied clients
- Pins/medallions awarded
- News articles about you or something you were significantly involved in
- Photographs of you in newspapers, magazines, or in-house publications, because of an accomplishment
- Sales reports documenting your success
- New accounts you opened
- New business activities you created that contributed to an organization's success
- Section from a business plan you created (with proprietary information deleted)
- Evidence of new products or services you created
- Evidence of inventions you patented
- Evidence of revenues or profits you were responsible for achieving
- Customer satisfaction reports
- Employee surveys you created
- Promotional materials you developed
- Designs or logos you created

*S.W.O.T. is an acronym for strengths, weaknesses, opportunities, and threats. Organizations frequently do S.W.O.T. analyses in order to identify appropriate strategies. If you are familiar with this technique you can perform a personal S.W.O.T. analysis to help you identify useful career strategies.

[+]S.T.A.R. stands for situation (challenge, problem, or opportunity) faced task to be undertaken, action taken (what decisions you made and actions you took in response to the problem), and results (the outcome of your action).

6. Task Accomplishments (cont.)

- Printouts from Web sites created for clients/employers
- Training manuals and programs you created
- Performance appraisals received, if highly favorable
- Evidence of a favorable 360-degree performance evaluation*
- Evidence of achievements in clubs, sports, hobbies, or other recreational achievements
- Tax return information (e.g., proof of past commissions/earnings; proof of profitable business)

7. Community Service

- Volunteer organizational affiliations, positions held
- Activities specified and illustrated: hours, photos
- Awards
- Thank-you letters for community service time or accomplishments
- Peace Corps service
- Pins/medallions awarded
- News articles about you or something you were significantly involved in

*Evaluations from a sample of all the people you work with and for.

Again, the above list is not meant to be all-inclusive. We provide it only to get you thinking about things you might have that could prove useful in your portfolio. Don't worry if you don't have many of the above items, or even any of them. The important thing is that the documents that you do eventually find give evidence of important P.E.A.K.S.

For further inspiration you might want to take a moment to thumb through some of the portfolio items in Part 2.

STRATEGIES FOR CREATING NEW DOCUMENTS FOR YOUR COLLECTION

When assembling your Master Portfolio, in addition to looking for documents you already have, you should be looking for opportunities to ask people for new documents and you should be on the lookout for opportunities to create some of these items yourself.

Ask people to create useful documents for you. Do not just wait for documents to come to you. If someone, for example a friend, colleague, professor, customer, or client, praises you or thanks you for something you recently did, you might ask this person: "Would you write me a short note restating that so I can include it in my portfolio?"

The chances are they will be happy to do so and may even be intrigued by the idea of a portfolio. If they reply that they'd like to write you a note but are very busy right now, you can offer to do a draft of the note, which they can edit, put on their stationery, and sign. (You may have observed that many, if not most, letters of recommendation get done this way!)

If the person is your current boss, you obviously don't want to create the impression that you are looking for a job unless he or she knows that you are and is supportive. However, you can tactfully say something like, "You know, Mary [insert your boss's name], I'm sure that someday, possibly quite soon, you are going to be moving on to a bigger position. When that happens, I want to make sure that I have a good portfolio ready so that I can get a good position, too."

The chances are your boss will want to learn more about putting together a portfolio for his or her own use!

You can (and should) create some of your portfolio documents yourself. In addition to asking for documents, you can also add to the items in your Master Portfolio by *creating* them. We are not talking about deceptive practices, such as fabricating fake letters of recommendation or creating bogus performance evaluations. Most assuredly, and we can't stress this too much, you should never include anything in your portfolio that lacks integrity. You won't feel good about inclusions that are, in point of fact, dishonest. And if you ever get caught using something that is not authentic, your credibility will be totally destroyed—the very opposite of what you are trying to achieve with your portfolio. You can and should, of course, make minor deletions to protect the rights of the authors of the documents you use. For example, you would need to delete proprietary information, such as confidential market share data, from copies of documents that you will be showing outside this organization.

Consider taking pictures and using the Web. You can create your own tailor-made documents by taking pictures of something you created or visiting Web sites that have pictures and other information that pertain to some important aspect of your life so far. One of the authors of this book used an Internet search engine to find the Web site for a school in Brazil where he once was an instructor. He was able to download pictures of this school in Rio de Janeiro, which he then combined with other pictures he found of Rio to create a colorful collage. Since there is no such thing as a bad picture of Rio, it didn't take much artistic ability to create a visually arresting prop for discussing his international experience.

Color sells. When creating your own documents or copying documents you already have, remember that color can lend appeal. Obviously you do not want to include a lot of gaudy colors that have the net effect of cheapening your own image. But you should be on the lookout for opportunities to include at least a little dash of color in your collection of portfolio documents. So, if you receive a letter of commendation and the person's name and address at the top of the letter are in color, you would do well to pay a little extra and have whatever photocopies are made done in color and on paper that matches the original stationery.

In this chapter our focus is on finding and creating documents that are based on your life so far. In Chapter 8, we will discuss activities you can pursue in the future that will generate a continuous flow of portfolio-worthy documents.

HOW TO ASSESS THE P.E.A.K.S. IN YOUR DOCUMENTS

Thus far we have discussed how you can go about finding and creating items to include in your Master Portfolio collection. Now, we will show you a strategy for evaluating the P.E.A.K.S. demonstrated by each of the documents in your Master Portfolio. If you do this well, when it comes time to actually select items from your Master Portfolio to take to an interview you will be able to quickly put your hands on useful documents. In Chapter 3, we will show you some techniques you can use to decide which of your P.E.AK.S. you should feature in the Can-Do Portfolios you take to particular interviews. But first, it is very useful to know just what P.E.A.K.S. you have in your Master Portfolio.

The Career P.E.A.K.S. Measurement Form

To demonstrate how you can assess the items in your Master Portfolio, we have created a worksheet called the Career P.E.A.K.S. Measurement Form. Prior to showing you how to use this form, we should make one thing very clear. *You do **not** have to fill out a Career P.E.A.K.S. Measurement Form for every item in your Master Portfolio.* Some of you will want to use this form for many of your items; and others of you will decide you would prefer to assess your documents without filling out this form. The important thing is that you understand the *thinking* that should go into analyzing your documents. Whether or not you use the Career P.E.A.K.S. Measurement Form to record your assessments of the relative strength of your documents is entirely up to you. We do recommend, however, that you read the next section so that you have a very clear idea as to what is involved when you assess the P.E.A.K.S. represented by a document.

An Example of Assessing the P.E.A.K.S. in a Document

Let us say, as a hypothetical example, that during the past year you were given the responsibility of leading a team of diverse people in raising productivity in your department by 10 percent. You had to deal with some very difficult personalities, but by the end of the year, the innovative ideas that your team recommended and subsequently adopted resulted in a 15 percent increase in productivity. In your annual performance evaluation your boss gave you a very favorable set of comments on your ability to get results.

To illustrate how you might describe and assess the P.E.A.K.S. that are featured in your annual performance review we have filled in a Career P.E.A.K.S. Measurement Form, which follows.

At the top of the Measurement Form, there is a place for the name of the document and a brief verbal description of the document. Under "Code" you can indicate where this document is located in your file. In this case, the document happens to be the third item in the "Task Accomplishments" section of your Master Portfolio file. The assignment of a code to identify your documents is totally arbitrary. Depending upon the filing system you choose to use, you may or may not have separate categories in your Master Portfolio. The important point is that you know where to find this document.

Next to each P.E.A.K.S. category, we give an example of what you might write, and a hypothetical numerical score that you might give each of the P.E.A.K.S., ranging from 1 (lowest) to 5 (highest). These scores are meant to reflect how strong you feel each of the individual

P.E.A.K.S. is. The worksheets are for your own personal reference, *not* for sharing with an interviewer. So be candid.

If you decide you would like to use the Career P.E.A.K.S. Measurement Form to assess the P.E.A.K.S. in some of your documents, we have included a blank copy of this form in the appendix.

But again, the key thing is that you understand how to assess the P.E.A.K.S in your documents, regardless of whether or not you actually use the Career P.E.A.K.S. Measurement Form.

Example Career P.E.A.K.S. Measurement Form

Name of Document: Annual Performance Evaluation

Description: 15% increase in productivity accomplishment

Code: Task Accomplishments: #3

	SPECIFY	RATE: 1 TO 5 (5 = highest score)
*P*ersonal characteristics that add value	Ability to handle diverse, often difficult personalities with skill	4
*E*xperience	Shows experience managing a new team	4
*A*ccomplishment(s)	STAR: Situation: Productivity flat, difficult personalities Task: To increase productivity by 10% Action taken: Brainstorm; everyone participated Results: Productivity increased by 15%	5
*K*nowledge	Good basic knowledge developed of our operations	3
*S*kills	Leading a team, leading change	4

Total: 20

DIFFERENT WAYS OF FILING MASTER PORTFOLIO DOCUMENTS

As the number of items in your Master Portfolio collection increases, you may want a filing system better than just tossing everything into a big box. The real issues are (1) knowing what you have and (2) retrieval. Knowing what you have can be accomplished by keeping summary sheets, a topic we will discuss in the next section of this chapter. The effectiveness and efficiency of your retrieval system will ultimately depend upon your ability to develop a filing system that not only works, but also is in tune with how you like to organize yourself. You have to be comfortable with your filing system or you won't keep using it.

Using tabs may help. You will likely find that it is easier to locate items if you have them stored in folders that have tabs on them for identification. There are, of course, many general categories you could use for these tabs. The following set of headings, which we reviewed earlier in this chapter, could prove useful for filing items in your Master Portfolio:

- Bio stats
- Targeted task skills
- People skills
- Learning skills
- Self-management skills
- Task accomplishments
- Community service

An obvious alternative to the above categories would be to file each document according to which of the following P.E.A.K.S. the documents best exemplifies:

- Personal characteristics that add value
- Experience
- Accomplishments
- Knowledge
- Skills

The problem with using the P.E.A.K.S. categories for initially filing documents in your Master Portfolio is that this filing system would require you to carefully analyze each document before filing it. Determining which of the P.E.A.K.S. a document best exemplifies can take a fair amount of time. And if it takes a long time to decide which category to file something under, the net result may be that you find yourself putting an excellent document aside somewhere, fully intending to file it in the future and losing it in the process.

Whatever nomenclature you do end up using for your Master Portfolio filing system, you will no doubt discover that some of your items could be filed under more than one heading. In these cases you can put copies of the same document in several different files or leave a note in each appropriate category that specifies the location of the actual document.

If you use Career P.E.A.K.S. Measurement Forms, don't lose them. If you use these worksheets, you will need some system for keeping track of where they are. You are unlikely to misplace them if you use paper clips to attach the filled-out forms directly to the original documents they assess. Alternatively, you can have a separate file or files for these worksheets.

Your filing system should suit your personal style for organizing things. With your Master Portfolio you can be as sloppy or as neat as you like to be. When you are shuffling through your Master Portfolio documents at home and at your leisure, you are not in an interview situation where you need to be able to find what you are looking for immediately.

Truthfully, one of the authors likes to just toss stuff into a big box and then periodically assess what he has and file it accordingly. The other author feels more comfortable if he can carefully file things into separate folders right up front. If the two of us were forced to use each other's approach to filing documents for our Master Portfolios, we'd probably both quit!

The key is to find a filing system you will continue to use. We have suggested some headings that might prove useful for filing and retrieving the items in your master collection of portfolio items. These are only suggestions.

If using the headings we have suggested for your Master Portfolio collection sounds like something you do not want to do, then chuck this system for filing your documents and try some other approach. The important thing with your Master Portfolio is that you keep collecting and evaluating potentially useful documents and that you file them in a way that allows you to retrieve them easily.

HOW TO KEEP TRACK OF THE CONTENTS OF YOUR MASTER PORTFOLIO

Whatever system you use for filing your documents, you will want to know what's actually in your Master Portfolio collection. Keeping track of all the different documents in your Master Portfolio may be fairly easy when you start out, if you haven't got many documents to include. However, if you are industrious about tracking down and soliciting items that you would like to include in your portfolio, it soon becomes difficult to remember everything you have in your Master Portfolio.

You can keep weeding things out, so that your Master Portfolio remains a manageable size. But, as noted earlier, this is not an advisable strategy, since you never know precisely what sort of work and jobs you will be going after in the future. If you decide to make a significant career shift, an item that seems of little use today may prove immensely useful at some point in the future. For example, there may be items you now have that document some esoteric knowledge that you have that is of little use in your present job but would prove to be just what an employer is looking for in a future job. We have often observed that people who are dissatisfied with their present job are able to make successful career shifts by marketing special skills and knowledge they have that they would love to use but are unable to do so in their present job. So your best bet is to keep all those documents that don't seem to fit into your present career, since you never know when they might prove useful.

Career P.E.A.K.S. Master Summary Sheets

To help you keep track of all the items in your Master Portfolio collection, we have created a Career P.E.A.K.S. Master Summary Sheet. You can use this form to list all of your items in this collection, along with your ratings of the P.E.A.K.S. associated with each of these items.

If your summary sheets are up to date, whenever you are putting together a Can-Do Portfolio for a particular job interview, you can run your eye down these summary sheets to see what you've got in your Master Portfolio that might be useful for this interview.

And perhaps even more important, these "snapshots" of the contents of your Master Portfolio will enable you to see patterns and themes with respect to the P.E.A.K.S. that have characterized your life. This sort of self-knowledge can be very useful, not only for a job interview but also for making important career decisions.

How to Use Career P.E.A.K.S. Master Summary Sheets

Recording items on this summary sheet is quite simple. Let us say, for example, that you want to list all the items in a Master Portfolio file you call "Task Accomplishments." The first thing you would do would be to write "Task Accomplishments" in the upper left-hand corner of the form. Refer to the example below to see how this would be done.

Example: Career P.E.A.K.S Master Summary Sheet for Portfolio Categories

On a scale of 1 to 5, rate each item for its P.E.A.K.S. (5 being most important)

Master Portfolio Category: Task Accomplishments	P Personal Characteristics That Add Value	E Experience	A Accomplish-ments	K Knowledge	S Skills	Totals
Printout figures: doubled advertising for student newspaper	3	3	5	2	4	17
Boss's letter: praising marketing plan	2	4	5	4	4	19
Annual performance evaluation: 15% boost in productivity	4	4	5	3	4	20
Etc.						

If your Master Portfolio does not have different files and headings, you can simply leave the "Master Portfolio Category" area blank.

Your next step is to create in the left-hand column a list of all the items that are filed in the category under consideration, using short, clear descriptions. Let's say, for example, that you have a computer printout that gives sales figures documenting your success in leading a team that doubled the amount of advertising for your school newspaper. You might list this as "Printout figures: doubled advertising for school newspaper," as we have done in the example.

After writing a short description of the document, record the P.E.A.K.S. ratings you would assign to it. These ratings are listed in the same row that the description is in, which for the "doubled advertising" example would be the first row. See the accompanying summary sheet illustrating how the ratings for these P.E.A.K.S. are recorded. (These ratings are the same as the P.E.A.K.S. ratings you assigned to this document on the corresponding Career P.E.A.K.S. Measurement Form if you used one.)

Your second item on the "Task Accomplishments" part of the Career P.E.A.K.S. Master Summary Sheet might be a letter from your boss congratulating you on the marketing plan you put together for a major account. Here you put "Boss's letter praising marketing plan" and record the P.E.A.K.S. ratings associated with this item.

In the accompanying example, we have also recorded a third item, "Annual Performance Evaluation: 15% boost in productivity." This is the document we analyzed earlier in this chapter, using a Career P.E.A.K.S. Measurement Form. As you can see, the same P.E.A.K.S. ratings would be recorded in the Master Portfolio Summary Sheet that were listed in the Career P.E.A.K.S. Measurement Form for this document.

For those of you who would like to have a go at using the above system for listing the items in your Master Portfolio, we have included a blank Career P.E.A.K.S. Master Summary Sheet in the appendix of this book.

Keeping a List of What You Have, Even If the P.E.A.K.S. Have Not Been Analyzed

Regardless of whether or not you use the above form, it is important that you keep a list of all the items in your Master Portfolio. This practice will enable you to see at a glance everything you've got so that when it comes time to actually select items from your Master Portfolio to take to an interview, you can feel confident that you haven't overlooked any important items.

This list will be most useful if it also includes a summary of how you have rated the P.E.A.K.S. featured in each document. But do not let the fact that you have not yet rated the P.E.A.K.S associated with a particular document prevent you from at least adding this document to your list.

FINAL THOUGHTS

In this chapter we have taken a close look at how you can assemble a master collection of portfolio-worthy documents. The worksheets, forms, and filing systems that we have suggested are strictly optional. What's important is that you begin collecting documents that demonstrate important things about you, and that you keep doing this.

As long as you are alive and well and have career-related ambitions, there really is no point in time at which you should stop collecting items for your Master Portfolio. The truth is you can never really know when a document that reveals something important about you could prove useful.

Continuing to collect items for your Master Portfolio is a good thing to do. But there's a danger here. You don't want to get so involved in perfecting your Master Portfolio collection, your filing system, summary lists, and so on, that you never get around to creating a portfolio you can actually use.

A Master Portfolio is most useful when it is put to use. In Chapter 3, we will show you how to select items from your Master Portfolio that you can use in specific situations, such as being interviewed for a job.

3

Targeting Your Portfolio

OVERVIEW

When the time comes to select items from your Master Portfolio to take to an interview, one strategy might be to simply sift through the items in your Master Portfolio and pull out the documents that you think might work. But will you hit the mark? In this chapter we will discuss strategies you can use to improve your aim so that you bring a well-targeted portfolio to every interview.

Specifically, we will review the following:

- What it means to target a portfolio and why you should do so
- When you should create a targeted portfolio
- How to select items that will appeal to your target audience
- How to organize the items in your targeted portfolio
- How to create the "right look" for your targeted portfolio

By the end of this chapter you should have a clear idea of how to create a well-targeted Can-Do Portfolio that will include the best items to bring to a particular interview.

In addition to having a great product, if you follow the suggested strategies, you are also likely to feel a great surge of confidence. Knowing that you will be bringing the "right stuff" to a meeting can actually inspire you to look forward to interviews that might otherwise fill you with dread.

If you would like to see some specific examples of targeted portfolios before learning how to create one, take a quick look at some of the examples we have provided of Can-Do Portfolios in Part 2 of this book.

WHAT IS A TARGETED PORTFOLIO?

A *targeted portfolio* is a collection of career-relevant documents that have been chosen because of their intended appeal to a specific audience. Simply put, these are the items from your Master Portfolio that you would bring to a meeting, hoping to impress the person or people with whom you are meeting.

As noted earlier, we call a targeted career portfolio that is designed to appeal to a particular audience a Can-Do Portfolio. It's called can-do because it gives evidence that you can do whatever is considered most important in the job or promotion under consideration. A strong Can-Do Portfolio enables you to make a convincing case that you are ready, willing, and able to get the job done. It helps you differentiate yourself from other candidates along important, job-relevant dimensions.

In addition to giving evidence that you can do whatever is considered most important in the job or promotion under consideration, a Can-Do Portfolio that has been properly targeted has the following two important features:

1. *It is targeted at a particular audience.* A properly targeted Can-Do Portfolio is not an all-inclusive scrapbook that captures everything you have done so far in your career. A chronological sequence of documents accompanied by a seemingly endless recitation of "and then I did this, and then I did that" is unlikely to hold the interest of anyone other than possibly your mother. The key is to select documents that will have a particular appeal to the person or people with whom you will be meeting.

2. *It is very selective.* In most situations where you might show items from your portfolio, you will have very little time to do so. You must be very efficient and show only those items that will have the greatest impact. When collecting items for your Master Portfolio, you should err on the side of collecting too much. But with Can-Do Portfolios the very opposite is true. If in doubt, leave it out, is a good rule to follow.

In the later sections of this chapter we will review techniques for identifying the specific kinds of items you should include in your targeted, Can-Do Portfolio, but first let's take a look at *when* you should target your portfolio.

WHEN SHOULD YOU TARGET YOUR CAN-DO PORTFOLIO?

You will want to have a targeted portfolio ready whenever you are about to go to a meeting during which you would like to show some of your portfolio items. In future chapters we will discuss techniques you can use to present your portfolio during different kinds of meetings. But prior to actually showing your portfolio, you first need to select a set of items that would be appropriate for presentation at the particular meeting you will be going to.

Wait until you have a specific situation in mind. There is no point trying to target your portfolio prior to having a specific kind of situation in which you might use it in mind. Since a properly targeted portfolio is focused on a specific position you desire, the odds are that for each position you interview for you will want to assemble a Can-Do Portfolio that has been specifically targeted in a somewhat different way.

Anytime you create a resume, consider also targeting your portfolio. As stated earlier, resumes should be used to get the interview and portfolios to get the job. So if you find yourself putting together a resume, the odds are you should also be targeting your portfolio. In Chapter 5, we show you how to create a P.E.A.K.S. resume that, in addition to improving your chances of getting an interview, also sets you up nicely to present your portfolio once you get there.

Try to target your portfolio prior to your first meeting. Typically, you are not required to bring a portfolio to an interview or meeting. But if you have a portfolio that demonstrates that you can do what the person with whom you are interviewing considers important, your chances of having a successful meeting are certainly improved. Therefore, your goal should be to have a targeted portfolio prepared prior to your first meeting. However, if you are not ready to bring a portfolio, then don't. Presenting a poorly organized portfolio is unlikely to make a good first impression.

If possible, assemble your Master Portfolio first. If an important meeting is coming up very soon, then obviously you will have to start assembling a Can-Do Portfolio for this meeting as soon as you can. And you may have to do this without first assembling a master collection of items. If, in fact, you find yourself in such a situation right now, you might do well to consult Chapter 10. But attempting to put together a targeted portfolio prior to assembling a Master Portfolio collection of potentially usable documents will dilute your efforts. As noted earlier, the more items you have to choose from, the better your targeted portfolio is likely to be.

Have a Can-Do Portfolio ready to close the deal. You may still be able to use a targeted portfolio, even if you were not able to put one together in time for your first meeting. During your initial meeting you should be able to pick up a lot of clues as to exactly what would impress the people with whom you are meeting. If you are invited back, you can bring a perfectly targeted Can-Do Portfolio to the next meeting. As you will see in future chapters, nicely targeted portfolios are very useful for "closing the deal."

A Can-Do Portfolio is always a work in progress. As you acquire new documents and gain more information on ways to impress the next set of people who will see your portfolio, you will want to make adjustments to your Can-Do Portfolio. It's best to think of a targeted portfolio as a work in progress. As a general rule, each time there is a significant change in the kind of opportunity you are pursuing or the type of people to whom you will be presenting your portfolio, you should consider making changes in your Can-Do Portfolio.

HOW TO SELECT ITEMS TO INCLUDE IN YOUR CAN-DO PORTFOLIO

The people with whom you will be meeting to discuss an opportunity may never have heard of the acronym, P.E.A.K.S., but it nicely summarizes the kinds of things most people are looking for when interviewing candidates for jobs and promotions. Interviewers are likely to respond favorably to documents that demonstrate that you have personal characteristics that they believe would add value to their organization. And they will be interested in items from your portfolio that indicate that you have relevant experience, accomplishments, knowledge, and skills for the job or promotion under consideration.

While we know that the people with whom you will be meeting are looking for desirable P.E.A.K.S. in candidates, the question remains, *which* P.E.A.K.S. do they value most in candidates? Which personal characteristics, for example, will they think are most important? Are they looking for people who are detail-oriented, as might be the case for some jobs in accounting, or are they seeking creativity, which might be considered a key trait of a successful copywriter in an advertising firm? And what kinds of accomplishments and skills would they find most impressive?

The challenge when targeting your Can-Do Portfolio is to identify ahead of time the kinds of P.E.A.K.S. that the people with whom you will be meeting are seeking in candidates. This will enable you to include in your portfolio the best items you have to demonstrate these P.E.A.K.S.

Here's a process you can follow to target your portfolio:

1. Describe the opportunity you are pursuing in *realistic* terms.
2. Identify the P.E.A.K.S. that the interviewer will consider desirable.
3. Select items that best demonstrate how you have the desired P.E.A.K.S.

Each of these steps is described in the sections that follow.

Step 1: Describing the Opportunity You Are Pursuing in Realistic Terms

The more accurately you are able to describe the real responsibilities, activities, and goals associated with a job or promotion, the easier it will be for you to identify the particular P.E.A.K.S. that are considered most desirable in candidates seeking this position.

Look for a job description. A good place to start is with a formal *job description*, if you can obtain one. Jobs that are advertised or posted often include a brief description of what the job involves and the qualifications that candidates are expected to have. To get a more comprehensive write-up, you can try contacting the people who will be interviewing you and ask them if you can obtain a copy of the job description prior to your interview. Making this kind of request has the added advantage of sending the message that you are doing your homework.

Get a realistic picture of the job. Regardless of how extensive it is, a formal write-up of a job can only tell you so much. You are not told what it is really like to be an incumbent of this particular job in this particular organization and industry. But a job description will give you a general idea as to what the job entails, so that you can start making inquiries into the specifics involved.

The key is to gather as much information as you can about what the job really involves. To learn more about the organization and the field in which it operates, you might first look at the organization's Web site, annual report, and promotional literature. But to get a less-biased, more up-to-date view on what's really going on in the organization and its industry, you should also search for relevant articles in trade journals and the popular press.

Play detective. Talk to people who might know something about this job, organization, or industry. Suppliers of the organization, former employees, customers, and competitors all have their biases, but they also have a lot of inside information that doesn't show up anywhere else. If you can't find anyone who knows something about this particular organization or job, you might still be able to find someone who has worked at an equivalent job in a different organization.

Do informational interviews. The best way to get a realistic picture of a job is to conduct informational interviews with people who can provide much of the information you are seeking. Unlike a *job* interview, in which you are the person being interviewed, when doing an *informational* interview *you* make the appointment and *you* do the interviewing. Informational interviews can be tremendously useful not only for getting a realistic picture of a job but also for assessing career directions you are considering. In the next chapter we will discuss everything you need to know about how to set up and conduct effective informational interviews.

Do as much research as you can. If you do not have time to do an informational interview, or do not wish to do one, it is still a good idea to do whatever research you can into the exact nature of the position for which you are going to be interviewed. Reading any material you can quickly put your hands on and having informal chats with anyone you can easily get a hold of who might know something useful is a lot better than not doing any digging at all.

The better you understand the real requirements of a job, the easier it will be to identify documents that demonstrate your ability to do this job well.

As you can see in the examples we provide in Part 2, you don't have to write a long essay on a job to prepare a targeted portfolio. A short paragraph will do, so long as you are catching the essence of what the job really requires. In fact, you don't have to write anything at all, though keeping some notes is helpful. The important point is that you understand what the incumbent of the job has to be able to do to be considered successful.

Step 2: Identifying the P.E.A.K.S. That the Interviewer Will Consider Desirable

Once you have a clear idea of the various job requirements, the next step is to identify the particular P.E.A.K.S. that the people who will be interviewing you are likely to be seeking in candidates.

Begin with the "customer's" mind in mind. Whenever you present items from your portfolio, you are engaging in self-marketing. And so, when preparing your presentation you would do well to heed the effective marketer's first rule: Begin with the customer in mind.

The "customer" here, of course, is the person to whom you will be showing items from your portfolio. And the important point is not what you think the customer *should* think is important, but what the customer actually *does* think is important. To do this effectively, you must have the customer's *mind* in mind, so to speak. Then consider what's on the customer's mind in terms of the P.E.A.K.S. they think a candidate for a particular job or promotion should have. The following are some strategies you can use.

Put yourself in their place. Once you have a clear idea as to what the job under consideration really requires, put yourself in the place of the interviewer and make your best guess as to the kinds of P.E.A.K.S. this person will consider desirable. The problem, of course, is that the real issue is not what you would think is important if you were doing the interviewing, but what they think. Putting yourself into someone else's position does not eliminate your own personal biases, nor does it take into account the mental processes of the person doing the interviewing.

Learn as much as you can about the mind-set of the people who will be interviewing you. The better you understand the mind-set of the people who will be interviewing you, the easier it will be to identify the kinds of P.E.A.K.S. they consider most desirable. By mind-set we mean the key assumptions and biases that shape a person's thinking on a particular topic. You might think it is nearly impossible to anticipate an interviewer's mind-set, particularly since the assumptions and biases that influence that person's thinking are often unspoken.

While it is true that without meeting someone, you cannot know for sure what this person's particular mind-set will be, it is also true that people in a particular field or profession are likely to share what we might call a professional mind-set. No two people in a field or a profession will have identical mind-sets, but they are likely to share certain assumptions about the P.E.A.K.S. that a person who is successful in their field should have. The fact is that certain kinds of people are attracted to certain kinds of fields. A person who is very outgoing and likes to meet and interact with people on a regular basis is more likely to be attracted to sales than, say, bookkeeping. And subsequent training and experience tends to reinforce a particular way of thinking. Salespeople learn to be very responsive to their customers and to accept rejection without letting it diminish their efforts. Bookkeepers are rewarded for being extremely well organized and detail-oriented.

Though it is not always possible to do so, it is particularly useful if you can learn about the background of the person who will be interviewing you prior to the interview. At the very least, you want to learn as much as you can about the *kinds* of people who are in the field in which you will be interviewing.

Have discussions with people who might know the interviewer's mind-set. The people who can give you a realistic picture of a job are also likely to be able to tell you about the typical mind-set of interviewers in this field.

Rather than ask about "professional mind-sets," which might require a fair amount of explanation on your part, you would probably do better to ask, "So what are the *personal characteristics* that interviewers are looking for in candidates for this kind of job?" You can make some suggestions as to what you think these personal characteristics might be, so that the person you are talking with knows what you mean by personal characteristics. And, of course, you also want to ask: "What sort of *experience* do you think the interviewer will be looking for?" "Please tell me about the kinds of *accomplishments, knowledge,* and *skills* that are likely to be most valued in job candidates."

It is particularly helpful if you can get the people you interview to specify which of the particular P.E.A.K.S. they have mentioned are of the highest priority.

Obviously, you can come up with your own variation on these questions, but these are the kinds of questions that are likely to elicit the information you need to target your portfolio.

Talk with assistants, if you can. It is not unreasonable to call the office of the person who will be interviewing you and ask if you can have a quick phone conversation with one of the interviewer's assistants to learn more about the job for which you will be interviewing. If you are able to get a hold of one of these people, in addition to finding out about the particulars of the job, you can ask about the particular P.E.A.K.S that are important to the person with whom you will be meeting.

Ask P.E.A.K.S. questions during informational interviews. If you are in a rush, then you may not have time to do formal, informational interviews. But if you can schedule an informational interview, definitely ask the above questions about the P.E.A.K.S. that are considered desirable. We explore ways you can do this in the next chapter, which focuses on techniques for conducting effective informational interviews.

Listen carefully for desired P.E.A.K.S. during job interviews. As noted earlier, in most cases you will want to be able to bring a targeted Can-Do Portfolio to your first job interview. But whether or not you are able to do this, you would do well to listen very carefully for clues as to what the interviewer and people in this organization think are particularly impressive P.E.A.K.S. If you are invited back, this knowledge will enable you to further refine what is included in your portfolio. And the knowledge of desired P.E.A.K.S. that is derived from actual job interviews could also prove useful if you will be interviewing for a comparable position in a similar organization.

Be sure to identify the personal characteristics that interviewers believe add value. Discussions that people have about jobs are often so focused on things like required skills, knowledge, and experience that it is easy to overlook an analysis of the personal characteristics of candidates that are believed to add value. But, as our research has shown, people who make employment decisions tend to rank the personal characteristics of job candidates as more important than their experience, accomplishments, knowledge, and skills. So remember to ask about the most desirable personal characteristics that a candidate could have. The beauty of having a targeted portfolio is that by selecting the right documents, you can make some of these all-important intangibles more real and tangible for the interviewer.

Make a list of desired P.E.A.K.S. It is very useful if, based on the research you have conducted, you make a list of the particular P.E.A.K.S. that the people to whom you will be showing your Can-Do Portfolio are likely to consider highly desirable. If possible, indicate which of the P.E.A.K.S. on your list are of the highest priority.

To assist you with this process we have included a Job P.E.A.K.S. Worksheet in the appendix, which you may find helpful. Whether or not you use this worksheet is up to you. What's important is that before selecting the items to include in your targeted portfolio, you have as good an idea as possible of the particular P.E.A.K.S. that the person or people to whom you will show your Can-Do Portfolio are likely to find most impressive.

Step 3: Selecting Items That Best Demonstrate How You Have the Desired P.E.A.K.S.

If you have followed the steps above and have a good summary list of what's in your Master Portfolio collection, the selection of documents to include in your Can-Do Portfolio should be relatively easy. The following are some considerations to help you make your choices.

Think link. The items in a properly targeted portfolio should provide links between what the person who will be conducting the interview is looking for and what you have to offer. And so, the first question to ask yourself is, "Does this document give evidence that I have one or more of the P.E.A.K.S. that the interviewer is likely to consider desirable?"

Identifying potentially useful documents to include in your targeted Can-Do Portfolio can be done very quickly if all of the documents in your Master Portfolio collection have been rated on Career PE.A.K.S. Master Summary Sheets.

Include good conversation pieces as well as documents that need no explanation. You should give strong consideration to any item that you can simply hand to an interviewer and, without further explanation, this person immediately understands that the document gives evidence that you have one of the P.E.A.K.S. that is being sought in candidates.

An example is a letter of commendation that explicitly praises you for a desired skill or personal characteristic.

But you should not limit yourself to documents that speak for themselves. As we will see in future chapters, the best way to show your portfolio is to do so in person. If you were to send your portfolio ahead or leave it behind, then every item would have to be self-explanatory. But since you will be presenting your portfolio in person, you will be able to explain why a particular item gives strong evidence that you have a desired qualification.

An example of a powerful document that might require some explanation is a spreadsheet that records impressive sales figures. Maybe you had the highest percentage increase in sales for three years running of all the salespeople in your company. To make sure that the interviewer is reading the figures correctly and understands what the spreadsheet indicates, you probably need to explain it to him.

A document that requires some explanation can give you a great opening to point out important things you want to convey about yourself. When presenting impressive sales figures, for example, you would have an opportunity to talk about the challenges you faced and the techniques you used to be successful.

Try to include only one or two pages of reports and other extended documents. So that you can include a number of different items in your Can-Do Portfolio, try to limit the number of pages associated with any one item. If, for example, you want to talk about a marketing report you compiled, you could include the executive summary and/or the title page. If you want to include a school paper that received a very favorable comment, include the page that has the professor's comments on it. If your interviewer expresses a strong interest in a report or paper you have done, you can offer to send him or her a copy after the interview, provided, of course, that information that should not be shared with this person can be deleted.

Your goal is not to go over a paper or report you did line by line, but instead to have a prop that enables you to discuss the key P.E.A.K.S. you demonstrated in doing this project.

Consider including pictures. A picture can be a good conversation piece for initiating a discussion of important P.E.A.K.S. that you have. For example, if you have a picture of yourself on a sports team, you can use this to discuss both your competitiveness and your skills as a team player. A picture of a volunteer event that you organized might be useful for discussing your organizational skills. If the picture showed up in a publication, so much the better, but having a photo from a newspaper or magazine is not necessary.

Make sure the items you include add *to your credibility.* If your explanation of how an item demonstrates one of your P.E.A.K.S. comes across as too much of a stretch, the interviewer might start wondering if other things you are saying about yourself are less than credible as well.

It is important to remember that a fundamental reason for showing your portfolio is to *add* to your credibility. With this in mind, you should be careful not to include items that might have the net effect of *undermining* your credibility.

In addition to refraining from including items that give only tenuous evidence of key P.E.A.K.S, you should also be careful to avoid choosing items that are, in essence, inauthentic. To protect against loss or theft, you should use photocopies, but they should be copies of the real thing.

Be careful to delete proprietary information. The documents you choose should not contain any misrepresentations. That said, you should make whatever deletions are necessary to protect the rights of the authors of the documents you use. Deleting proprietary information from company documents is necessary if you will be showing these documents to another company in the same industry.

Do not limit yourself to items drawn from the world of work. While it is desirable to include as many items as you can that are drawn from actual work experience, it is entirely appropriate to include items drawn from your nonprofessional life, such as hobbies or even family or other social events you have organized. The important thing is that these items give evidence of desired P.E.A.K.S. that would impress an employer or client.

Your education, work, and personal history will determine the menu of items you will have to choose from. The younger you are, the more likely it is that the majority of items in your Can-Do Portfolio will be drawn from skills learned and achievements made during your school years.

Whenever possible, include your most recent documents. Generally speaking, whenever you have a choice, you should include your most recent documents. Documents from the past five years are likely to have the greatest impact. That said, a document from long ago that suggests you have always had a desired talent or personal characteristic could also be quite powerful.

Try to cover each of the P.E.A.K.S. categories. Having a perfectly balanced portfolio, with an equal number of entries under each P.E.A.K.S. category, is not necessary. The odds are that you will *not* be showing your entire portfolio during an interview, and your prior research is likely to reveal that certain P.E.A.K.S. are far more important than others for each job you apply for. Still, if you can have several documents in each of the P.E.A.K.S. categories, you will have more options during your interview. You cannot know ahead of time what will happen during the interview, but if you have a wide variety of entries in your portfolio, you are likely to have more opportunities to show the right item at the right moment.

If there is a particular personal characteristic or a specific kind of experience, accomplishment, knowledge, or skill you know is considered highly desirable in a candidate, you should try to include several different documents that give evidence that you have this special something.

You may not be able to include entries in all of the P.E.A.K.S. categories, but you should give a high priority to identifying documents that indicate that you have the personal characteristics that the interviewer is likely to consider highly desirable. Remember, your portfolio gives you the opportunity to make these key intangibles tangible.

Be wary of featuring skills and knowledge that you do not *enjoy using.* If you have a skill or area of knowledge that you feel an interviewer would value but you do *not* enjoy using, look out! You may well find yourself getting a job you can't stand.

The more you are able to use skills and areas of knowledge that you enjoy developing and using, the happier you are likely to be. Assembling a Can-Do Portfolio will give you a great surge of confidence, but only if it features the P.E.A.K.S. that you value.

Include documents that enable you to lead from strength. Documents that demonstrate any of the desired P.E.A.K.S. that are *particular* strengths of yours should be considered strong candidates for inclusion in your targeted portfolio.

Use documents to address important concerns about your qualifications. Is there something about your candidacy that makes you vulnerable? An example of a vulnerability that can be effectively addressed with a good portfolio item would be the gender issue that a male obstetrics/gynecology physician would face. See, for example, the career situation of Zachary Schwartz, an OB/GYN, in Part 2. Roughly 80 percent of the doctors he would be competing against for a position in the women's health field would be female physicians. The burden was on him to overcome the presumption that female patients would find a female doctor far more sensitive to their needs and concerns than he, as a male, could ever be. For this reason he included in his portfolio a letter from a female patient that thanked him for his caring manner and sensitivity to her concerns and needs.

Try to include no more than twenty items in your Can-Do Portfolio. We would suggest that you first decide which items you feel make good entries in your Can-Do Portfolio, and then cut this list back, based on the physical capacity of the carrying case you choose to use and the number of documents that you feel is manageable. As a rule of thumb, we suggest that twenty documents is the absolute upper limit. And you certainly do not need this many items. In Part 2, we give examples of how nicely targeted portfolios can be assembled with only eight documents.

One thing to bear in mind is that the more documents you bring with you to an interview, the more time it will take to put your hands on a document that you suddenly decide you want to present. This brings us to our next subject, how best to organize the items in your Can-Do Portfolio.

HOW TO ORGANIZE YOUR CAN-DO PORTFOLIO

There is only one rule you must follow when choosing a system to organize the items in your Can-Do Portfolio: *Items must be easily retrievable under pressure.* With this rule in mind, the following are some things to think about.

Consider using some form of three-ring binder for your Can-Do Portfolio. Loose items that are stuffed into a briefcase can be hard to find when you are in the middle of an important conversation. Alternatively, these same items can be readily retrieved if they have been filed under headings in a three-ring binder. Furthermore, a person who is calmly flipping through the pages of a binder appears to be a lot better organized than someone who is fishing about with his head stuck in a briefcase! For this reason, we recommend that you use some form of three-ring binder for your Can-Do Portfolio items. We will discuss the look of this binder later in this chapter under "Getting the Right Look for Your Can-Do Portfolio."

Try using tabs with P.E.A.K.S. headings. We suggest that organizing the entries in your Can-Do Portfolio using the following six headings is very useful:

- Resume
- Personal characteristics
- Experience
- Accomplishments
- Knowledge
- Skills

If your Can-Do Portfolio is organized in the above fashion, you will find that it is very easy to put your finger on the document you need to highlight one of your P.E.A.K.S.

Clearly, some of your items could be filed under more than one of the above categories. In these cases you can put extra copies of the same document in several different sections, if that helps you locate it quickly.

The above organizational system is only a suggestion. You should use whatever filing system you find works best for easily retrieving examples of your P.E.A.K.S.

Include extra copies of your P.E.A.K.S. resume. Note that "Resume" is one of the tabs suggested above. Having several extra copies of your resume filed under this tab is extremely beneficial. This way, if some of the people with whom you are meeting do not have a copy of your resume, you can hand them one. Even if you sent your resume in advance of your interview, they may not have it.

A well-thought-out resume can give you openings to present key items in your portfolio. In Chapter 5, we will show you how to put together a P.E.A.K.S. resume that encourages interviewers to focus on your key P.E.A.K.S.

You can use a digital format for your Can-Do Portfolio in certain situations. In most face-to-face interviewing situations you will want to hand people documents that they can touch. They are more likely to trust an item they can hold than something they see on a screen. But in some situations having your Can-Do Portfolio stored on a disk can be quite effective. If you believe the digital option is appropriate for you, refer to Chapter 9 for ways to prepare and present a digital portfolio.

GETTING THE RIGHT LOOK FOR YOUR CAN-DO PORTFOLIO

When it comes time to use your Can-Do Portfolio, the effectiveness of your presentation will be determined not only by what you say and what you have in your portfolio but also by how everything looks. The following are some strategies you can use to get the right look for the portfolio you take to an interview.

Getting the Right Look for Your Carrying Case

As noted earlier, the carrying case for a portfolio that is taken to a meeting is typically an enclosed three-ring binder that can be zippered shut. The kind of impression you wish to make will, of course, determine the particular look you are trying to achieve with the carrying case for your Can-Do Portfolio.

Consider using a carrying case that looks like a briefcase. For most situations we recommend a binder that looks like a thin, leather briefcase. The beauty of carrying your portfolio items in what appears to be a briefcase is that it is not intrusive. In most cases you cannot know ahead of time whether or not the right opportunities will come up to present items from your portfolio. If your portfolio looks like a briefcase, you have the option of not using it, without drawing attention to the fact that you have brought a collection of portfolio items along. It's perfectly reasonable for you to show up for an interview carrying a briefcase. And you can, in fact, use your portfolio carrying case as a briefcase, as well, in which you might carry business cards, an appointment book, and a pad of lined paper for taking notes. Alternatively, a loose-leaf binder that is not zipped shut is likely to catch the interviewer's eye. If the interviewer asks what you have brought along, you have just lost control of when and how you present the items in your portfolio.

If a certain kind of carrying case is expected, use it. The nature of the field in which you will be interviewing is an important factor when choosing a carrying case. People in design fields are expected to have portfolios, and typically the carrying case is quite large to accommodate artwork that needs to be bigger than a sheet of notebook paper to be properly appreciated. On the other hand, if you are applying for an accounting or sales position, an 8½- by 11-inch format is probably just right.

Use a carrying case that blends. Another thing to bear in mind is that the carrying case for your portfolio can look very ordinary or quite sophisticated, depending upon the color and texture of the material used for its outside cover. You will want to avoid bringing to a meeting something that does not support the image you are trying to project. So, as a general rule, the design and look of your carrying case should be compatible with the kind of clothes you intend to wear. The less obtrusive your portfolio is, the more control you have over when you use it.

Getting the Right Look for Your Portfolio Items

As we will see in future chapters, typically when you present your portfolio, you hand a person one or two documents at a time. The following are some ways to increase the visual impact of these documents.

Photocopy your documents. To protect yourself in case you misplace your targeted portfolio, we recommend that you include only photocopies in your Can-Do Portfolio. Using photocopies has the added advantage of giving you more creative freedom with regard to the layout you use for presenting these documents.

Size your documents consistently. Provided that you do not alter the fundamental essence and integrity of a document, you can make certain adjustments like alteration in size when you photocopy the originals. Little photographs or memo-pad notes of appreciation can be enlarged to give them greater impact, and huge spreadsheets can be reduced in size to fit comfortably in your carrying case.

Try using collages. In addition to being able to make documents bigger or smaller than their original size, photocopying also makes it easy to create a collage of several documents on a single piece of paper. For example, you could photocopy several cards containing customer service comments onto a single notebook-sized page. And if you have several degrees or certificates that you would like to present, you could first photocopy each of them at a reduced size. By cutting and pasting, you can combine them all on one page that you then photocopy. If you are trying to make the point that you have been well educated or trained, this presentation could have quite an impact. For added effect, you might add to this paper the seals or logos of the institutions from which you received these degrees. But be careful! Documents must be presented clearly and not appear cluttered.

Remember, color sells. Items are visually most appealing and seem most authentic when they are copied in a way that captures their original color and texture. Pictures, logos, and other graphics that were originally in color should be copied with a process that captures the color and texture of the original document. It will cost a bit more to make photocopies in high-quality color, but as we have said before, color sells.

Use sheet protectors. Sliding your portfolio documents into clear plastic sleeves, known as sheet protectors, keeps the documents from becoming damaged or worn with frequent handling, and it can give them a nice, fresh look and feel. Three-ring sheet protectors have the further virtue of enabling you to store your documents in a binder, without having to punch holes in them.

We have found that heavy-duty, three-ring sheet protectors that are clear on both sides and can hold 8½- by 11-inch documents work quite well in most Can-Do Portfolios. You can find these items at most office supply and stationery stores.

Use the front and back of a sheet protector to link documents.
Using sheet protectors that are clear on both sides gives you the option
of displaying with one plastic sleeve two items that are linked. For example, if you did an important report that was well received, you might
put the executive summary or some other key page on the top side of
the sheet protector and a note or e-mail that praises this project on the
back. A page protector that is clear on both sides can also be used to
show both the front and the back of two-sided items, like brochures.

Store extra items behind displayed documents. Extra copies of documents can be stored behind the items that are displayed in sheet protectors. If, for example, there are several pages from a report that you
would really like to have available in the event that the interviewer is
intrigued by this project, you can store these pages behind the title
page or executive summary that you have displayed. Sandwiched between an executive summary on one side and a letter of commendation
on the flip side of the sheet protector, these pages are out of sight, but
easy to retrieve. You might also store extra copies of your resume behind the resume in your sheet protector.

FINAL THOUGHTS

The following are a few final suggestions.

*Have someone in the industry take a look at your proposed Can-Do
Portfolio.* Once you have put together what you think is a good Can-Do
Portfolio, it is very helpful if you can have someone who is knowledgeable about the job for which you are interviewing give you a critique of
your portfolio. Although in an actual job interview you are unlikely to
show more than a couple of items from your portfolio, you cannot know
in advance which of your items you will have an opportunity to present.
This limitation means that you would do well to have someone assess
the appropriateness of *all* of the items that you intend to include in
your Can-Do Portfolio.

Earlier in this chapter, we suggested that an excellent way to learn
about the desired P.E.A.K.S. for a job is to do formal, informational interviews with people who are in a position to know. Informational interviews are also useful for getting feedback on your Can-Do Portfolio
prior to using it in an actual job interview.

Do the best you can and then go with it. Don't be discouraged if you
feel that despite your best efforts your Can-Do Portfolio doesn't include
everything you think it should. Maybe there's an elusive document that
you can't seem to put your hands on. Or it could be there's an important skill that you haven't yet developed. In Chapter 8, we will discuss
strategies you can use to generate new P.E.A.K.S. that you can document in future portfolios. But no matter what you do, the fact is there
will always be something you wish you had in your portfolio but don't.

Missing some items is not the problem you may think it is. As
we've said, the best way to use your portfolio in an interview is not to
show the whole thing, but instead to present a few items at the right
moment. You may be aware that you are missing an item or two that

you would like to have, but the person to whom you are presenting your portfolio will not know this. Just because you are missing an arrow or two from your quiver doesn't mean you can't hit the target with the arrows you do have.

Let the P.E.A.K.S. in your Can-Do Portfolio give you confidence. The process of targeting your portfolio should make you very aware of the particular P.E.A.K.S. you have that are right for the job under consideration. Focus on these strengths and you will start looking forward to going to interviews that will give you opportunities to discuss these P.E.A.K.S.

You will know that whatever claims you make about yourself, you can back up. You will know this because you have a Can-Do Portfolio.

In the next chapter we will discuss everything you need to know about how to set up and then conduct an effective informational interview. You might want to at least skim this chapter to see if an informational interview is something you would like to do. Clients tell us that they find informational interviews not only very useful but also fun to do. But if you are pressed for time, you should proceed directly to Chapter 5.

4

Using Informational Interviews to Perfect Your Portfolio

OVERVIEW

In this chapter we will show you how to use informational interviews to get the precise information you need to create a portfolio that is tailored specifically for a future meeting. In the previous chapter, we alluded to the fact that informational interviews are a great tool for learning about the particular P.E.A.K.S. that an employer is likely to be seeking in job candidates. And we also suggested that informational interviews are useful for getting feedback on drafts of your Can-Do Portfolio. In this chapter, we will show you some strategies for getting and conducting informational interviews that are both fun and productive.

Specifically, we will review the following:

- What informational interviews are and why they are important
- Key things you can learn in an informational interview
- How to identify and then contact the right people to interview
- The homework you should do prior to these interviews
- How to conduct an informational interview

We noted in the past chapter that this is an optional chapter. You can, in fact, create a targeted portfolio without doing informational interviews. But you will get your best information for targeting your portfolio if you make the effort to do some informational interviews.

And here's an added bonus. In this chapter you will learn how informational interviews can be used for targeting your career. Do one, and you will probably want to do some more!

INFORMATIONAL INTERVIEWS: WHAT THEY ARE AND WHY THEY ARE IMPORTANT

Informational interviews are interviews that are used for gathering information. In the context of managing your career, informational interviews are primarily intended to generate information about industries, organizations, and jobs so that you can both make informed career decisions and learn how to present yourself effectively in future job interviews.

Whereas the primary reason for going on a *job* interview is to get job offers, the primary purpose of conducting an *informational* interview is to learn more about careers and jobs in a particular field and to learn what employers are looking for.

The more you can learn about what a particular field or job involves and what potential employers are looking for, the easier it is to select the documents to include in your targeted career portfolio. For this reason, it's a good idea to begin conducting informational interviews well ahead of the time you intend to actually start applying for jobs. Doing so will give you more time to prepare yourself and collect the documents you need to put together a strong portfolio. For example, you might discover that doing volunteer work or engaging in further training is necessary for enhancing your portfolio. If you've started early enough in the process, you'll have more time to attain these goals.

Unlike in a job interview, in an informational interview you will be asking most of the questions, and, therefore, the person you are interviewing should be doing most of the talking. Nevertheless, the person with whom you are speaking is likely to ask you about yourself. And so, as in a job interview, you will want to be prepared to share some key highlights about your background and, more importantly, be prepared to talk about your career goals.

It is decidedly bad form to appear to be angling for a job when your announced purpose is to have an informational interview. Nevertheless, the possibility always exists that the person you are speaking with may have a particular job in mind that you could be a candidate for. Whatever the circumstances, you can be sure that the person you are interviewing will be assessing you, even as you ask the questions. Therefore, you will want to make a good impression. Your desire to make a good impression doesn't necessarily mean that you are likely to show your portfolio during an informational interview. The informational interview is intended to give you some guidelines for developing and targeting a portfolio that you will use in the future. However, if your portfolio is in reasonable shape, you may decide to show it during an informational interview as a way of making a good impression and of getting useful feedback.

In addition to the obvious focus on information gathering, another important objective of an informational interview can be to build your network of contacts. The person you are interviewing could very well learn at some future date about jobs that might be just right for you. If you made a good impression and are still in his or her mind, this person will likely bring these opportunities to your attention. And, if you have established a good relationship, this person could also prove a useful advisor when you are assessing future job offers.

Another benefit you will get from doing an informational interview is practice describing yourself in a situation that is less pressured than a formal job interview. Clearly, becoming adept at informational interviewing is a skill that can prove valuable to you throughout your career.

KEY THINGS YOU CAN LEARN IN AN INFORMATIONAL INTERVIEW

As noted above, the main reason for conducting an informational interview is to gather information about jobs and careers in fields in which you might be interested. Having this information will enable you to make informed career decisions and will enable you to present yourself effectively in future job interviews. The following are some specific things you can learn in an informational interview.

Realistic Job Previews in Fields You Are Considering

First of all, you will want to learn as much as you can about what it would be like to be employed in the particular field you are exploring. Instead of focusing on learning about just the positive aspects of the field, you would do well to encourage the person you are interviewing to give you what is known as a realistic job preview. A *realistic job preview*, or RJP, is meant to be a complete and balanced picture, warts and all, of what to expect in a particular job. With an RJP, you are hoping to gain an understanding of the job that is closer to reality than the descriptions you are likely to read in promotional literature put out by employers and professional organizations. An RJP can both supplement and rebut the information you have already gathered.

The literature on realistic job previews primarily focuses on the desirability of recruiters giving job applicants a balanced picture of what the job will be like, so that the person who ultimately accepts the job is less likely to be subsequently disappointed. For more on this, see, John Wanous, *Organizational Entry: Recruitment, Selection, and Socialization of Newcomers,* 2nd Ed. (Addison-Wesley, 1992). People who conduct informational interviews would also do well to make sure they get a realistic job preview.

The P.E.A.K.S. That Employers Are Looking for in Your Intended Field

Once you determine that you are indeed interested in pursuing a job in the area you've been discussing, you will then need to know what qualities employers are looking for in job candidates.

Learning about the specific P.E.A.K.S. that employers are seeking in candidates can also provide guidelines for selecting items to include in your targeted Can-Do Portfolio. You will also learn about areas where employers might perceive you as weak or even unqualified. This information will give you the opportunity to make some improvements before actually applying for the job you have your heart set on. You may need to do more training in a particular skill area before going on a job interview. For example, your computer skills could fall short of what employers in your chosen field are looking for, and so you would do well to take an appropriate computer course before applying for a job in this field.

An Insider's View of Desirable Personal Characteristics for a Particular Job

If the person you interview is working in the field you are considering, an informational interview can be particularly useful for learning more about the personal characteristics of people who are currently in demand for the particular kind of job that you are considering. Job postings and formal job descriptions typically focus on the skills, knowledge, and experience that a candidate should have and reveal little about the desired personal characteristics. But, as we have said several times before, the majority of employers that we have surveyed in many different fields have indicated that, when assessing candidates for a job, they give highest priority to personal characteristics that add value.

The precise definition of what these personal characteristics are will vary with industries and employers. Informational interviews can help you learn more about the specific characteristics that are most valued for the kind of job you are considering. This knowledge will enable you to decide which of your personal characteristics you should try to feature in your Can-Do Portfolio.

Of course, if the personal characteristics that employers are looking for are not a good description of the real you, and you hear this from more than one person that you talk to, you may want to reconsider your career choice. You will never be happy trying to be someone you are not. You want to develop a portfolio that not only resonates with potential employers but is also in tune with the real you!

What a Person Like You Should Know about Jobs You Are Exploring

The ideal informational interview is with a person who not only has firsthand knowledge of the field and type of job you are exploring but is also like you in some significant way. Maybe this person has already made the kind of career shift you are now considering. Or she might have had an education that is similar to yours. When there are significant points of similarity between you and the person you are interviewing, there is a particularly good chance that you will get insights that are relevant to your situation.

Feedback on Drafts of Your Can-Do Portfolio

If you have prepared a draft of your targeted Can-Do Portfolio, informational interviews are a great place to get low-risk feedback on the appropriateness of the items you are thinking of including. The odds are that the person you are interviewing will be intrigued by the fact that you have a portfolio and will be interested in taking a look at it.

Further Leads

If the interview goes well, the person you are talking with is likely to suggest further people you should talk to and may even provide you with some job leads. You may also be able to get an insider's view of the next steps you should take to get the kind of job you are seeking.

HOW TO GET USEFUL INFORMATIONAL INTERVIEWS

To get good information about a job or field in which you are interested, you need to talk to people who are both knowledgeable about the field or type of job that you wish to learn more about and willing to talk to you.

The following are some strategies to set up informational interviews with people who can help you.

Think broadly about people who might be knowledgeable. The kinds of people who might be particularly useful to interview are not limited to current incumbents of the kind of job you are looking for. Here are some other categories to consider:

- People who have entered the field you are interested in recently (in the past couple of years) and who can tell you what it's like
- Senior people who have pursued careers in the field and can provide some perspective
- People who have recently left the field
- People who work with people in the field—consultants, suppliers, and so on.

Contact the least intimidating people first. This step will get you started. Comfortable initial contacts might include friends, extended family members, parents' friends, friends' parents, professors, former employers, teammates, classmates, alumni of schools you went to, trusted colleagues, and so on. Your initial contacts may not be the people you wish to interview but, instead, be people who can refer you to people to interview.

Seek out friends of friends. When developing contacts, you should know that your most promising leads are most likely to come from friends of friends rather than from the people you actually know at the beginning of your search. So, if you don't know anyone in the field in which you'd like to do an informational interview, that's not a barrier. The odds are that someone you know will know someone in your chosen field. And most certainly a friend of a friend will know someone who would be a good interview for you. The key thing is to get the word out among people you trust that you are looking to do some informational interviews in a particular field.

If a person you want to interview is a friend of a friend, your chances of getting an interview are improved if your friend makes the first contact. If this arrangement cannot be made, you will at least want to refer to your friend when you initially contact this person.

Try writing first, then following up with a phone call. The most polite and probably easiest approach to obtain an informational interview is to write a letter (or send an e-mail) and then follow up with a phone call. When you write, be sure to mention how you got that person's name—for example, "My uncle John Doe recommended that I write to you." Include your resume and mention that you are in the process of learning more about careers in that person's field. It doesn't hurt to tell him you understand that he has had a lot of interesting experience and you would be very appreciative if he could spend a little time with you sharing his thoughts on what it's like to be in the career he is in. Most people like to talk about themselves; let them know this will be an opportunity to do so.

When you do your follow-up phone call to ask for an appointment, be sure to convey to this person that you're *not* looking for him to spend half a day with you. Tell him that you know he's "incredibly busy," and so, any time he can give you would be "truly appreciated." You might say something like: "I know you've got a tough schedule. I'd love to meet with you whenever it's convenient for you, maybe for cup of coffee, or whatever works best for you."

Although it is preferable to meet in person, an informational interview can take place over the phone.

Make an extra effort to meet with busy people. A busy person is an active person who is typically "in the know" about the very things you are most interested in. If the person you are trying to get an appointment with starts grumbling about her busy schedule, you can say something like: "You know, it's busy people like you who can give me the best insights into what it's like to be in your field. I'd really love to talk to you. I'm ready to meet you anywhere, or, if you'd prefer, we could talk on the phone sometime." If she still doesn't seem at all intrigued or interested, it's best not to push it.

Tell that person you're sorry she won't be able to talk to you personally, but that you can certainly understand why this is the case, given her busy schedule. You might then ask, "Is there someone else you could recommend that I might talk to, so that I can learn more about your field? Maybe someone in your organization?" You may be able to salvage a lead out of this otherwise dying conversation! And, of course, remember to thank the person in a gracious manner. You don't want to burn any bridges!

Try to interview someone in this field who is like you in some significant way. As noted earlier, particularly useful are people with whom you have something in common and who have been successful in a field that you are interested in. The more similar the person is to you, the better the read you will get on what it would be like for you to be in this job or field.

Try to set up appointments with at least three different people. You will want to make sure that you are not relying on just one person's opinion. For this reason it is a good idea to have informational interviews with at least *three* different people for each job area that you are exploring.

Talk to people in the target organization last. If you are able to find a contact at a place where you might really like to work, you may want to wait a bit to arrange an interview. Information you gather from other interviews along the way will enable you to ask just the right questions of this insider.

Of course, if you only have time for one informational interview, then your top choice should probably be someone from the target organization.

HOW TO PREPARE FOR AN INFORMATIONAL INTERVIEW

Although the purpose of an informational interview is to obtain information, prior research and preparation are still essential. The more you know going into an interview, the better your questions will be. And if you have done your homework, you won't have to burn up valuable time asking basic questions about things you could have found out on your own. In an informational interview you want to focus on picking up insider information that you are unlikely to get from a printed source.

Remember, the better prepared you are for this interview, the better the impression you are likely to make on a person who has the potential to help you. The following are some ways to prepare for an informational interview.

Do prior research on the person and the organization. Learn something about the person you are going to see, beginning with his or her title. You also need to have information about the company or organization, along with its products or services, size, and place in the market. You should not have to ask for information that is easily available elsewhere. In particular, make sure you have studied the organization's Web site and that you have skimmed newspapers, weekly news magazines, and trade journals for current information on the organization.

Prepare key questions ahead of time. Write down the key questions you want to ask. It is not inappropriate to bring this list. In fact, it's a good way of letting the interviewee know that you have done your homework and are well prepared. Later in this chapter, in the section on conducting interviews, we will suggest some key questions you might consider asking.

Be prepared to talk about yourself. While you will be responsible for conducting the interview, the person with whom you are speaking is, nevertheless, likely to ask you about yourself. In fact, it is a good idea to talk a little bit at the beginning of the interview about your background and to articulate your current career goals. Having this knowledge will enable the person with whom you are talking to give you the kind of information and advice that would be most helpful to you.

It is a good idea to practice giving a 2- to 3-minute summary of your background and the career direction that you are now considering. Learn how to get to the point quickly. The more you practice, the less rambling and more focused you are likely to be.

Consider preparing a resume for this interview. Being able to bring a good resume to informational interviews offers some advantages. You can hand your resume to the people whom you are interviewing and in a matter of seconds they can get a quick overview of your background. And if the interview goes well, they can use this resume to describe you to other people and maybe even send it to a job lead that occurs to them. You might also ask them to give you feedback on your resume.

On the other hand, you may decide that you would prefer to create a resume after an informational interview, so that you can use what you learn to further target and hone your resume. If your interviewees ask you for a copy of your resume, you can always tell them you are in the process of reworking it and that you would be happy to send them a copy. In fact, you can include a copy of your revised resume with your thank-you note and mention that the interview gave you the precise information and insights you needed to get your resume into its current form.

So, whether or not you prepare a resume in advance of an informational interview is up to you. But bear in mind, an informational interview does give you an excellent opportunity to get constructive feedback on your resume.

Assemble a careful draft of your Can-Do Portfolio, if you are ready to do so. As noted earlier, informational interviews can also be used to get constructive feedback on drafts of your Can-Do Portfolio.

If you intend to bring a draft of your targeted portfolio to an informational interview, the items that you include should be carefully selected according to the criteria discussed in earlier chapters. The carrying case should be the one you intend to use on a job interview. And the items should be well organized and have the look that you intend to achieve when you present them in a job interview.

Showing up at an informational interview with a big stack of disorganized, loose items and asking, "So, which of these do you think I should include in my portfolio?" would be inappropriate. For starters, the person you are interviewing might not know much about career portfolios, and so it would be unreasonable to expect her to show you how to put together a good portfolio. More importantly, you would be wasting that person's time by having her sift through potential portfolio items. What you are trying to do is get feedback on the impact of your best effort at assembling a convincing portfolio.

So, if you wish to get useful feedback on the latest draft of your Can-Do Portfolio, it should be as good as you can make it at that point in time. And it should look exactly the way you think it should look if you were taking it to a job interview.

HOW TO CONDUCT AN INFORMATIONAL INTERVIEW

It's important that you have a clear idea of how to proceed when you conduct an informational interview. If you go about the interview in a well-organized fashion, you will give yourself your best chance of getting what you want from the interview. And you will come across as being very professional.

Creating a good impression can pay dividends. There are many reasons why you should strive to make as good an impression as you can, just as you would if you were interviewing for a job. Here are just a few:

1. You have asked someone for a favor. You would certainly like this person to remember that you were gracious and appreciative, as well as enthusiastic, bright, and articulate;
2. The person might be thinking of hiring someone in the near future;
3. Your interviewee might be told the next day that his or her company would like to hire someone;
4. A professional colleague of this person might ask if he or she can recommend any good candidates for an opening;
5. You might work with this person in another capacity, as a client, customer, or colleague, sometime in the future;
6. You might want this person to be someone you can turn to for future advice.

The Stages of a Successful Informational Interview

To get the information that you need and to create a good impression in the process of doing so, it is helpful if you think of an informational interview in terms of the following four stages:

- <u>I</u>ntroductory stage
- <u>N</u>eed-to-know stage
- <u>F</u>inding further leads stage
- <u>O</u>bliging stage

Note that we have underlined the first letter of the word that describes each stage of the interview and that together the letters create the acronym I.N.F.O. If you can remember that you are seeking I.N.F.O. in an informational interview, this acronym will help you keep focused on what you want to accomplish during each stage of a well-conducted informational interview.

The following are some things to think about as you pilot the interview through each of the above stages, beginning with the introductory stage.

Introductory Stage

First impressions can be lasting impressions. Ordinarily, you should dress and behave exactly as you would for a regular interview. However, if the person suggests that you meet, not at his or her office, but at home or at a coffee shop or other informal location, then it would be acceptable to dress a bit more casually, but never in blue jeans, shorts, sundresses, or other distinctly "play clothes." The following are some points to keep in mind during the introductory stage of the interview:

- Thank the person for making time for you.
- Confirm the amount of time the person can give you, so that you don't overstay.
- Talk a little about your mutual contact, if a friend helped you set up the interview.
- Explain why you asked for an interview. Give a *short* explanation of who you are and why you want to talk to this person: "To determine if this job/organization/field would be right for me. And to find out what employers are looking for in candidates."
- If you have prepared a resume, this is a good time to hand it to your interviewee. Even if you've already sent the person one, you should bring extra copies to the interview, as it might have been misplaced. Your resume is particularly useful at this stage of the interview for giving a quick summary of your background. Moreover, if the person with whom you are speaking asks to keep your resume, it can serve as a reminder of you and also be something he can show to others.
- Do not give the people you are interviewing the impression you are looking for them to give you a job or help you get a job. If you do, they will most likely resent the fact that you have, in effect, deceived them. You said you wanted to get advice from them and now you're pestering them for a job! They know you're looking for a new job; if they want to mention some possibilities in their firm, fine. But let them make the first move.

Need-to-Know Stage

Once you have completed the brief introductory phase, you will want to spend the bulk of the time you have asking the interviewee questions about what it's really like to be in the job or organization or career you've come to learn about. And, as noted earlier, you will want to learn more about what employers are looking for when they interview candidates for positions in this field.

As a result of your research, you may have developed some industry-specific questions for your discussion. It is usually helpful, however, to begin the discussion with a few broad or general questions. And, remember to be sensitive to the age and title of the person with whom you are speaking. Certainly, you will ask different questions of a chief executive officer than of a marketing assistant.

Feel free to take notes. Writing down what they say usually flatters interviewees. A tape recorder, however, might upset them and could put a damper on candor. What follows are the specific topics you will likely need to know.

Try to get a realistic job preview (RJP). Once you've covered the general issues, you can tell the interviewee that you would like to get as realistic a picture as possible of what it's like to be in this job/organization/career. To begin to get a balanced view, you can ask questions like the following:

- "What did you do this past week that you see as typical of a career in this field?"
- "What do you wish you'd known more about before entering this career?"
- "What would you say are the two things that are really great about this organization and what two things do you wish were different?" Listen carefully for the real message, then probe with questions like: "Can you say more about . . . ?"

You will also want to discount the biases of the person you are interviewing. If this person was recently fired or demoted or is a competitor of the organization you are trying to learn more about, certain biases are likely to surface, despite the interviewee's attempts to be objective.

The goal of an RJP is not to linger on the negatives but to get a balanced picture so that you can make an informed career choice. And please bear in mind that whatever job you take, you will have to, as the expression goes, "dig some dirt." In other words, you will always have to do some unpleasant things you don't really want to do, if you hope to be successful.

One final point about RJPs: Learn as much as you can about the "culture" of the organizations for which you think you might want to work. By organizational culture, we mean the often tacit, but nevertheless very real, rules and shared understandings that seem to govern behavior in a particular organization. You will want to know what sort of behavior gets rewarded (risk-taking? conservative analysis? team efforts? individual contributions?), and what kind of behavior is frowned upon, despite what you might read in the promotional literature.

Ask questions that will tell you if the organizations you might work for are the kinds of places you would like in terms of the "climate" and "feel" you desire. People's happiness in their jobs often has a lot to do with the fact that they are comfortable with the culture of the organization they are working for. Yet this area is the one where job seekers often do the least due diligence. Many job seekers get so focused on things like salary and job content that they don't make a sufficient effort to find out what the organization is like to work for day in and day out.

Ask about the P.E.A.K.S. that employers are looking for in candidates. The second major task in the need-to-know stage is to find out what employers are looking for in candidates for the type of job you have been discussing.

The P.E.A.K.S. acronym can be helpful here. Each letter of P.E.A.K.S. suggests a question you might ask:

P: "What *personal characteristics* are highly valued by employers?"

E: "What *experience* is highly valued?"

A: "What kinds of *accomplishments* are employers looking for?"

K: "What *knowledge* is highly valued?"

S: "What *skills* are employers looking for?

It is helpful to know which of the above P.E.A.K.S. is most important to employers in a specific field: Personal characteristics? Experience? Skills? And why do employers feel this way?

As noted earlier, the answers to these questions will give you some good guidelines for selecting items to include in your targeted Can-Do Portfolio. And you can learn if there are areas where employers will perceive you as weak or even unqualified, so that you can make some improvements before actually applying for a job in this field.

Ask about which personal characteristics that add value are perceived as key. As noted earlier, the P category, personal characteristics that add value, is typically perceived as very important by employers. However, the precise definition of what these characteristics are will vary with industries and employers. So asking the interviewee questions like the following is important:

■ "Which of the personal characteristics that you mentioned are most important?"

■ "What would you say are the top three personal characteristics that add value in the eyes of potential employers?"

Ask "why" questions to understand the mind-set of the people in the organization and field you are considering. You want to understand not only *what* employers in a particular field and organization feel is important but also *why* they feel this way. The better you understand the key assumptions and biases that shape the mind-set of the people you will be showing your portfolio to, the easier it will be to select the right items and present them in the right way.

Unless your interviewee happens to know the particular person with whom you will be meeting for a job interview, there is no way to know for sure what the particular biases of the individual will be. But there do tend to be certain professional biases that practitioners are likely to acquire in their field. Organizations can have a particular corporate culture that is likely to influence the thinking of all of their employees.

Rather than talking about mind-set, which might be an unfamiliar concept, the best way to learn more about the professional biases of practitioners in a particular field and organization is to ask your interviewee a lot of "why" questions. As your interviewee answers the various P.E.A.K.S. questions, you can probe with follow-up "why" questions, such as the following:

■ "*Why* are people in this organization likely to give such importance to this particular personal characteristic?"
■ "*Why* do they feel that this kind of experience is particularly valuable to have?"

Get feedback on your Can-Do Portfolio, if it is ready to show. A good time to get feedback on the latest draft of your Can-Do Portfolio is after you have covered the key RJP and P.E.A.K.S. questions. Both you and your interviewee will have fresh in your minds the key things that employers in your intended field are likely to be seeking in candidates.

Provided that you are not asking your interviewee to sift through a huge pile of items, you should feel comfortable showing your interviewee a select group of items that you are considering for inclusion in your portfolio. What you are hoping to get is feedback from someone who is in a position to know about which items are likely to be most impressive and which documents you should probably leave home.

Explain to your interviewee that in an actual job interview, you would probably show only a few of these items. And then ask her which would be the best ones to try to show. As noted earlier, the odds are that your interviewee will be intrigued by the fact that you have a portfolio and will be very interested in taking a look at it.

Get feedback on your resume, if it is ready to show. As with drafts of your targeted portfolio, you will also want to get feedback on your resume. The key issue is to find out if it is properly targeted. Your interviewee is unlikely to want to spend a lot of time editing your resume line by line, but you can ask questions like these:

■ "Will this resume help me get job interviews in the field we have been discussing?"
■ "What sort of changes would you recommend that I make to improve my chances of getting job interviews?"

Finding Further Leads Stage

Although it is important not to appear to be asking your interviewee for a job, it is entirely appropriate for you to ask in an informational interview what the interviewee thinks your next steps should be. You might ask:

■ "Is there anyone else that you think I should talk to?"
■ "How might I contact this person?"
■ "Is this a person I should call directly, or would you like to speak to him first?"
■ "Can I use your name when contacting this person?"

Finally, without saying or even implying that you want this person to either give you a job or even help you get a job, it is perfectly appropriate to ask for advice on how you should go about getting a job in this area. Good questions might be:

- "Knowing what you know about me, what do you feel would be the best way for me to get a job in this field?"
- "If you were me, what would you do next to get a job in this field?"
- "Is there something I should have asked you that I haven't?"

Obliging Stage

As noted earlier, although you are not being evaluated with respect to a specific position, you can be sure that the person with whom you are speaking is forming impressions of you. If you make a good impression, this person might be able to help you sometime in the future. To make a good impression, you do not want to just focus on selling yourself. You also want to make the other person feel *appreciated* by you. The more this person feels appreciated by you, the more likely he or she will be to help you in the future.

Here are some ways to make your interviewees feel appreciated:

- *Be a good listener.* Listen attentively, sympathetically, and don't interrupt.
- *Nod appreciatively when your interviewees think they've made a good point.* Nodding doesn't mean you necessarily agree with them, it just means you understand what they are saying and why they feel the way they do.
- *Show that you respect how important and busy they are by not over-staying your welcome.* Because you requested the meeting, it is your responsibility to monitor the time. If you asked for a half hour, you should point out that you are asking your final question as it gets close to that time. If the person with whom you are speaking encourages you to continue or says that she would be willing to talk for another twenty minutes, thank her and continue. Otherwise, stick to the original plan and take responsibility for bringing the interview to a close: "This conversation has been most helpful to me, Ms. Smith. I know you've got a lot of important things to attend to. Thank you very much for your time."
- *Continue to be obliging **after** the interview.* If you've been polite, listened carefully to everything that has been said, and been appropriately appreciative along the way, the chances are you will get some very useful information during the interview. You will also be well on your way to making a friend who could prove very useful to you. So it is important to keep in touch.
- *Write a thank-you note **immediately** after the informational interview.* If you can, pick up on something they said or advised you to do and tell them how you intend to follow through.
- *Write thank-you notes when you get a job.* Your contact should not cease with a post-interview thank-you note. It is courteous, and can also be helpful, to keep the people you meet informed of your

progress, by writing to let them know when you find a new job. You may write a handwritten note if you wish, but make sure the tone is professional. Include, if you can, something that they said or did that helped you in the process. When someone has assisted you, he or she becomes a stakeholder in your success and will, except in rare instances, be delighted and interested to know what happens to you.

- *Keep in touch periodically.* Most everyone has something they are passionate about. Keep a file in which you note next to each interviewee's name at least one strong interest that he has, at work or in his personal life. In the future, whenever you come across something that might be of interest to people on your list, let them know about the article, event, or whatever. The best way to maintain a network of useful contacts is to *make yourself useful* to others. You don't want to be in the position of only calling people when you need a favor. The more reciprocal the relationship, the stronger the link. Of course, you don't want to overdo this, either. A periodic note is a lot more powerful than "weekly updates"!

FINAL THOUGHTS

The above suggestions are just that—suggestions. It would certainly be unwise to blindly follow any predetermined outline. If you have a clear idea of what you would like to get out of the interview and are mindful of the I.N.F.O. outline, you can feel free to capture the moment and "go with the flow," when the interviewee feels like getting expansive on a particular topic. Since you know what you want to achieve, you will be able to use appropriate junctures to return to the key questions you want to ask.

In the appendix we have included an Informational Interview Debriefing Form. We recommend that you review this form as you prepare for doing an informational interview and that you fill it in after the interview to summarize the key things you learned about the job you are considering. Whether or not you choose to use this form, you should bring your own specific questions to the interview and take notes on the key points your interviewee makes.

5

Creating Resumes That Work with Your Portfolio

OVERVIEW

In this chapter we will show you how to create a P.E.A.K.S. resume that not only sets you up to show key items from your portfolio during an interview but also improves your chances of *getting* that interview in the first place.

Specifically we will review:

- What you should be able to achieve with your resume
- How a P.E.A.K.S. resume format can help you achieve these goals
- How to create a "master resume" that puts the right stuff at your fingertips
- How to target your resume for going after a particular job

If you are wondering whether you should put in the extra effort to create a P.E.A.K.S. resume, here are some things to consider.

Special bonus: You can get more job interviews with a P.E.A.K.S. resume. The fact that a P.E.A.K.S. resume format is unusually effective for getting job interviews was a discovery that occurred during the development and testing of our portfolio system.

As we began showing people how to create and then use a Can-Do Portfolio that demonstrates P.E.A.K.S., we were often asked what kind of resume would work best with this portfolio. We knew that a traditional resume would be perfectly adequate, and so for a while we suggested that our portfolio clients simply use any of the traditional approaches for creating their resume.

But as we thought about it more, we realized that you could use P.E.A.K.S. subheadings in your resume to prompt questions about activities associated with items in your portfolio. And so we developed a P.E.A.K.S. resume format that was designed to create openings to show portfolio items. It worked. But it did something else as well. Our clients told us they felt they got more job interviews when they used a properly targeted P.E.A.K.S. resume.

You can use the work you've already done for your portfolio. As we will see in this chapter, the system for creating a P.E.A.K.S. resume parallels the process used for creating a Can-Do Portfolio. This means you can use whatever research you've already done in connection with putting together a Can-Do Portfolio.

If you are in a big rush to get a resume together, you can take a shortcut. You are most likely to create your best resume if you follow the recommendations in this chapter. But if you are in a huge rush, you can study the examples of targeted resumes in Part 2, and then do your best to try to emulate what you see there for your own resume.

RESUMES: WHAT THEY ARE AND WHY THEY ARE IMPORTANT

A resume is typically a one- to two-page summary of the highlights of a person's education, work experience, and career-relevant *non*work experience. As noted in the previous chapter, you can use a resume in an informational interview to give the person from whom you are seeking advice a quick overview of your background. But the key use for a resume is in connection with going after a particular job.

When you are seeking a job, the fundamental purpose of a resume is to help you get job interviews. Once you've made it to a job interview, a resume can also serve as a starting point for reviewing your credentials for a particular job. And after this interview is over, your interviewer may very well use your resume as a quick way of describing you to other people in the organization. So having a resume that's just right can make a big difference.

Your resume can create opportunities to show your portfolio. In addition to the traditional reasons for putting together a well-thought-out resume, here's another thing to consider. If you have created a targeted portfolio that you would like to use during a job interview, handing your interviewer a resume that highlights key things about you that you can support with items from your portfolio is likely to create opportunities for you to show some of these items.

A good resume directs the reader's attention to your key qualifications for a job. Clearly, what you put in a resume is very important. You will want to include the things that are most likely to receive favorable attention from a prospective employer. But it's not just a matter of finding the right things to include; it's also important that you properly direct people's attention to the very things you want people to know about you. And do so quickly.

Typically, when a person first receives your resume, you will not be there to explain it, and the recipient will spend no more than ten seconds looking at it. You can't assume that if something that you think is very important is included in your resume, the recipient will see it. Nor is it reasonable to assume that just because you've listed something, the reader will understand its relevance to the job you are seeking. For example, listing the title and duties of a position you once had does not guarantee that the reader will instantly recognize the key *skills* you displayed in this job. And yet, the skills you used in this job may be just the skills the recipient of your resume is looking for.

Your resume will be most effective if the "format" of your resume—the organization and arrangement of the information it includes—directs the reader's attention to key things you have that a prospective employer is hoping to find in a job candidate. A P.E.A.K.S. resume format can do just that.

THE BENEFITS OF USING A P.E.A.K.S. RESUME

Definition of a P.E.A.K.S. resume. A P.E.A.K.S. resume is basically any resume that categorizes key items according to the kind of *personal characteristic, experience, accomplishment, knowledge,* or *skill* they exemplify and is achieved by using P.E.A.K.S. subheadings.

Instead of just listing the things you did within a job, in a P.E.A.K.S. resume you would organize what you have done according to the P.E.A.K.S. categories. If, for example, the job required the mastery of certain computer skills, you would list the particular computer systems you used under the subheading "Computer Skills." If the job also required you to work directly with customers, you would list this skill under the subheading "Customer Service Skills." The key things you achieved within a job would be listed under the subheading "Accomplishments." Special knowledge of a market or industry would be so identified under the heading "Knowledge." Each of these subheadings would be listed under the job where these P.E.A.K.S. were developed or exemplified.

To get a quick idea of what P.E.A.K.S. resumes look like, see Part 2 and examine some of the examples there of P.E.A.K.S. resumes.

You can, of course, use any resume format you like to pursue job interviews. And there is no one format you must use for your resume in order to introduce your portfolio. We would suggest, however, that you are likely to get your best results if you use a P.E.A.K.S. resume. Here's why.

A P.E.A.K.S. resume format can be used to highlight desired qualifications. In a properly targeted P.E.A.K.S. resume, the subheadings that specify particular P.E.A.K.S. would be determined not just by what you have done but also by your best guess as to what the prospective employer to whom you will be sending your resume will be seeking in a candidate.

So if, for example, the person who will be receiving your resume is likely to believe that multitasking skills are very desirable in a job candidate, and you have demonstrated these skills in a particular job, you would include the subheading "Multitasking Skills" beneath your listing of this particular job. You could then list several activities or projects that required multitasking skills.

By making connections very explicit, P.E.A.K.S. resumes leave less to chance. You might say, isn't it obvious that a particular job or project requires certain kinds of skills or knowledge? Maybe to you, but the person who reads your resume might not make the connection between what you did and the key P.E.A.K.S. that are being sought in a job candidate. Remember, the recipient of your resume is unlikely to spend more than a few seconds reviewing its contents.

By making very explicit the connections between what you have done and the key P.E.A.K.S. that are being sought in job candidates, you do not leave it to the reader's imagination to determine the possible relevance of items in your resume to the job under consideration. For this approach to be successful, of course, you need to have done some research and have a clear idea as to the desired P.E.A.K.S. for this particular job.

Extra work is required on your part to categorize key items in your resume according to P.E.A.K.S. they exemplify, but the effort is worth it. A properly targeted P.E.A.K.S. resume leaves it less to chance that the reader will understand why the skills and experiences you listed in your resume make you a strong candidate for the job under consideration.

P.E.A.K.S. resumes are particularly useful for identifying transferable skills. People who are attempting to make a substantial shift in the direction of their career are under a particular burden to make the case that some of the things they learned and achieved in their previous jobs are relevant to the new field they wish to enter. Adding to this challenge is the fact that prospective employers often do not know enough about what was required in a career-switcher's previous jobs to quickly understand that these jobs involved important transferable skills. A P.E.A.K.S. format can highlight useful transferable skills that a prospective employer might otherwise miss in a more traditional resume.

P.E.A.K.S. resumes are easy to speed-read. Recipients of resumes typically get annoyed when a resume contains a tangle of information that is hard to slug through. They want to get the key points quickly so that they can decide whether or not this person is, in their opinion, worth talking to.

Because a P.E.A.K.S. resume uses headings that specify the relevance of key items, it's an "easy read." The format enables readers to get the important points quickly. And because a P.E.A.K.S. resume is easy to digest, its length can be extended to more than one page.

P.E.A.K.S. resumes can be constructed to create openings to show portfolio items. You can use P.E.A.K.S. headings in your resume to draw attention to things you have in your portfolio that interviewers are likely to be interested in learning more about. Using P.E.A.K.S.

headings is likely to prompt questions that will give you openings to show key portfolio items that give tangible evidence that you, indeed, have these desired P.E.A.K.S.

P.E.A.K.S. resumes get noticed—in a positive way. Using a P.E.A.K.S. format gives your resume a distinct look that improves the chances that it will get noticed in a stack of traditional resumes. It's different, but not in a silly way like, say, using shocking purple paper that will definitely get noticed but is likely to achieve nothing more than making the print much harder to read!

The P.E.A.K.S. resume format is distinctly different in a way that is helpful to the reader. The extra effort you put into highlighting your P.E.A.K.S. is effort the reader does not have to make to figure out just what it is you have that might be relevant to the job under consideration.

As we noted at the start of this section, you can certainly use any resume format you like to pursue jobs. But we do believe that a P.E.A.K.S. resume format works best in all phases of the job-seeking process. Our clients and students keep telling us that when they use a P.E.A.K.S. resume they get more job interviews and during the interview they often get compliments on their resume, such as, "Hey, this is great! Where did you learn to do this resume?"

In the following sections we will show you how you can create a P.E.A.K.S. resume that works.

CREATING A P.E.A.K.S. MASTER RESUME

The actual resume you use for a particular job should be a succinct synopsis of your experience and education, presented in a format that highlights the very things that are most likely to receive favorable attention from the people who will be receiving your resume. This would be your "targeted" resume, and you should expect over the course of time to target your resume in many different ways, as you take aim at many different audiences.

One of the problems associated with creating targeted resumes is that typically you are not given a lot of time to put them together. When people ask you for a copy of your resume, you don't want to take a long time getting it to them, as this might suggest you are not particularly interested in the opportunity they have in mind for you. You could send along a copy of an old resume, but this may not include your latest information, and it's not likely to be properly targeted for pursuing a new opportunity.

Create a master resume that you can cut and paste. So that you are always ready to put together a great resume on short notice, it's extremely helpful if you can have on file a periodically updated master resume that lists everything you might want to consider when creating a targeted resume. This master list becomes a resource from which you can select particular items for inclusion in a resume that is targeted at obtaining a particular job or work assignment.

If you save this master resume in your computer as a template, you will have the ability to quickly create a shorter, targeted resume without danger of losing the original. To create a targeted resume, you would simply make a copy of your master resume, delete the items you don't want to use, and then edit the rest.

Use the P.E.A.K.S. categories for your master resume. The creation of a targeted portfolio will go a lot faster if the things you want to use from your master resume are already in a P.E.A.K.S. format. Filing the items in your master resume according to the P.E.A.K.S. they exemplify also makes it easier to quickly identify the best things to use for a targeted resume.

In early drafts of your master resume, stress length, not strength. It doesn't matter if you include marginal things in your master resume that ultimately prove to be weak items. This isn't a resume you will show to anybody; it's just a file that itemizes things you might conceivably use. Your goal should be to make your master resume as complete as possible, so that when it comes time to pick and choose items for a targeted resume, you will know that you have considered everything that might work.

Use the items in your Master Portfolio collection for inspiration. The items that you have collected for your Master Portfolio will remind you of things you have done that should be included in your master resume. If you have already categorized these items according to the P.E.A.K.S. they best exemplify, that too will be helpful, as it will suggest which of the P.E.A.K.S. subheadings the activities associated with these documents should be listed under.

SUGGESTED CONTENT FOR YOUR P.E.A.K.S. MASTER RESUME

A good way to begin putting together your master resume is to keep it simple and use the following basic categories that are found in most resumes:

- Name, address, telephone number, and e-mail address
- Overview
- Work experience
- Education
- Additional information
- References

You can change these categories any time you want, but you've got to start somewhere.

When creating a rough first draft, do not be concerned with tidiness and getting everything just right. The important thing is to get something down on paper that you can develop and change as more ideas occur to you.

Please note, too, that if you are in a field that uses a curriculum vitae format for resumes, you will be expected to provide a complete record of all of your professional activities, including a list of all of your publications, major presentations, and professional honors.

As we review what should go into each of the above categories, we'll point out some of the places where you can use P.E.A.K.S. subheadings to highlight your key qualifications.

Name, Address, Telephone Number, and E-Mail Address

Typically the name you use on your resume should include your full first name. If you like to use a shortened version of your first name in formal situations, you can use this on your resume, but obvious nicknames should be avoided. One of the authors uses Frank instead of his full first name, Franklin, for his resume. But he does not include nicknames that his friends from school still use, which he prefers to leave to your imagination.

You should use an address where you are easily reachable and *want* to be reached. If you have a job and don't wish to be contacted at work (which is usually the case), you can use your home address.

If you are a student and have a campus address that does not apply during vacations or after graduation, you should give both a college and a permanent address. You might use your parents' home address, a post office box, or the address of someone who will know where to contact you at all times. Also, always include phone numbers with area codes. If you have an e-mail address, you will most likely want to include this information as well.

Overview

The Overview should include both your *"Professional Objective"* and a brief *"Profile"* that gives top billing to your "personal characteristics that add value," along with other P.E.A.K.S. that prospective employers are likely to consider important.

If you are currently considering more than one career direction, you would do well to develop several different versions of your overview statement. This way you will have a useful draft on file to work with when it comes time to create a targeted resume for one of the areas you are considering.

A professional objective can be one of the most important parts of a resume and should not be overlooked. It informs potential employers that you have a focus and are moving in a certain direction, states your work preference(s), and serves as a focal point for reviewing and analyzing your resume. It should be brief and clearly stated.

Your profile gives you the opportunity to present your strengths at the very beginning of your resume. This is a good place to mention several key P.E.A.K.S. you have that are likely to be considered particularly desirable by recipients of your resume. And most importantly, you should include here personal characteristics you have that prospective employers are seeking in candidates. As noted earlier, our research indicates that the majority of employers put particular emphasis on personal characteristics of candidates. Your informational interviews should give you a good indication of the particular personal characteristics that recipients of your resume will value most highly in a candidate.

You can combine your "profile" with your "professional objective" statement, as is done in the following example:

Overview

A well-prepared professional with solid academic background and experience in marketing, seeking a marketing management position where he can make a difference. A team player who is creative, enthusiastic, and likes to get things done. Strong background in sports marketing.

Alternatively, you can list "Professional Objective" and "Profile" as separate subheadings under the general heading, "Overview":

Overview

Professional Objective: *Professional sales representative with a diverse range of successful sales experience, seeking institutional manager position within the pharmaceutical industry.*

Profile: *Enthusiastic, dedicated, persistent, able to build lasting relationships. A leader who is a team player.*

Further examples of overview statements can be found in the resumes included in Part 2.

Work Experience

You might call this section "Professional Experience," if you have been working as a professional or your work experience has been preparing you for a professional career. Bear in mind that the term "professional" is used pretty broadly these days. Work that was once considered clerical, for example, can now be referred to as professional.

Many students have limited paid work experience but have been involved in volunteer work, internships, practicums, student teaching, or other forms of student work such as being an advertising director for the school newspaper. These experiences should be included in the resume if they involve P.E.A.K.S. that would be important to a potential employer. It is particularly important that candidates for teaching positions include their student teaching experience in their resumes.

Homemakers and others who have taken time off from a "paid work career" can list volunteer activities here, under "Work Experience," or under a separate "Community Service" heading. Whatever you decide to do with your headings, the most important thing to remember when first putting together a master resume is to list these unpaid work activities somewhere, as they give ample opportunity for demonstrating P.E.A.K.S. that employers are seeking in candidates.

List all work experience in reverse chronological order. In other words, list the most recent things you did first.

Each job or other work experience you have had can be listed using the following format, which highlights your key P.E.A.K.S. Wherever you see *italicized font*, you would replace it with the relevant information. So, for example, in the first line, you would type in the actual job title or role you had, but do *not* preface this with *Title or Role*. The phrases below in **bold** font, such as **"Experience,"** should be typed on the resume as subheadings for P.E.A.K.S. categories.

Title or Role   *Name of organization where you worked*
                                           Location; Dates of employment

Personal Characteristics Demonstrated:

- *Insert short phrases and adjectives that describe key personal characteristics you demonstrated.*
- *Use bullets if necessary.*

Experience:

- *Insert brief description of valuable experience that you gained from this job.*
- *Use bullets, if necessary.*

Accomplishments:

- *Insert a brief description of important accomplishments.*
- *Use bullets, if necessary.*

Knowledge:

- *Insert a brief description of useful knowledge gained.*
- *Use bullets, if necessary.*

Skills:

- *Insert a brief description of important skills.*
- *Use bullets, if necessary.*

Since your personal characteristics that add value are featured prominently in your initial overview, you will most likely want to focus on your other P.E.A.K.S. in the "Work Experience" section of your resume. In particular, you will probably want to focus on your skills and accomplishments. You do *not* have to include all categories of P.E.A.K.S. for each work experience that you list, nor should you.

The P.E.A.K.S. subheadings might include modifiers to highlight the specific type of P.E.A.K.S. that were demonstrated in a job. For example, you might use "Customer Service Skills," if that is a good description of the kind of skills that are listed under this subheading. If you use subheadings that have modifiers, you can have more than one subheading for any of the P.E.A.K.S. categories. So in addition to "Customer Service Skills," you could also use "Computer Skills" for the same job, if you had something to list under each of these categories.

A good way to get a feel for how P.E.A.K.S. subheadings might be used in a resume is to take a look at the examples of P.E.A.K.S. resumes in Part 2.

Education

This category is particularly important if you have not had a great deal of work experience. As with your work experiences, you should list your educational achievements in reverse chronological order, so that your most recent degree or certificate is listed first.

Include your degree (AA, BS, BA, MBA, MA, etc.), college or university attended, date of graduation, minors or concentrations, and any special workshops, seminars, related coursework, or senior projects. A grade point average (G.P.A.) of higher than a 3.0 (either overall G.P.A. or G.P.A. in major) might also be noted here.

You might use "Knowledge" or "Skills" subheadings to highlight areas of academic concentration and particular skills developed.

Additional Information

This category is useful for displaying information that doesn't fit in any other category. Although Interests, Computer Knowledge, and Activities can be separate categories, especially if you have items that would be included under these that are very strong, alternatively, items that would otherwise be listed under these categories can be listed here. Languages spoken, or any extra, relevant bit of information can also be placed here.

Again, you can use P.E.A.K.S. subheadings for each of the things listed under "Additional Information."

References

It's a good idea to start creating a list of people you might want to use as references. In particular, you will want to identify people who can and will vouch for your key P.E.A.K.S.

TARGETING YOUR P.E.A.K.S. RESUME

A targeted resume is intended to appeal to a particular audience. When seeking a specific job, the target audience for your resume would be the people who review the resumes of candidates for this job.

If you use a P.E.A.K.S. format for your resume, the targeting process should focus on including the particular P.E.A.K.S. that would most impress your target audience.

When used in connection with seeking a particular job, a targeted P.E.A.K.S. resume is really a can-do resume, in that it gives the reasons why you "can do" the key things that the job under consideration requires.

What follows are steps you can take to target an effective P.E.A.K.S. resume.

The Ten-Step Process for Targeting a P.E.A.K.S. Resume
  1. Describe the opportunity you are pursuing in *realistic* terms.
  2. Identify the P.E.A.K.S. that the people who will be interviewing you are likely to be seeking in candidates.
  3. Create an "Overview" section that (a) clearly defines what you are seeking in the context of the targeted opportunity and (b) presents

the "best you" in terms of the P.E.A.K.S. you have that are desired by employers.

4. Select from your master resume the things from your "Work Experience," "Education," and "Additional Information" sections that will give a picture of you that (a) is sufficiently complete and (b) presents your most relevant P.E.A.K.S.

5. Decide on an overall plan and layout for organizing the above material for your resume.

6. Use P.E.A.K.S. subheadings to demonstrate that you have desired P.E.A.K.S.

7. Edit for language, length, and visual presentation.

8. Get feedback on your resume prior to distributing it.

9. Choose references who can verify your key P.E.A.K.S. And brief them on the P.E.A.K.S. employers are seeking in candidates.

10. Prepare cover letters that refer to key P.E.A.K.S.

Each of these steps is discussed in the paragraphs below.

Step 1: Describing the Opportunity You Are Pursuing in Realistic Terms

The more accurately you are able to describe the real responsibilities, activities, and goals associated with a job or promotion, the easier it will be to identify the things that should be included in your targeted resume.

You can, and in fact should, use the same statement or notes you used for targeting your portfolio to target your resume.

You don't have to write a long essay on a job to prepare a targeted resume. A short paragraph will do, so long as you are catching the essence of what the job really requires. In fact, you don't have to write anything at all, though keeping some notes is helpful. The important point is that you understand what the incumbent of the job has to be able to do to be considered successful.

Use Can-Do Portfolio research methods. To generate an accurate description of the opportunity you are pursuing, you can use the same research methods that are used for targeting a Can-Do Portfolio:

■ Look for a job description.
■ Get a realistic picture of the job.
■ Play detective.
■ Do informational interviews.
■ Do as much research as you can.

You can find further descriptions and explanations of the above techniques in Chapter 3.

Step 2: Identifying the P.E.A.K.S. That Interviewers Believe Are Most Important

Once you have a clear idea as to what the job under consideration really requires, the next step is to identify the particular P.E.A.K.S. that the people who will receive your resume are likely to be seeking in candidates. The real issue here is not what you would think is important, but what *they* think is important.

If you already have a list of desired P.E.A.K.S. that you prepared in connection with targeting your portfolio, you can use that list here. If not, you can use the techniques reviewed in Chapter 3 to generate a useful list. Be sure to identify the "personal characteristics" that are highly valued.

Step 3: Creating a Targeted Overview for Your Resume

As noted earlier, the "Overview" section in your resume should include both your professional objective and a brief profile that gives top billing to your personal characteristics that add value, along with other P.E.A.K.S. that prospective employers are likely to consider important.

Because it goes at the top of your resume, right after name and address information, your overview is your opportunity to make a good first impression. It should clearly define the kind of opportunity you are seeking, stated in a way that makes you seem appropriate for the job you are going after. And, equally important, your "Overview" section should give a quick synopsis of the P.E.A.K.S. you have that will likely impress the recipient of this resume, giving particular emphasis to your personal characteristics that add value.

If you have created a draft of your overview for your master resume, you can rework and refine it in light of the P.E.A.K.S. that you believe are considered most important for the particular job you are seeking.

Step 4: Identifying the Key Things to Include from Your Master Resume

If your master resume is in a computer file, you will have the ability to quickly create a draft of your targeted resume by (1) copying your master resume and pasting it into a new document, (2) deleting the items you don't want to use, and then (3) editing the rest. Here are some guidelines for identifying what to include in your targeted resume.

Include activities that give evidence of desired P.E.A.K.S. As you review your work experience, education, and other activities, use your understanding of desired P.E.A.K.S. as your guideline for selecting the particular things to include in your targeted resume.

Make sure your resume is sufficiently complete. Certain things are expected in a resume such as relevant *work experience* and at least something about *formal education*. If you are using a curriculum vitae format for your resume, you will be expected to give a complete record of all of your professional activities, including a list of all of your publications, major presentations, and professional honors.

If you are a student seeking a first full-time job, the recipient of your resume will expect your resume to be mostly focused on formal education, school activities, and work experience acquired through student types of work, which could include jobs held while at school, internships, and summer jobs.

On the other hand, if it has been a while since you have been in school, the recipient of your resume is likely to be more interested in what you have done since you were in school. If there have been long periods of time when you haven't held a job or been otherwise engaged in paid work, you should be sure to include your volunteer activities, and present them in a way that demonstrates desired P.E.A.K.S.

As we will see in the next section, you can also divert attention from gaps in your employment history by using a "functional" format for the overall plan of your resume.

Consider portfolio documents you would like to present. In addition to reviewing your master resume for useful material, you would do well to also review the key documents in your Can-Do Portfolio so that you can be sure to include in your targeted resume activities associated with documents you would like to present during an interview.

Step 5: Deciding on an Overall Plan for Your Resume

There is no one best way to organize a targeted resume. The major headings that you decide to use, such as "Professional Experience" and "Community Service," and the decision as to whether the overall plan will be chronological or functional will depend upon a number of factors, including your objectives, the material you would like to present, and your personal preferences. Here are some things to consider as you make these decisions.

Name and address information should go first, followed by the overview. A standard practice is to place name and address information right at the top of a resume, followed by some form of overview. You would be wise to follow this practice.

The reader of your resume needs to know within a couple of seconds the basics of who you are, what you are seeking, and the essence of why you may be well qualified for the job or position. These are the things that recipients of resumes typically want to know first, so that they can decide whether or not it's worth their time to read the rest. And if they can't find this basic information quickly, they very well may not read the rest.

Consider whether a chronological or functional overall plan works best for you. The material in most resumes is organized according to a chronological or functional overall plan, or some combination of the two. Since P.E.A.K.S. subheadings can be used within either organizational scheme, you can use either approach and still have a P.E.A.K.S. resume. But it is important, nevertheless, to consider the relative merits of these two organizational plans for your own situation.

A *chronological resume* typically lists jobs and other work experience you've had in reverse chronological order, beginning with the most recent job you have had first. Educational achievements are also listed in reverse order, so that your most recent degree is again listed first.

A *functional resume*, on the other hand, clumps jobs and other work experiences according to the different functional areas they represent. If, for example, you have had jobs in both the public relations and sales fields, in a functional resume you might use these functional areas as "Public Relations Experience" and "Sales Experience" headings and list your work experience according to the appropriate category.

A functional resume has the advantage of quickly communicating to the reader a person's general areas of expertise. People who have been out of the workforce for long periods of time might use a functional format to direct attention away from these gaps in their employment history. And people seeking to make substantial shifts in their career often use functional resumes to highlight the basic skills they have that could be readily applied to their new field, even though these skills were developed in an unrelated field. A chronological format, on the other hand, enables people who have steadily worked their way up in a particular field to underscore the continuity and progress of their work career.

It is beyond the scope of this book to explore the many other considerations that might go into deciding whether to use a chronological or functional format for your own resume. If you are struggling with this decision, consult one of the many how-to books on creating resumes that will tell you all you need to know to decide whether you should use a chronological or functional format.

Develop major headings that are good descriptions of content areas. The nature of the material that you have decided to include in your targeted resume and the overall plan that you have chosen (chronological, functional, or a hybrid of the two) can be used to determine the major headings for the content areas of your resume. If you are having trouble coming up with headings you like, reviewing the headings used in the examples of targeted resumes included in Part 2 should give you some inspiration.

Step 6: Using P.E.A.K.S. Subheadings for Items You Want to Feature

P.E.A.K.S. subheadings enable you to highlight the elements that are likely to impress the recipients of your resume. As noted above, P.E.A.K.S. subheadings can be used within either a chronological *or* functional resume.

Here are some guidelines you can follow.

Use P.E.A.K.S. subheadings throughout your resume. Earlier in this chapter we explained how to create effective P.E.A.K.S. subheadings for your work experience. You can and should also use P.E.A.K.S. subheadings under all of the major headings of your resume. The targeted resumes in Part 2 give nice examples of how this can be done.

Refine the P.E.A.K.S. headings from your master resume. If you have created a master resume that already has P.E.A.K.S. subheadings, these subheadings provide a good *first* draft for the headings you might use in your targeted resume. But once you are able to learn more about which P.E.A.K.S. are considered most important for the particular job you are now pursuing, you should take another look at the subheadings you have created.

You may wish to add modifiers to your P.E.A.K.S. subheadings so that these headings describe the specific kinds of P.E.A.K.S. being sought in candidates. If, for example, a prospective employer is looking for someone who has superb people skills, and you have done work or performed a service that required particular finesse in working with people, list these as "People Skills" rather than just calling them "Skills."

Use P.E.A.K.S. subheadings to create opportunities to show your portfolio. Headings that accurately describe desired P.E.A.K.S. are likely to prompt questions that will give you opportunities to show documents in your portfolio that give evidence of these P.E.A.K.S.

Step 7: Editing for Language, Length, and Visual Presentation

Here are some things to think about as you edit your targeted resume for its look and language.

Use language that recipients of your resume will understand and like. Do not use jargon that the readers of your resume are unlikely to understand. And try to use terms that they will like. For example, if the people who will be reviewing your resume are looking for aspiring leaders, use leader instead of manager and led rather than managed when describing your supervision of activities.

Check for correctness of spelling, usage, and grammar. Misspellings and poorly constructed sentences create a very negative impression. Recipients of resumes have very little patience for resumes that are poorly written, and they are likely to have even less patience for authors of such resumes. Remember that computer programs designed to catch spelling, grammar, and usage errors do not always identify every mistake. If possible, ask someone who is a good writer or editor to proofread your resume.

Use terms, fonts, and a format that computer programs will properly read and print. Keep in mind that resumes are often scanned first by computers for key words and phrases. So be sure to use correct terms when describing the kind of job you are looking for, and when you are describing your P.E.A.K.S. try to use words and phrases that computers are likely to have been programmed to pick up. Make sure that you use fonts that computers are likely to be able to "read."

When you e-mail a resume that is in a word processing format, such as Microsoft Word, the document may not print exactly as you sent it. For example, a one-page resume that is forwarded in a word processing format may come out as more than one page when the recipient prints it. For this reason you may decide to e-mail your resume as an attachment in a PDF (Portable Document Format).

Do not exceed two pages. You may have heard that resumes should only be one page. The real issue with a resume is not its length but its perceived ease of reading. Since a P.E.A.K.S. resume can be read quickly, you can extend its length to two pages. You never want to leave out vital information that would be supportive of your candidacy.

If your resume is in the form of a curriculum vitae, there is no limit to its length. Since a "C.V." is meant to include all of your publications, presentations, and professional honors, the game here, in fact, is to make it as long as possible.

If you have been out of school for some time, you are likely to want to use both sides of a page. You should probably use only one side of a page if you are fresh out of school, but do not use narrow margins and miniscule print to fit everything in.

Whether you use one or two pages, be sure to include lots of "white space" so that the text does not appear to be too crowded.

Be consistent. Make sure that whatever approach you use for presenting your information, you keep with this approach throughout your entire resume. The order in which you present information should be consistent. And visual things like patterns of spacing and fonts used for highlighting should not vary.

Make certain that your resume is visually appealing without being flashy. If you wish to make a "statement" with your resume, do it with words, not with flashy paper and unusual fonts. Use high-quality paper in white, off-white, or other conservative colors. Use standard fonts that are easy to read. Avoid smudges when printing copies. Have the final version of your resume professionally reproduced, if that's what it takes to get the copies looking right.

Step 8: Getting Feedback on Your Resume Prior to Distributing It—and After

It is extremely helpful if prior to showing your resume to a prospective employer you are able to get some feedback not just on how it looks and reads but also on whether or not it is properly targeted for the situation in which you want to use it.

As noted in the last chapter, you are likely to be able to get particularly useful feedback on drafts of your resume in informational interviews. If you can't show it in an informational interview, at least show your resume to some people who receive and assess resumes from time to time. If there is a glaring gap or mistake, they're likely to flag it for you.

The key test for a resume is simply this: Does it generate invitations to job interviews? People do not get invited to job interviews for many reasons, including a downturn in the economy. But if you keep sending a particular resume and you never get any nibbles from the people who receive it, you should again ask people who are knowledgeable about resumes and will be absolutely candid with you if there isn't something basically wrong with the way you have targeted this resume.

You can also get useful feedback on your resume if a person who is interviewing you for a job uses your resume to review your credentials. Does this person seem impressed by the P.E.A.K.S. you have featured in your resume? If so, your resume is working for you. On the other hand, if the interviewer keeps mentioning the importance of some P.E.A.K.S. that you have not referred to in your resume, this emphasis suggests that you might want to try to work these P.E.A.K.S. into your next draft.

Step 9: Choosing References Who Can Verify Your Key P.E.A.K.S.

You do not have to list in your resume the names of people who will serve as references for you. You can simply put "References furnished upon request" at the end of your resume. Or you can just ignore this topic.

What you can't ignore is that if someone is interested in possibly hiring you, this person is likely to ask you for references. And so, you will want to have at least a mental list of several people who will serve as your references.

One rule you must follow is to never say someone is a reference without first checking with this person to see if he or she would be willing to provide this service for you. It's just plain good manners to do so, and furthermore, you're likely to get a good read on just how favorable a reference this person is likely to be when you ask this person if he or she will serve as your reference.

We would strongly encourage you to choose as references people who can verify that you have the particular P.E.A.K.S. that the recipients of your resume are likely to believe are highly desirable. And when people agree to be one of your references, give them a copy of your resume and brief them on the particular P.E.A.K.S. that you would like them to verify that you have.

Step 10: Preparing Cover Letters That Refer to Key P.E.A.K.S.

It is beyond the scope of this book to discuss in any detail the many factors to consider when composing cover letters that accompany the mailing of a resume. There are, in fact, many good books available on this topic.

The one point we would like to make here is that a cover letter gives you an opportunity to quickly mention one or two P.E.A.K.S. you have that the recipient of your resume is likely to find particularly impressive. Your goal is to get them to look at your resume.

You don't have to go on and on about your P.E.A.K.S. in your cover letter. If you have followed the above guidelines for preparing a targeted resume, your resume will give a strong synopsis of the key P.E.A.K.S. you would bring to a job, without your having to say or write another word.

FINAL THOUGHTS

As we mentioned up front, the resume you use in conjunction with your portfolio does not have to have a P.E.A.K.S. format. But if you do make the extra effort to feature your desired P.E.A.K.S. in your resume, we believe you will discover, as our clients have, that you will get more job interviews and have more opportunities during these interviews to show key items from your portfolio.

If you have prepared a targeted portfolio that you are hoping to show, you might put the following statement at the bottom of your resume:

Portfolio available upon request.

Now that you know how to create a resume that will get you to an interview and create opportunities to show your portfolio, it's time to take a look at how you can put your portfolio to work once you get there. We'll do just that in the next chapter.

6

Using Your Portfolio to Get That Job

OVERVIEW

Once your Can-Do Portfolio is assembled and ready to be shown, the time has come to put it to good use. In this chapter we will show you how you can use your portfolio to get attractive job offers.

Specifically we will review:

- What you should be able to achieve in a job interview
- The advantages a portfolio can give you in an interview
- How to prepare yourself to use a portfolio in an interview
- How to use a portfolio during the different stages of an interview
- How to use your portfolio in follow-up interviews and when responding to a job offer

To many people, interviewing for a job does not come naturally. In fact, it can feel like a form of torture! Selling yourself, or more politely, drawing attention to your strong points and qualifications may not be a role with which you are comfortable.

You may have dreaded job interviews in the past, but, as we will see in this chapter, having a well-targeted portfolio and knowing how to use it effectively can be a great confidence builder. Equipped with the right tools and techniques, becoming very good at presenting who you are and what you can do is possible. Once you learn how to do this, you may even start looking forward to job interviews. And most certainly you will get results.

We call this "the portfolio advantage."

WHY EMPLOYERS CONDUCT JOB INTERVIEWS

A job interview is a conversation between a person who has applied for a job and another person (or committee) who, on behalf of the employing organization, directs this conversation in a way that is intended to assess the merits of the applicant's candidacy for the job. As a result of a job interview, a candidate may be offered a job, denied a job, invited back for further interviews, or told that his or her name will be kept on file should an appropriate position open up in the future.

The hiring organization's goals normally include the following:

- Assessing how well the candidate's qualifications match the job requirements
- Assessing the likelihood that the candidate will be a well-motivated, successful performer within the organization
- Assessing the candidate's potential for growth and advancement within the organization
- Determining if the candidate is likely to be a good fit for the culture of the organization
- Assessing the likelihood that the candidate will remain with the organization long enough for the organization to get a reasonable return on its investment in the person
- Hiring the best person available for the job on mutually acceptable terms
- Conducting the interviewing process in a manner that enhances the reputation of the organization

The people who conduct job interviews are typically employees of the hiring organization, though in some cases consultants or board members conduct job interviews on behalf of the organization. The job applicant may be someone from within the organization who is applying for a transfer or promotion or someone "from outside" who is not affiliated with the organization.

The timing of an interview usually gives a good indication as to whether it is meant to be used for "screening" or "selecting" candidates.

Early job interviews are often used for "screening" candidates. The screening interview is used to weed out unqualified candidates as well as applicants who are considered overqualified or overpriced. These interviews are often performed by outside consultants, such as headhunters, or by professional interviewers from within the organization. The goal of the screening interview is to quickly assess whether or not an applicant for a particular job is sufficiently promising to justify being interviewed in greater depth at a later time.

Typically, a screening interview is quick and follows a set format consisting of questions designed to determine if the applicant has the basic requirements for the job, such as the right level of education and experience. More often than not, screening interviews are conducted over the phone. At the end of the screening interview, applicants may have some idea of whether or not they will be invited for another, more in-depth interview.

Obviously, if a screening interview is conducted over the phone, there is no opportunity to show your portfolio face to face. However, if you have done the research that is necessary to create a Can-Do Portfolio, you will be well prepared to talk over the phone about the P.E.A.K.S. you have that would make you a well-qualified candidate. You do not need to show portfolio items to speak confidently about the things you have done that generated these items. In Chapter 9 we will discuss digital options for sharing your portfolio electronically.

Later interviews are used for "selecting" candidates. One or more rounds of *selection interviews* follow the screening interview. As the name implies, the goal of a selection interview is to make a selection. Actually, both the interviewer and the person being interviewed are engaged in making a selection. The interviewer is trying to decide which candidate is best for the job. And the interviewee, in addition to trying to make a good impression, is also attempting to determine if this job is a good opportunity.

Typically there is more than one round of selection interviews. A human resource specialist may be involved in early rounds of selection interviews. People who would be associates of the person who eventually fills the job may also conduct selection interviews. But in the final round of selection interviews, typically the person whose opinion is given the most weight is the supervisor or manager of the position that is being filled. In fact, it is usually this manager who conducts the final round of selection interviews.

The focus of this chapter will be on selection interviews where you meet face to face and therefore will have the opportunity to show your portfolio.

WHAT YOU CAN ACHIEVE IN A JOB INTERVIEW

Prior to going on a job interview, your first task is to decide what you want to achieve in this interview. As a candidate for a position, your goals probably include the following:

- Acquiring enough information about the job and the organization to make an informed decision as to whether or not you want to work there. Is this position right for you? Is this organization's culture what you had hoped it would be? Will this job put you in a good position to capitalize on future opportunities?
- Communicating information about yourself in a way that makes you a strong candidate for the job.
- Learning more about the P.E.A.K.S. that the prospective employer is seeking in candidates, so that you can further refine both your re-

sponses to questions and the content of your Can-Do Portfolio, should you be invited back for further interviews.

- Receiving a job offer, if you believe this job is right for you, or, if this is premature, to at least move on to the next round of interviews.
- Being able to get the specific things that might come with this job that are most important to you (the salary, title, authority, and so on that you are seeking) should you be offered this job.

You might also decide to go on a job interview even though you are not initially interested in the particular job for which you will be interviewed. Your goals here might include:

- Bringing yourself to the attention of this employer in a favorable way so that you will be considered a viable candidate should a more desirable job open up in the future.
- Developing your skills as an interviewee.
- Getting some practice showing your portfolio.
- Testing yourself in the marketplace so that you can benchmark your P.E.A.K.S. and determine your current market value.
- Seeing if there are jobs available that might be more appealing to you than the one you currently have.
- Getting a job offer on the outside so that you can attempt to leverage a better deal or opportunity with your present employer.

As we will see in the following sections of this chapter, your Can-Do Portfolio will help you achieve many of the key objectives of a job interview. Most importantly, it can help you get the job!

THE PORTFOLIO ADVANTAGE

Here are some of the advantages that having a well-targeted Can-Do Portfolio can give you during a job interview, if it is used properly:

- The simple fact that you bring a portfolio to the interview distinguishes you from candidates who did not bring a portfolio; this shows initiative on your part.
- Having a nice-looking portfolio suggests that you are the kind of person who is well prepared and well organized.
- Having a portfolio that contains documents that verify P.E.A.K.S. that are relevant to the job under consideration suggests that you have a very serious interest in this job, and that you have a clear idea as to what is required to be successful in this job.
- The items in your portfolio enable you to give tangible evidence that you, indeed, have important qualifications for this job.
- Your portfolio enables you to give tangible evidence that you have the key personal characteristics being sought in a candidate.

- You can discuss your qualifications for the job with confidence, with or without showing items from your portfolio. Even when you do not show documents from your portfolio, just knowing that you can verify the claims you make about yourself allows you to talk in a very confident and convincing manner about your qualifications.
- You come across as a can-do candidate. You give the overall impression that you are very much a candidate who is ready, willing, and able to get the job done.

HOW TO GET READY TO USE YOUR PORTFOLIO DURING A JOB INTERVIEW

To make your best case with your portfolio during an interview, you need to have gathered information beforehand about yourself, the job, the organization, and the industry. And, of course, you will also want to know ahead of time as much as you can about the P.E.A.K.S. that your interviewers are likely to consider highly desirable.

The research you have already done in connection with targeting a portfolio for a particular interview should help with the preinterview preparation. But to be well prepared to use your portfolio effectively, there are some further things you can do as well. The following would be particularly helpful.

Have extra copies of a targeted P.E.A.K.S. resume ready to bring to the interview. Even if you have sent your resume ahead, you should still bring several copies to the actual interview. The interviewer may have misplaced your resume, and more than one person may show up to interview you. If you are able to hand to each of your interviewers a copy of a resume that features P.E.A.K.S. that that person is likely to find desirable, there's a good chance you'll get questions that enable you to show items from your portfolio. Putting "Portfolio available upon request" at the bottom of your resume also improves the chances you will be able to show items from your portfolio.

Be ready to give a brief description of yourself that features your key P.E.A.K.S. A standard practice for many interviewers is to get candidates to describe themselves by asking open-ended questions like, "So tell me a little bit about yourself and what you've done."

You should be ready to give a two- to three-minute synopsis of your resume, making sure to include the key P.E.A.K.S. that the interviewer is likely to want to know more about. Again, this information is likely to prompt questions that will give you a chance to show documents from your portfolio.

A good way to practice this synopsis is to do so out loud without referring to any notes. Time yourself to see if you can get it under three minutes without rushing, and consult your resume at the end of each recitation to make sure you have covered your key P.E.A.K.S. If you can do this with a friend, so much the better. Listening to a tape of yourself doing this can also be quite useful.

Know your portfolio. It is very important that you are intimately familiar with what is in your portfolio. You need to know how to find key documents quickly and what each document is saying about you.

It's helpful to leaf through your portfolio as often as you can, mumbling to yourself the reasons why each document was included. It is particularly important to do this the day of the interview, making sure one last time that you know where each document is located.

Do role-playing with a friend, if possible. In addition to going over your portfolio by yourself, it is particularly helpful if you can practice presenting key items to a friend. Or lacking an available partner, do so with a tape recorder.

Documents that give evidence of skills, knowledge, or experience are typically pretty easy to explain. People often feel awkward, however, when talking about their desirable personal characteristics, so you will want to practice doing so out loud to another person.

Although it may make you a bit self-conscious, you should also be sure to practice talking about items that give evidence of your achievements. Many interviewers are likely to want to know if you have had any significant accomplishments, believing, quite rightly, that past performance is a good predictor of future performance.

An effective way to discuss your achievements is to use the S.T.A.R. acronym that may be familiar to the interviewer. S.T.A.R. stands for: **s**ituation (challenge, problem, or opportunity) faced, **t**ask to be undertaken, **a**ction taken (what decisions you made and actions you took in response to the problem), and **r**esults (the outcome of your action).

Make copies of items you may wish to leave behind. You might want to give a few items in your portfolio to your interviewer, if the opportunity arises. Before making copies of these documents, be sure to remove any information that should not be distributed.

Make sure your portfolio is in good shape physically. Prior to showing your portfolio, make sure that the carrying case looks good and that the items and tabs have not become bent or torn.

HOW TO USE YOUR PORTFOLIO DURING A JOB INTERVIEW

In order to make the very best use of your portfolio during a job interview, it's useful if you know how to use your portfolio effectively during each of the stages that a job interview is likely to pass through.

The Stages of a Job Interview

A job interview that goes well typically advances through six key stages. To help you remember these stages and the order in which they are likely to occur, we have created the acronym H.E.R.O.I.C., which stands for:

- **H**elloing
- **E**ngaging
- **R**esponding
- **O**pportunity finding
- **I**nvolving

■ Closing

The order may vary, and stages may be skipped. The helloing stage of a job interview will happen at the beginning of every job interview, and the closing stage will inevitably come at the end. The other stages of the job interview process, however, may not come in the above order. One or more of the engaging, opportunity-finding, or involving stages, in fact, may not happen at all.

But if you are able to recognize the stages that *do* occur in an interview and you know what can be achieved with your portfolio in each of these stages, you should be able to make good use of your portfolio.

Help the interviewer through each stage. It is important to know that while the interviewer is responsible for conducting the interview, and as such, is ostensibly in charge of the process, you, as an interviewee, can play an important role in assuring that the interview proceeds smoothly and successfully. Perhaps it is best to think of yourself, not as being interviewed, but instead as *participating* in an interview.

The idea is certainly not to try to seize control of the interview in any obvious way. Much to the contrary, you will want to make the interviewer feel that he or she is in control of the process at every step of the way. Never lose sight of the fact that the person who is interviewing you wants to feel that he or she is being a skillful interviewer. Anything you can do to subtly help the interviewer achieve a feeling of competence can only work to your advantage. The interviewer is likely to conclude that the easier it is to interview you, the easier it will be to work with you.

The person who interviews you will most likely have a particular approach that he or she wants to take during the interview. And more often than not, the interviewer will have a specific set of topics that he or she will want to cover, and a specific set of questions that all candidates will be asked to respond to.

The interviewer will probably not be thinking about the "stages" of the interview in any conscious way. But if you understand the different stages that job interviews typically pass through and the order in which these stages are likely to occur, you will be able to discern which stage you are in. You will know what you hope to achieve in each stage and how your career portfolio can be used to best advantage during job interviews.

How to Use Your Portfolio During Each Stage of the Interview

Let's take a look now at how you can make the best use of your portfolio during each of the stages that are likely to occur during a job interview, beginning with the *helloing stage*.

Stage 1: <u>Helloing</u>

Many interviewers will admit that they have largely made up their minds about a candidate within the first five minutes of meeting the person. So it is very important to make a good first impression. As noted earlier, looking professional with regard to your clothes and grooming is a good start. Here are some more things to think about during the *helloing stage*.

Be courteous and attentive to everyone you meet. Make sure to be very polite, not just to the senior people you meet, but also to the secretaries, administrative assistants, and other people in the organization. If junior people feel slighted, they won't forget it, possibly to your detriment.

Do not push your career portfolio. Have your portfolio, but don't show it during the helloing stage, unless asked to. Do not hold up your portfolio and announce, "I have something I want to show you." Use this ammunition selectively throughout the interview.

If asked what you are carrying, you can say it's a portfolio, but don't hand it to the interviewer. Instead, describe very quickly what's in it. You might hold it up briefly, and say something along the order of: "This is my career portfolio. It has materials in it that document some of my accomplishments." Smile, put it back on your lap or at your side, and then proceed with the interview.

If the interviewer insists on having a look at your portfolio right then, instead of just handing it to him, get up and walk your portfolio around to his side and show it to him. This enables you to retain control of how your career portfolio is presented. It is helpful to practice this response beforehand with a friend.

Let the interviewer lead the transition to the next stage. The interviewer will give the cue as to when the greeting stage is over. Your job is not to lead to the next stage. Sit quietly and politely await the interviewer's next move. A professional or job-related question is typically the signal that the helloing stage is over.

Stage 2: Engaging

As noted above, the usual signal that you are no longer in the helloing stage is when the interviewer progresses from small talk to more pointed questions aimed at getting to know you better professionally. In addition to trying to find out more about you, typically the interviewer will also want to talk about the organization and the position that you are seeking.

We call this the *engaging stage* of the interview, because your goal, as a candidate, is to *engage* the interviewer's interest in you, both intellectually and emotionally.

On an intellectual level, you want the interviewer to start thinking that you are a promising candidate based on your qualifications and the way you present them. On an emotional level, you want the interviewer to start feeling that you are a strong candidate because the interviewer is starting to feel some rapport with you. During the engaging stage you want the interviewer to start thinking and feeling, "This might be the candidate we've been looking for. There's something about this candidate I like."

If it's a group interview, be responsive to everyone. If you are being interviewed by more than one person, it's natural to focus your attention on the senior members of the team. But it is important that in doing so, you do not in any way ignore or treat disrespectfully the junior members of the interview team. You can bet that at the end of an interview, the top person will turn to a trusted junior person and ask, "So what do you think?" If you offended this person during the interview, it's unlikely that a glowing recommendation will be forthcoming! And this less-than-glowing opinion can be devastating to a candidate. Managers are unlikely to hire someone whom they feel would have difficulty getting along with peers and subordinates in their organization.

Offer a copy of your resume to interviewers who do not appear to have it in front of them. You can say, "I've brought along a copy of my resume," (an "extra copy," if you already sent one) and hand it to the interviewer. If your resume is in a P.E.A.K.S. format and the interviewer uses it to review your qualifications, you are likely to get a number of questions that will give you opportunities to show key documents from your portfolio.

If asked to describe your background, you can introduce your portfolio. If you are asked to give a synopsis of your career, you can give the two- to three-minute self-description you have prepared that features your key P.E.A.K.S. At the conclusion, you have a good opportunity to hold up your Can-Do Portfolio and say something like: "I have brought along my career portfolio. It has materials in it that document some of the things I've just talked about."

Hold on to your portfolio. As noted earlier, if the interviewer asks to see the portfolio, instead of just handing it over, and thereby losing control of it, turn to relevant entries and show her these items, while holding on to the portfolio. This enables you to direct the interviewer's attention to the key documents in the order you want to present them.

Hand individual items to your interviewer. The best way to show an item from your portfolio is to take it out of your portfolio case (but not out of its translucent sheet protector) and hand it to your interviewer. This focuses the interviewer's attention on the particular item you want him to see.

Err on the side of showing too few entries from your portfolio. You are trying to use your portfolio to do the following:

1. Support a few points you've made about yourself
2. Demonstrate that you have initiative and are well organized
3. Leave the impression that your portfolio is full of impressive information

Of course, if the interviewer insists on grabbing the portfolio from you, you can't really say, "Hands off, Buster!" But your goal is to retain control of your portfolio, so that you can use it selectively to emphasize points you want to make throughout the interview.

If the interviewer reaches for the portfolio, you can respond by asking, "May I show this to you?" and, without waiting for a response, start opening your portfolio to a relevant entry.

Stage 3: <u>R</u>esponding

The *responding stage* of the interview occurs when you, as a candidate, begin fielding questions that are specifically intended to determine the extent to which your qualifications and personal qualities match up with what the hiring organization is looking for. Unlike the general questions you are asked during the engaging stage of the interview, these interview questions are sharper, more specific, and more intense.

Typically, the interviewer and/or the hiring organization has developed a list of questions, the answers to which, they believe, will give a very strong indication as to whether or not a candidate is right for the job. These are the questions you will be asked to respond to during the responding stage of the interview.

If the engaging stage of the interview is characterized from the interviewer's perspective as "getting to know each other," the responding stage is the "let's see if you've got what it takes" phase of the interview.

Although not all interviewers do so, an obvious tip-off that you have entered the responding stage is if the interviewer suddenly starts reading questions from notes and begins taking more careful notes when you respond.

Whether or not the interviewer intensifies his or her note taking, when you have entered the responding stage you are likely to feel that the responses you are giving are being very carefully scrutinized. You are likely to feel a greater amount of stress during this stage.

The responding stage can be pretty intense, as it is meant to be the "moment of truth." But it is also a phase of the interview when your Career Portfolio can be particularly helpful, if used skillfully. Here are some things to think about:

Look for clues about which P.E.A.K.S. most interest the interviewer. You should be able to tell from the kinds of questions you are asked and the responses you get which P.E.A.K.S. the interviewer seems to feel are most important.

Getting a better read on the interviewer's mind-set will enable you to zero in on the particular P.E.A.K.S. you should be focusing on as the interview progresses. And, if you are invited back for further interviews, knowing more about the P.E.A.K.S. that this organization particularly values will enable you to further refine the targeting of your portfolio for these interviews.

Keep in mind your desirable P.E.A.K.S. when responding to questions. Many of the "standard" interview questions that are asked during the responding stage of a job interview are really attempts to learn more about a candidate's P.E.A.K.S. As you respond to these questions, try to refer to specific P.E.A.K.S. you have that the interviewer is likely to find desirable. As you work your key P.E.A.K.S. into your responses, you will be reminded of items in your Can-Do Portfolio that you might want to show.

Show your portfolio very selectively. You should absolutely avoid whipping out your portfolio every time you speak. However, if a question comes up about your accomplishments or something else for which you have a particularly strong portfolio item, it is appropriate to ask, "May I show you something in my portfolio that illustrates this?"

If you know that your interviewer is interested in seeing items from your portfolio, rather than asking for permission to show your portfolio, you can simply open your portfolio and hand the interviewer the relevant document. You will know pretty early on in the interview whether or not the interviewer is receptive to seeing entries in your portfolio. But even if the interviewer is excited about documents in your portfolio, don't overdo it. It's a rule of show business: You always want to leave 'em hungering for more!

Most of the time, use portfolio items as confidence builders that you don't actually show. If you spend too much time during the responding stage waiting to pounce with portfolio items, you run the risk of not being very responsive to the questions you are asked.

The fact is, if you have done a good job of researching and putting together a well-targeted Can-Do Portfolio, you don't really have to show portfolio items to get good value from them. Just knowing that you can produce documents that verify claims you make about yourself will enable you to talk about your P.E.A.K.S. in a very confident and convincing manner.

Be sure to explain the portfolio items you do show. When you do show something from your portfolio, you need to point out why this document is important. Tell the interviewer quite explicitly the relevant P.E.A.K.S. that this document illustrates or verifies. You don't have to be a big boaster. You can say something like: "This illustrates, I believe, my ability to take responsibility and accomplish a big job in a short period of time."

Use portfolio items to demonstrate desirable personal characteristics. Personal characteristics that are desirable in candidates but are hard to prove when discussed in the abstract can be nicely illustrated with your portfolio. When asked to describe some of the personal qualities you bring to the workplace, it's okay to say, "I have a lot of initiative." But it's far more impressive to be able to say, "I think I show a considerable amount of initiative. For example, here's a letter of appreciation I received for a project I initiated." Use your portfolio to give tangible evidence of these hard-to-measure intangible qualities that can make all the difference in the hiring decision.

The responding stage is typically the longest phase of the interview. As noted above, this is the stage when interviewers typically ask the questions they believe will get at whether or not you are a strong candidate. But this is *not* your final chance to make a good impression. Once interviewers have finished asking the questions they intended to ask, the interview is certainly not over, unless, of course, one or both of you decide there is an obvious misfit between you and the position for which you are interviewing.

Stage 4: <u>O</u>pportunity Finding

Opportunity finding can happen at any stage of the interview. However, a particularly good moment to pursue opportunity finding occurs when the interviewer has finished asking his or her list of set questions. The interviewer might ask, "Do you have any questions?" or, "Is there something you would like to tell us about yourself?" This is a good chance to nudge the interview process toward the *opportunity finding stage.*

The odds are that the person who is trying to fill this job has a problem. Possibly the previous incumbent was fired or left unexpectedly. Or, perhaps a new project for which the interviewer has no qualified staff is looming. This is the time in the interview when you attempt to explore with the interviewer ways in which you would be particularly well qualified to solve the interviewer's problem.

Maybe the position is new and they're not quite sure how the job should be performed. Or there could be a sticky political situation in connection with this job, and the interviewer is afraid that the person who is hired might behave in a manner that only makes the situation worse. If you can discover precisely what the problem is, you, as a candidate, may have uncovered a big opportunity.

You must take a proactive role here. During the opportunity finding stage you want to zero in on what the critical issues are in the interviewer's mind, and then make the case that you are the person "to get the job done." Your Can-Do Portfolio can help you do this. Here's how.

Ask about the particular opportunities and challenges associated with the job. You need to know exactly what the interviewer *believes* are the issues and opportunities associated with the job. You may have been able to pick up a lot of this information during the earlier, engaging and responding stages. If you feel you now have a solid understanding of the opportunities and challenges, then you'll want to verify that you've got it right.

However, if you are still uncertain as to exactly what the opportunities and challenges are in the job, this is a good time to ask questions about the specific problems that an incumbent in this job must deal with effectively to be successful.

Paraphrase your understanding of the job's particular problems and opportunities. As a way of making sure you understand what the interviewer *perceives* the issues and problems to be, repeat to the interviewer what you believe you have heard are the job's particular challenges.

Make every effort to be polite here. You can begin your statement with a phrase like, "If I understand correctly, the three big challenges associated with this job are. . . ." And then ask, "Have I got it right, or is there something else that is more important?"

Use your portfolio to show how you are the right person for this job. Rather than just saying something like, "I think I can get these things done for you," use your portfolio to give the interviewer tangible evidence that you can perform as desired in this position.

You might say something like, "Based on what you have told me about this job and what I know about myself, I think I could do a good job for you." Briefly state your case, and then ask, "May I show you some entries in my portfolio that support what I am saying?"

Explore opportunities not associated with the job that intrigue you. Possibly the interviewer has said something along the way that is not directly related to the job you are being interviewed for yet you feel you could make a substantial contribution in this area. It can't hurt to discuss this possibility during this stage of the interview.

You might say something like: "I know this isn't part of the job I am being interviewed for, but I was intrigued when you mentioned [the particular opportunity]. I think I could make a substantial contribution in this area. Is this something that perhaps we should discuss?"

Be enthusiastic! With your choice of words, tone of voice, and body language, beam the message that you see many opportunities here. Interviewers are looking for highly motivated candidates. Enthusiasm is a personal characteristic that all interviewers are likely to appreciate.

Stage 5: Involving

The *involving stage* follows naturally after the opportunity finding stage. Here your goal is to get the interviewer truly excited about seeing you in the position for which you are being interviewed. If opportunity finding is an intellectual exercise, involving is a matter of the heart.

During the involving stage, you want the interviewer to be talking, not about the job, but about *you* in the job. And doing so in a caring way. This can be achieved by asking the right questions. Since you are trying to get the interviewer to do most of the talking, you probably will not be showing your portfolio during this phase of the interview.

Here are some examples of the kinds of questions you might ask during this stage:

Ask the interviewer to describe how you could be particularly useful to the organization. It is always best when the interviewer articulates why you might be a good fit for the job under consideration. You can encourage the interviewer to do this by asking a question like, "From what you know about my qualifications, what projects are you planning that, in your opinion, would be a good fit for me?"

You can then support positive suggestions the interviewer makes by showing an item or two from your portfolio that confirms that you have what it takes to do this project. But you should be wary of overselling, and you should be careful not to disrupt the flow while the interviewer is making your case for you.

Get the interviewer to describe you in the third person. Interviewers always have less trouble talking about candidates in the third person. If you ask, "what do you think of me?" you may get a very noncommittal answer or you might make the interviewer feel awkward. An alternative approach is to ask a question about yourself, referring to yourself by your first and last name. For example, you could say:

I am very enthusiastic about everything I've heard here today. I'd like to know some of the ways you think Joe Candidate [use your first and last name here] might be able to help you in this job?

Of course, if you feel awkward talking about yourself in the third person, don't do it.

Get the interviewer selling the job to you. Here's a question that can increase the interviewer's involvement in your candidacy:

If this position were to be offered to me, what in your view would be the main reasons for my accepting it?

This gets them telling you why you should take it!

Stage 6: Closing

Finally, the interviewer begins to close the interview. A signal that the interviewer is thinking of winding down the interview occurs when the interviewer begins to summarize what has been said, often accompanied by an elaboration of certain points that were made.

If you are interested in further pursuing this position, this is the time to make it known. Just stating that the position is of interest to you and then quickly reviewing the points that you have made which qualify you for the position can accomplish this. If there are other applicable skills or experience that you believe would be helpful in your being chosen, these points must be made now.

You may be able to show one more entry from your portfolio during the closing phase. But as a general rule, this is not the time to show your portfolio. The emphasis as you leave should not be on your portfolio, which is a sales aid, but on you, the person they might hire.

Here are some things to think about during the *closing stage.*

Supply the interviewer with a few words that summarize why you are a strong candidate. Based on what you know about yourself and what you now know the interviewer is looking for, give the interviewer a few words that summarize why you believe you are a strong candidate. In other words, supply the interviewer with the language she can use to describe you in a positive way to other people in their organization.

Do not *leave your entire portfolio behind.* You never want to leave your entire portfolio with an interviewer. By doing so, you lose total control over how it is used. What you can do is bring extra copies of entries that you think are particularly useful for advancing your candidacy. Then, if the interviewer indicates he or she would like you to leave the portfolio behind, you can say, "I can't leave this behind. However, I do have copies of a few of the key entries that I'd be happy to leave with you."

Try not to commit to a salary number. The issue of your salary expectations may come up now or even earlier in the interview. As a basic negotiating strategy, you do not want to be the first to commit to a specific number. Any figure you mention will put a ceiling on what you

HOW TO USE YOUR PORTFOLIO TO IMPROVE A JOB OFFER

As noted earlier, the first offer you get from prospective employers is usually not their best offer. Even if the position is an entry-level job that has a locked-in, nonnegotiable salary, there are usually some other aspects of the job offer that are negotiable. Your portfolio can give you a big assist when negotiating for an improved offer. Here's how.

Schedule a meeting to discuss your future with the organization. When you first get the offer, you may feel like reacting immediately to some of the specifics, but there's usually more to be gained if you do not. Try to limit your emotions to a very pleasant "Thank you for making this offer," unless, of course, the offer is so good or so bad, you are prepared to immediately accept or reject it. In either case, you will want to first make sure you understand exactly what the offer is. Take notes and repeat back to them your understanding of the offer.

If you want to try to improve the offer, tell them you'd like to take a few days to think about it, and then meet with them again to discuss both the offer and your future with the organization. When scheduling this meeting, you should give yourself at least several days to get prepared.

Identify the key things you want to improve in their offer. Your first task is to determine which of the things in the job offer you are most interested in trying to improve. Salary and benefits are of concern to most people, but these are not the only issues that should be discussed when responding to a job offer. Other key issues to consider include a signing bonus, coverage of moving costs, paying off school loans, your starting date, the date of your first salary review, equity opportunities, professional development opportunities, the flexibility of your work hours, the length of your vacation, your title, your level of authority, the specifics of who you report to and who reports to you, and the resources available to you.

Some of the additional benefits of a job offer may not be even remotely possible for you to negotiate or bring up. The important thing is to identify the features that you care about that you might be able to negotiate. To know what is, in fact, negotiable you need to do a reality check.

Do a reality check. If you have not done this already, find out as much as you can about the employment packages that recent hires are getting for comparable jobs in the industry. You can use Internet search engines to get printouts of salary ranges for jobs in most established fields, and you can use the Web to search for postings for comparable jobs. Job ads in regional newspapers and industry publications can also yield useful information. Articles in the press may also spell out the kinds of deals that people in comparable jobs are getting.

To learn about aspects of employment packages that are not likely to show up in job postings and publications, you need to talk to industry insiders who are in a position to know who gets what and why. You want to know what's the least people are getting, what's the most they are getting, and why some people are getting more than others. And here "getting" refers not just to salary and benefits, but to all the

might get. And if the number you give is on the high end for them, they may not be prepared to think of you as worthy of this salary. As we will see later on, salary negotiations are best conducted in a separate interview, after the organization has made you an offer. You are in a much stronger bargaining position, once the organization has committed to you. And, you can prepare your portfolio especially for a salary negotiation.

If at any point during the interview you are asked, "What are you looking for in terms of money?" you can respond, "What is the salary range you have budgeted for this position?" And if commissions are involved, ask about the median salary of the person holding a position comparable to the one you are seeking.

If your interviewer tells you, for example, that the position is rated at $42,000 to $46,000, you can then say why you think you deserve to receive the higher end of the scale, based on your knowledge and experience.

If you are asked what you are making now, don't lie, though you can say (when your salary is, say, $51,000 and you want an offer in the $60,000 range) "I'm earning in the fifties right now, though I'm hoping to improve on that."

If you are given an offer, schedule a meeting to discuss it. Do not accept or reject an offer when it is first presented, unless, of course, it is outrageously good or bad. Prospective employers' first offer is rarely their best offer. Thank them. Make sure you understand exactly what you are being offered. And tell them you would like to think about it and meet with them again to discuss both their proposal and your "future with the organization." When scheduling this meeting, give yourself at least several days to prepare your portfolio, for as you will see later, your portfolio can be used to great advantage when responding to a job offer.

Don't overstay your welcome. The interviewer most likely has other appointments to keep. Err on the side of leaving a little early. If you've made a good impression, they'll want you back.

End on a high note. The close of an interview most always ends with "Do you have any further questions?" The odds are the interviewer doesn't really want to field a question now that would require a lengthy answer. The interviewer is trying to send you a polite signal that the interview is over.

Instead of asking a question, you can say something like: "No, I think we've really covered it. I just want you to know that I appreciate your spending this time with me. I'm really excited about this opportunity and hope you feel the same way about my candidacy for this job."

Ask about next steps. Before leaving an interview you should be clear about the next steps. If the interview has gone well, you may want to press for an indication of where your candidacy stands. Depending upon where you are in the interviewing process, you might even ask for the job. At the very least, you will want to find out when you can expect to hear from your interviewer. To broach the subject of next steps, you might ask:

Let me reiterate my strong interest in the position we have been discussing. I am very impressed with everything I have heard here today. What's the next step? How do we progress from here?

Don't Worry If Interviewing Stages Get Skipped or Scrambled

As noted earlier, except for helloing and closing, the above stages may not go in their prescribed order, and some of the stages we have described may not happen at all.

But if you know what can be achieved with your portfolio in each of the stages that do occur, you should be able to use your portfolio to your advantage during the job interview.

HOW TO FOLLOW UP AFTER THE INTERVIEW

A week or so after the interview, it is perfectly appropriate for you to call (or e-mail) your interviewers about the status of your candidacy, provided you do not contact them on or before the date they said they would get back to you. But well before you make any follow-up calls, there are some things you must do almost immediately after the interview.

Make some notes on what happened. As soon as you can after an interview, jot down some notes. This is particularly important if you are going to another interview in the same day. You certainly do not want to confuse one interview with another. You might think you can keep everything straight in your head and don't need to write things down until the evening. But at the end of a long, tense day, the events can all seem like a blur. You don't need to write pages, just jot down enough key words and phrases to bring the conversations back to you.

These notes will become crucial if you are invited back for a second interview. Your notes should include key things you learned about the company and its future, your impressions of the people with whom you met, and what you would like to learn more about.

Were there any topics raised during the interview that seemed to elicit very strong positive or negative emotions? What seem to be the particular interests of each interviewer? How does each of them view the future of their organization?

Be sure to note when you can expect to hear from them, whether or not you promised to send something, and if you agreed to make a follow-up call on a certain date.

If you did not receive business cards from the people you met, you may call the company directly when you get home and ask the receptionist for the correct spellings of those people's names and their titles.

Record P.E.A.K.S. they are seeking and portfolio items that most impressed them. It is particularly useful to write down your impressions of what the people you met are looking for and which of your P.E.A.K.S. seemed to most impress each person. Were there items they particularly liked in your portfolio?

Promptly send a thank-you note. Your note should express your appreciation, reconfirm your interest in the job, and *briefly* note how you think your key P.E.A.K.S. would enable you to succeed in the position. It should be sent within a day or two of the interview.

Send promised portfolio items with *explanations.* If you promised to send some items from your portfolio, do so with your thank-you note. Remove any information in these documents that should not be distributed. And be sure to explain, as you did in the interview, the context for these items and their relevance.

HOW TO USE YOUR PORTFOLIO DURING SUBSEQUENT INTERVIEWS

If you are invited back for further interviews, the approach you take to these interviews should parallel what you did in the first interview. You should, of course, take advantage of the fact that you now know more about the organization, about the potential opportunities there, and about the specific P.E.A.K.S. being sought in job candidates. Here are some specific things to think about if you are invited back for another round of interviews.

Prepare a more targeted portfolio. Use the information you gathered in your first interview to adjust your portfolio so that it is more precisely targeted at the opportunities you would like to pursue. This may mean adding or subtracting items and possibly rearranging the order in which they appear. You should now have a better idea of the kinds of P.E.A.K.S. they are looking for. Choose your items accordingly.

Make copies of portfolio items you might leave behind, based on what you now know. Since you now have a better idea of what the prospective employer is looking for in a candidate, a second interview is a very good time to bring extra copies of several items you believe would particularly impress the person who will interview you.

Assume your next set of interviewers will know nothing about you. Do not assume just because you have been invited back for further interviews that the new people who interview you will already know all about you and be favorably disposed toward your candidacy. The first person who interviewed you may have done nothing more than forward your resume to your next interviewer with a note that said something like, "I think it's worth taking a second look at this candidate." In fact, your first interviewer might refrain from describing you at this stage so that the next interviewer can take an unbiased look. There's also the possibility that your next interviewers have interviewed some other candidates and already have their own favorite, so your challenge will be to win them over. Your portfolio can help you do so.

Remember that the ideal interview is still H.E.R.O.I.C. Once there, you will again want to be aware of which stage of the interview you are in so that you can get your best results by using your portfolio appropriately in each phase.

other features of the employment package that are of interest to you. An insider can tell you what's negotiable and what's not.

Particularly important is to try to find out from industry insiders why some people get much better deals than others, beyond the fact that they may have had great negotiating skills. What P.E.A.K.S. do they have that make them worthy of the best offers? You may have gotten a good answer to this question when you were initially targeting your portfolio. If not, get it now.

Your reality check should help you decide what things you can legitimately try to improve upon and what you cannot.

Add documents to your portfolio that will help you negotiate a better deal. Once you have decided on how you want the job offer to be improved, add the following kinds of documents to help you make your best case.

- *Documents that reveal obvious shortcomings in their offer.* If you have seen a chart that demonstrates that others in the industry are typically getting far more than you are being offered for the same job, make a copy for your portfolio.

  If the job offer does not significantly improve upon what you already have in your present job, try to find documents that will verify your current arrangement. You can use copies of things like organizational charts and job descriptions to demonstrate the level and responsibilities of your current job. A copy of the last W-2 form you received can document your current compensation.

- *Documents that reaffirm that you can contribute in the ways they are hoping you will.* Review your notes from earlier interviews to identify the ways in which your interviewers seem to feel you can make your biggest contribution to the organization. Then take a look at your Master Portfolio collection to see if there are some documents not yet in your Can-Do Portfolio that can give further evidence that you have the P.E.A.K.S. necessary to add value in the way that the interviewers hope you will. If they have you slotted for, say, bringing a better sense of organization to a department, then add to your portfolio everything you've got that demonstrates your ability to organize people and processes.

- *Documents that show you can add value in the way the people who get the best deals do.* Add to your Can-Do Portfolio any documents you might have that demonstrate you have the key P.E.A.K.S. that the people who get the best employment packages in a comparable position seem to have. If, for example, people with good sales skills seem to get the best deals in comparable positions, try to include evidence that you can be an effective salesperson. Obviously, if you can't stand selling, even though you may be good at it, you would be better off not trying to emphasize this skill or you may find yourself landing a high-paying job you can't stand!

Use your portfolio to demonstrate you are worthy of their best offer. When you meet to discuss their offer, you can use your enhanced Can-Do Portfolio to help you make the point that because you can add a lot of value to their organization, they should give you an improved employment package.

Unlike in earlier interviews, if you have the right ammunition in your portfolio, you can use it extensively when negotiating for a better deal.

You should not shy away from presenting whatever evidence you have that the deal you are being offered does not measure up to industry standards; or that it does not significantly improve upon what you are getting in your present job. This provides a reality check for them.

But your main focus during this meeting and the principal use of your portfolio should be to demonstrate that you have the P.E.A.K.S. that will enable you to add value to the organization in the very ways they have indicated they hope you will. And stress that the value you will add qualifies you for the very best deal available.

If you have done your homework, you can say something like, "I know that the salary range for this kind of position is typically [*quote the range*]. Here's why I think I deserve [*cite the highest figure*]." And then support this statement by making use of your portfolio.

When negotiating, it doesn't hurt to keep throwing at them one more example of why you are the very person they must have for this job. Negotiators are expected to keep giving more and more evidence to support their position.

One of our clients recently used this "total portfolio" strategy to negotiate for a better starting salary. The company offering her a job ended up not only matching her salary request but also threw in a generous benefit package that made the offer all that more attractive. She accepted.

Using portfolio items in your negotiations will take a lot of the awkwardness and discomfort out of going after what you want. And you will give yourself your best chance of getting all the good things you deserve!

FINAL THOUGHTS

Your portfolio can be a great asset in a job interview, if you use it properly. To help you remember the key dos and don'ts for using your portfolio in a job interview, we've prepared the following checklist that you might want to review each time you are planning to use your portfolio to get that job.

Portfolio Dos and Don'ts
1. *Do not let go of your portfolio.* If it leaves your hands, the whole direction of the interview will change. Instead, hand individual items to your interviewer.

2. *Keep the focus on **you**, not on your portfolio.* Your portfolio should be viewed as something that enhances the presentation of your qualifications for the job, not as the central feature of the interview.

3. *Do not keep your portfolio continuously open.* To do so would put too much focus on your portfolio.

4. *Use the peek-a-boo technique when showing your portfolio.* Take your portfolio out to make a point, then close it and put it aside.

5. *Do not use your portfolio as a crutch.* Do not use it to fill awkward silences or to remind you what to say next.

6. *Look for opportunities to use your portfolio in response to key questions.* Your portfolio can really come alive when you use it to substantiate a point you want to make about yourself in response to a question that is obviously very important to the interviewer.

7. *Always explain the relevance of the documents you present.* When you show an item from your portfolio, tell the interviewer quite explicitly the relevant P.E.A.K.S. that this document illustrates or verifies. "I included this document to illustrate my ability to. . . . It also, I believe, shows that I. . . ."

8. *Use portfolio items to demonstrate desirable personal characteristics.* Personal characteristics that are desirable in candidates but are hard to prove can be nicely illustrated with your portfolio.

9. *Use most of your portfolio items as confidence builders that you don't actually show.* Remember, you do not need to show items to speak confidently about the things you have done that generated these items. Just knowing that you can verify claims you make about yourself will enable you to talk in a very confident and convincing manner about your qualifications.

10. *Bring extra copies of items that your interviewer is likely to find particularly impressive.* And make doubly sure all proprietary information has been carefully deleted from anything you intend to leave behind.

11. *Do not leave behind items that have not been explained during the interview.* And do not send things from your portfolio that were not discussed during the interview.

12. *Be careful not to show your portfolio too much.* Less is truly more when presenting your portfolio. As noted earlier, follow the old show biz maxim, and "leave 'em hungering for more."

Once you get your job, don't throw your portfolio away and forget about all this portfolio stuff! As you will see in the next chapter, a portfolio can also be used to great advantage after you are on the job—during performance reviews, when applying for new work assignments, and when going for raises and promotions.

7

Getting That Raise and Other Important Uses for Portfolios

OVERVIEW

Thus far we've focused on how you can use a career portfolio to get the job you want. But, as we pointed out in the first chapter, that's not the only thing a strong portfolio can do for you. In this chapter we will examine some other particularly good ways that a portfolio can be a real career booster. And we will review several ways that career counselors and organizations can achieve important goals by encouraging the use of career portfolios.

Specifically, we will review how the Can-Do Career Portfolio system, targeting career P.E.A.K.S., can be put to good use in the following ways:

Personal Use:

1. To have a successful performance review
2. To get a raise
3. To get a promotion
4. To make lateral moves within your organization
5. To make a radical change in your career
6. To get consulting assignments
7. To get into college or graduate school

Organizational and Career Counseling Use:

1. In career counseling, placement, and outplacement activities
2. In staffing and other human resource management activities
3. In academic settings

As we'll see in the following sections, the criteria used for selecting items to put in your targeted portfolio and the strategy for presenting it should vary with its intended use.

FURTHER USES FOR CAREER PORTFOLIOS

The following are seven important ways to use the Can-Do Portfolio system to boost your career that we haven't discussed yet in any detail. Note that a somewhat different strategy is associated with each use of your portfolio.

Use 1: To Get a Favorable Performance Review

Get started early. In order to create a portfolio that gives you an edge in your next performance review, it is important for you and your boss to have an explicit understanding of the criteria on which your performance will be judged. If you have recently been hired, you should have a conversation with your boss concerning these criteria. And whenever you have a performance review, you should get a clear statement of what areas your boss wants you to focus on in your job. Once you understand the basis on which your performance will be judged, you can collect documents along the way that give evidence of your meeting (or exceeding) these expectations. The actual assembling of your portfolio for a performance review should begin several weeks before your review, so that you have time to collect whatever documents you are missing and can put the finishing touches on your portfolio at your leisure.

Assemble a portfolio that shows you have met or exceeded your boss's expectations. Here are some things to think about when you are assembling your portfolio:

1. *Identify the key performance criteria in your boss's mind.* List the performance criteria on which you will be judged. If you and your boss agreed to a business plan, that would be "an important" source for your performance criteria. The key issue is, "What will my boss be judging me on, and in what order of priority?" If you are having difficulty determining this, talk to a person you trust who has had successful performance reviews from your boss in the past.

2. *List the particular P.E.A.K.S. your boss considers most important.* Sort this list of performance criteria according to the P.E.A.K.S. they exemplify. These performance criteria may not have been identified as P.E.A.K.S. during your last performance review, but you can identify them as such. If, for example, your boss informed you in your last performance review that you were perceived as "abrasive" by your

peers and you "should do something about this," you might list "perceived as cooperative and empathetic by peers" under desired "Personal Characteristics."

3. *Collect documents that demonstrate that you have met or exceeded expectations.* Performance figures, letters of appreciation, awards, citations, certificates—*any* document that gives evidence of one or more of the high-priority P.E.A.K.S. you have demonstrated since your last performance review should be collected. To review the techniques for getting documents you've earned that you don't already have, refer to "Strategies for Creating New Documents for Your Collection," in Chapter 2.

4. *Organize your portfolio using a P.E.A.K.S. format.* Sort the above documents according to their P.E.A.K.S. categories.

5. *Select the best documents to show.* Choose the documents that give the strongest evidence that you have met or exceeded important expectations. Since, unlike on a job interview, you will be trying to show *most*, if not *all*, of the documents in your portfolio, try to select no more than a dozen documents.

6. *Assemble* two *copies of your entire portfolio.* Since you may be leaving a copy of your entire portfolio with your boss, you should create a second copy. The copy you leave with your boss should be something that can be easily slipped into a briefcase—a light, cardboard binder that has metal clips that you fold back is probably preferable to a heavier, three-ring, loose-leaf binder. Your boss's copy should be organized in the same way that yours is, with dividers and P.E.A.K.S. headings. There is, of course, no need to delete proprietary information from internal documents.

Try to show the entire *portfolio.* Using a portfolio for an annual performance review is different from using it for a job interview in that you want your portfolio to become the center of attention. Obviously you would like to linger on the P.E.A.K.S. that are most important to your boss, but if you can, you should show every item in your portfolio. Your goal is to demonstrate that you have met or exceeded as many of your boss's expectations as you can.

The kind of presentation that you are hoping to be able to make would go something like this:

> *Last year, these goals were identified:*
>
> *We agreed I would accomplish this [list goals here]. Here is what I did [list accomplishments here].*
>
> *We agreed I would work on these skills [list deficiencies here]. Here is what I did [list improvements here].*
>
> *We were looking for a 125% increase in production and according to the latest production report we are at 145%.*

In order to control the flow of your presentation, do not give your boss a copy of your portfolio until after you are finished discussing the items in your portfolio.

You will also want to make sure that by the end of the review you have a clear idea of the P.E.A.K.S. that your boss wants you to focus on in the future. With this knowledge you can begin preparing for your next performance review.

Use 2: To Get a Raise

Using a portfolio to get a raise is quite similar to using a portfolio to get a good performance review. In both cases, you will want to *show everything* in your portfolio that gives evidence of your having met your boss's expectations. And you should prepare a *second copy* of your entire portfolio to leave with your boss. If you have not done so yet, it would be helpful to first review the suggestions made above for using a portfolio to get a good performance review.

Here are some further things to think about.

Know the reasons why you might qualify for a raise. You will want to include documents in your portfolio that help you make your case. But first you need to know what your case is. Why might you qualify for a raise? Were you promised a raise if you met certain expectations? Does your organization offer merit increases if certain criteria are met? Do industry salary figures reveal that other people are being paid more than you are for essentially the same job? Have you taken on new responsibilities in your job that should qualify you for a raise? Are you offering to take on new responsibilities?

Talk with someone who has been successful at getting a raise from your boss. If you are going for a raise, it's helpful to talk with someone in your organization who has been successful at getting a raise from your boss. Find out about the particular P.E.A.K.S. that most impressed your boss.

In addition to P.E.A.K.S. documents, gather other key evidence that supports your case. In addition to documents that demonstrate the P.E.A.K.S. your boss considers most important, get documents that support the particular case you are making. If you believe you are underpaid, get a document that quotes industry salary levels for your kind of job. This data can usually be found using an Internet search engine. If you have taken on additional responsibilities not originally assigned to you that you believe qualify you for a raise, include a copy of your original job description along with your write-up of your present responsibilities.

Use 3: To Get a Promotion

Using your portfolio to get a promotion is quite similar to creating and using a Can-Do Portfolio to get a job with a new employer, particularly if the promotion is not controlled by your present boss. However, there are some differences that can work in your favor when you are competing against people from outside your organization.

Being inside an organization means you are well placed to find out about the precise P.E.A.K.S. that the people who will be interviewing you consider most important. And you are in a good position to demonstrate your ability to meet expectations in ways that are very meaningful to the people who interview you. When going for a promotion, here are some things to think about, in addition to the suggestions made earlier in Chapters 3 and 6 on creating and using a portfolio to pursue a job with a new employer.

Demonstrate that you are a reliable performer who is ready for a new challenge. Your goal is to show that you can be relied upon to do what you are asked to do *and* you are ready for a new challenge. You should include documents that demonstrate you have consistently met past expectations during your tenure in this organization. Including these items is particularly important if someone who does not know you very well is evaluating you for this promotion. But, unlike a portfolio that you use to get a good performance evaluation, you do not want to have in this portfolio mostly documents that demonstrate your ability to handle your present job. If you do so, you might come across as being indispensable in that job! The focus of your portfolio should instead be on the P.E.A.K.S. you have developed that make you ready to take on the new job.

Use your access to insiders to learn as much as you can about the new job and boss. Here's where you have a big advantage over outsiders applying for the job. Talk to the people in your organization (or to friends of friends in the organization) who can tell you about the expectations associated with the job. What are the specific responsibilities, activities, and goals associated with the job? What are the particular P.E.A.K.S. that the person to whom you would report is seeking in a candidate? Are there people from human resources who will also be interviewing you? If so, what are their biases? If there was a problem in the past with how this job was done, what was it, and how can you present yourself as someone who can make significant improvements?

Get documents that verify relevant P.E.A.K.S. you have developed in your current position or elsewhere. When collecting documents for your portfolio, you should not limit yourself to items associated with your present job. You are trying to demonstrate that you have what it takes to succeed in a new job, which means that the desired P.E.A.K.S. are likely to be somewhat different from those required for your present job. Any document that gives evidence of one or more of the desired P.E.A.K.S., regardless of where or when you developed these P.E.A.K.S., should be considered. It could be a document associated with a job you once had at a different company, or maybe an item from a volunteer or school activity that demonstrates one of these key P.E.A.K.S.

Show more portfolio items than if you were going for a job outside your organization. When you are applying for a promotion, the people who interview you are typically still thinking of you as someone in your present job. The burden is on you to demonstrate that you have important dimensions that your interviewers may have overlooked. To counter current biases, you may wish to show more items from your portfolio than you normally would if you were interviewing for a job at a different organization. You want to make sure that you can present concrete evidence that you have the very P.E.A.K.S. that are being sought in a candidate. And you will want to keep focusing on the future, or the interviewer might think you are too good to lose in your present position.

You might wish to leave a full copy of your portfolio behind, so that the people who are evaluating you can be reminded that your abilities are far more extensive than they might have initially thought.

To see an example of how a portfolio might be targeted for a promotion, you can refer to the Amanda Ferraro case in Part 2.

Use 4: To Make Lateral Moves within Your Organization

A portfolio can be very helpful if your goal is to make a *lateral move* in your present organization. Here we are talking about moving sideways without necessarily moving up in the chain of command. Getting a substantially different work assignment or a new kind of job in a different department are examples of lateral moves. Reasons for pursuing such a change may include wanting to gain broader experience within an organization, wanting to work with different colleagues, or wanting to work on a specific assignment.

To assemble a useful portfolio, you should do many of the things that we suggest you do if you are seeking a promotion. However, you should also remember that the further the lateral move would take you from your present setting, the more likely you are to be misinformed about the key P.E.A.K.S. and responsibilities associated with the new job. Therefore, it is particularly important that you learn as much as you can about the new opportunity from people in the organization who can give you reliable information about both the job and the person to whom you will be reporting. Here are two other things to consider as well.

Try to include evidence in your portfolio that you are a quick and dedicated learner. You want to be able to make the statement "I can learn new things quickly" and be able to back it up—particularly if the new job is perceived as a real stretch for you. Documents that refer to successful projects you have done in the past that required a lot of on-the-spot learning demonstrate that you are a "quick study." Evidence that you have continually engaged in professional development activities, like attending workshops, could demonstrate that you are oriented toward continually learning new things.

Feature P.E.A.K.S. from your present job that would be useful in the new job. Rarely are two jobs entirely different. Any of the P.E.A.K.S. that are important in your present job that would be considered very useful in the new job should be demonstrated in your portfolio—especially if these P.E.A.K.S. are particular strengths of yours.

Use 5: To Change Careers

Changing careers means making a radical shift in the work you do. Examples of a career change include taking on a totally different kind of job in the same field, like transitioning from being a stage actor to becoming a marketing person for a theatrical company. Or, even more challenging, changing careers could involve changing both the kind of job you have *and* the field in which you will be doing the new job. An example is switching from being a schoolteacher to being a computer salesperson.

If you want to get a job that is completely different from what you are doing now, a properly targeted Can-Do Portfolio can help you to convince a potential employer to take a chance on you. Since lateral moves within the same organization can sometimes represent a fundamental career shift, the advice given earlier in this chapter on making internal lateral moves applies here as well. It must, however, be adjusted to the fact that you are also seeking to move to a new organization, if that's what you are trying to do. Here are some further things to consider if you are seeking to make a truly radical shift in your career.

Explain your "translatable skills" that will be useful in the new job. Skills that you have developed in one context that can be used in a new arena are often referred to as *transferable skills.* You probably have already developed and demonstrated a number of skills that could ultimately be used in the new career you are trying to enter. The problem is you may need to do some "translating" so that your potential employer understands that you, in fact, do have relevant transferable skills.

If, for example, you are a nurse who is applying for a position in an advertising agency, you can't expect your interviewers to immediately understand the relevance of your nursing background for being a successful account executive or office manager. But, you can show your interviewers a picture of disgruntled and anxious faces in an overcrowded physician's waiting room and explain how you have to use your people skills to calm these patients down and establish rapport with them. And you can show your interviewers letters you have received from grateful patients and say: "You know, people are people. Given the way I've been able to handle patients with very distressing medical problems, I think I could be quite effective working with some of your most demanding clients."

Use a P.E.A.K.S. functional resume. A resume that has P.E.A.K.S. headings and uses a "functional" approach to organizing its items can highlight useful transferable skills and other important "translatable" P.E.A.K.S. that a prospective employer might otherwise miss. If the items in your portfolio verify the P.E.A.K.S. you feature in your resume, handing your interviewer a copy of your resume at the start of the interview will set you up to show these key items from your portfolio.

To review the particulars of why a P.E.A.K.S. functional resume makes sense for career-switchers, and how to create one of these resumes, refer to Chapter 5. For a quick overview, see "P.E.A.K.S. resumes are particularly useful for identifying transferable skills" and "Consider whether a chronological or functional overall plan works best for you," in Chapter 5.

Be prepared to show many items from your portfolio. Since you may have to overcome initial skepticism about your ability to add value in your new career, be prepared to show more of your portfolio than you would if you were not trying to make a radical shift.

For an example of a career-switcher's Can-Do Portfolio, see Karen Cresson's in Part 2.

Use 6: To Get Consulting Assignments

If you are a consultant seeking to build your practice, a properly targeted portfolio can be a very useful marketing tool during meetings with potential clients. Brochures and Web sites are excellent vehicles for making people aware of who you are and what your basic services are. They can also help you get appointments with potential clients. But when it comes time to sell your services to a potential client, a targeted portfolio can help tremendously.

When you meet with a potential client, two essential things have to be established if you are to get the assignment. The client needs to believe that you have the right *expertise* to help him or her and the client must feel a *rapport* with you. A properly targeted and presented portfolio is a wonderful vehicle for establishing both your level of expertise and a feeling of rapport. Here's how it's done.

Prepare a portfolio that demonstrates you have the expertise this person is seeking. A client's perception of your "expertise" will be determined not just by the technical skills you are perceived to have, but by assessments of your other P.E.A.K.S., as well. Prior to assembling your portfolio, try to find out as much as you can about your prospective client's problems and opportunities and about what kinds of P.E.A.K.S. this person thinks a useful consultant should have. To get this information you can use the same basic techniques described in "How to Select Items to Include in Your Can-Do Portfolio" in Chapter 3. If possible, try to have a phone conversation with this person prior to your meeting to learn as much as you can about the reason why this person is considering using a consultant and the desired P.E.A.K.S. of the consultant being sought. Talk to people who either know this person or are familiar with the kind of business and situation this person is in.

The better you understand the kinds of P.E.A.K.S. that your potential client believes an expert consultant should have, the easier it will be for you to select the right documents to include in your portfolio.

Present your portfolio in a way that establishes a feeling of rapport. A feeling of rapport—a sense that you and your potential client are "connecting" in a very positive way—is most likely to come if you place the emphasis, not on your portfolio and not on yourself, but on your potential client. Focus on being responsive to her hopes and fears. Ask questions. Listen very carefully and with empathy. And then *selectively*, in response to particular comments made or questions asked, show some documents from your portfolio. Show enough documents to establish your credibility as an expert who can help this person. But beyond that, you run the danger of overselling. You are better off leaving your potential client with the feeling that you have a lot of impressive things left in your "bag of tricks" that there just wasn't enough time to go through. A potential client who wants to see you again can very well become a paying client.

Use 7: To Get into College or Graduate School

As noted in Chapter 1, a properly targeted portfolio can give you a significant advantage if you are competing for admission to a school that interviews its applicants. The items in your portfolio can bring to life and make credible the things you say about yourself in your written application. And the fact that you have gone to the effort of assembling a portfolio to bring to an interview conveys the impression that you are strongly motivated, well organized, and "have your act together," so to speak—provided, of course, that the items you show from your portfolio do not undermine or contradict statements you have made in your written application! Here are some further things to consider.

Learn about the P.E.A.K.S. the school particularly favors and likes to develop. Talk to someone closely associated with the school about the P.E.A.K.S. that are most valued in candidates for admission and the particular P.E.A.K.S. that the school prides itself on being able to develop. Ideally, you should talk to someone in the admissions department prior to your interview. But you can also learn a lot about valued P.E.A.K.S. by talking to successful students, professors, and recent graduates. This step really should be done prior to sending in your application, as it will help you decide if this school would be a good fit for you.

Use your portfolio to establish your distinct identity. You should include documents that demonstrate P.E.A.K.S. that are clearly valued by the school. But there should also be a focus to your portfolio that establishes a clear identity for *you*. You want to be remembered in a positive way after the interview is over, and this is most likely to happen if you can present a set of items that establishes you as a certain kind of person who can make a certain kind of contribution. If you want to be remembered as being a natural leader, then make sure you have a set of documents that demonstrates this quality. If you have a special interest that you have developed, include three or more items that demonstrate your interest. Or, if you have a personal characteristic like resourcefulness or persistence in the face of adversity, be prepared to prove it. You can have several areas of concentration or themes in your portfolio, but if there is no distinctive way of summing up what you are presenting, you can't expect to get a forceful endorsement from an interviewer.

Try to "stay on message" when presenting your portfolio. Since your goal is to have the interviewer be able to sum you up in a very positive way in a few sentences, you should try to show as many items as you can that support the distinct identity that you are trying to establish. You will, of course, want to be responsive to the questions you are asked. And you don't want to be so focused on the points you are trying to make that you are boringly repetitive. But it's not a bad thing to be remembered as being passionate about your interests.

If you are very confident of your portfolio and most of the items are self-explanatory, you should bring along an extra copy of your portfolio that you can give to your interviewer as a way of keeping you in his mind.

ORGANIZATIONAL AND CAREER COUNSELING USES

As noted earlier, in addition to individuals using Can-Do Portfolios to boost their own careers, *career counselors* and *organizations* can also make good use of this portfolio system. The following three ways show how.

Use 1: Career Counseling, Placement, and Outplacement

If you are engaged in some aspect of the career counseling/placement business, having clients develop and use a career portfolio will increase your ability to help them achieve their career goals and make sound career decisions. Your role here is to coach your clients through the process of creating and using portfolios. A structured way to do this is to have your clients read sections of this book to get started and then discuss with them what they have come up with. Here are some of the expected benefits.

Your clients will have a power tool for getting jobs, raises, and promotions. Hopefully, by now you're in agreement with the proposition that a well-targeted career portfolio can be a very powerful tool for marketing oneself in the world of work. Making your clients aware of this power tool and encouraging them to use it properly will enhance their ability to get what they want in their careers.

Your clients will be better able to bounce back from adversity. A career portfolio, as we will see in the next chapter, is not just a tool for moving ahead, it's also an excellent weapon for fighting back from adversity. Not only does having a portfolio enable clients who have been "beaten up" in the workplace to regain a competitive edge. The process of assembling a portfolio is, in itself, a great confidence booster, since it requires a person to review documents that demonstrate his or her admirable P.E.A.K.S.

Your clients will be able to make better career decisions. As they create their portfolios, your clients will gain knowledge about themselves and the work world, which will help them make career choices that are right for them.

The process of identifying and assessing documents for their Master Portfolio is likely to give your clients a strong sense of what they like to do and the situations that seem to bring out the best in them.

The process of doing informational interviews to target their portfolios will help your clients determine which jobs and fields are most appealing to them and whether or not they have the P.E.A.K.S. to succeed in these areas. Armed with this *self-knowledge* and *marketplace knowledge*, your clients will be in a good position to make career decisions that work for them.

Use 2: Staffing and Other Human Resource Management Activities

In earlier sections of this chapter, we discussed using Can-Do Portfolios, targeting career P.E.A.K.S., for performance reviews, raises, promotions, and job changes within an organization, all from the individual's point of view. Here we'd like to make the point that organizations can benefit from having their employees use the Can-Do Portfolio system, as well.

An organization can use this system to do the following:

- Encourage employees to continue to develop themselves in productive ways
- Get the right people in the right jobs

Here are ways you can use the Can-Do Portfolio system to do this.

Encourage P.E.A.K.S. informational interviews within your organization. Employees who are encouraged, even required, to do a certain number of informational interviews in their organization are likely to become more proactive in managing their careers within the organization. Conducting informational interviews will enable them to develop a better idea of what kinds of jobs and activities would be most appealing to them in the future. And, if they ask P.E.A.K.S. questions, they will improve their understanding of the P.E.A.K.S. they will need to develop to get desired work assignments and promotions.

If the culture of an organization does not explicitly encourage employees to go on informational interviews, few people will feel comfortable doing so. To have a successful program, managers must be encouraged to grant informational interviews. Managers who do so are likely to find that responding to questions during these interviews sharpens their own thinking about the key things involved in the positions being discussed.

*Require portfolios for annual reviews that cover **all** of the P.E.A.K.S. categories.* Requiring employees to present portfolios that have documents from each of the P.E.A.K.S. categories during annual reviews improves the chances that professional development issues will be worked on throughout the year and properly discussed during the performance review.

During annual reviews, in addition to discussing an employee's accomplishments, progress made developing useful skills and knowledge and the extent to which relevant experience has been gained may be looked at as well. Personal characteristics can also be discussed to the extent that they are relevant to the employee's performance of her job. For example, if an employee has demonstrated a greater patience with customers during the past year, this could be commended. And if more work needs to be done in this area, this room for improvement can be noted and discussed.

For this "Total P.E.A.K.S." portfolio approach to be successful, managers should be required to unambiguously specify the particular kinds of P.E.A.K.S. that their subordinates should seek to develop and demonstrate in the upcoming year.

Create a P.E.A.K.S. master resume database. As noted in Chapter 1, firms that are most adept at reshuffling their employees to capitalize on emerging opportunities can gain a significant competitive advantage by using P.E.A.K.S. master resumes. Requiring employees to periodically submit updated resumes that feature the full range of their P.E.A.K.S. can help management identify the right people for promotions and internal reassignments.

The key is to get employees to include not only the P.E.A.K.S. demonstrated during their most recent job or jobs at the organization but also strong P.E.A.K.S. developed outside the organization. You can achieve this by having employees keep their P.E.A.K.S. master resumes on file. To review the technique for assembling this kind of resume, refer to "Creating a P.E.A.K.S. Master Resume" in Chapter 5.

Require Can-Do Portfolios in promotion and other staffing interviews. Requiring people who are applying for promotions, lateral transfers, and other new work assignments to present their portfolios gives management the opportunity to test the extent to which these applicants have the P.E.A.K.S. considered most desirable in candidates for these positions.

Use 3: Academic Settings

Schools and universities can use the Can-Do Portfolio system in a number of useful ways, including:

- Helping students get jobs
- Assisting students in getting into advanced academic programs
- Aiding students in setting career goals
- Assessing student progress
- Evaluating the effectiveness of the school's curricula

Here are some steps to follow to achieve the above goals.

Identify the desirable P.E.A.K.S. for the students' next steps. When designing curricula, schools should take responsibility for identifying the particular P.E.A.K.S. their students need to develop to get into advanced academic programs and to get the jobs they will be seeking. One-on-one interviews and focus groups with desired employers and graduate schools can be used to accomplish this goal.

Students should be encouraged to do informational interviews as early as possible in their academic careers so they can set realistic career goals and identify the specific P.E.A.K.S. they will need to develop to achieve their goals upon graduation.

Encourage and help students to prepare Can-Do Portfolios. This service can be coordinated by a school's career services office, or, even better, the process can be embedded in the school's curriculum. The career services office can offer workshops and counseling on how to prepare and use a Can-Do Portfolio that will help students achieve their career goals. On the academic side, students should be encouraged, or required, to assemble a Master Portfolio as they progress through their programs.

We have included an example of a student's Can-Do Portfolio in Part 2. It was developed by Peter Evans, who is graduating from community college and applying for his first job.

Help students get feedback on their portfolios before they use them in job interviews. Alumni and others who are already in the fields that students aspire to enter can be recruited to evaluate student portfolios before the students present their portfolios in actual job interviews. The feedback from this evaluation process is of tremendous value, not only to the students whose portfolios are being critiqued but also to those in charge of developing university curricula. Those responsible for fund-raising at the school are likely to be supportive of the idea of getting alumni involved in the process of advising students, as it is a nice way of keeping alma mater alive in the hearts and minds of alumni.

Use student portfolios for assessing student progress and quality of curricula. Periodically assessing the quality of the portfolios that students create within a particular academic program is a useful way of evaluating not only the progress of individual students but also the effectiveness of the curriculum.

FINAL THOUGHTS

We've been reminded in this chapter that there are many good uses for career portfolios. Nevertheless, it is important to remember that a portfolio is only as good as the documents in it. And, if you only concern yourself with your portfolio at the times when you might need it, you are not likely to be able to come up with all of your best material. Not on short notice.

In the next chapter we will explore ways you can continue to develop your Master Portfolio, so that you will have on tap the very documents you need, when you need them.

8

Developing Your Portfolio to Protect and Advance Your Career

OVERVIEW

This chapter focuses on how you can continue to develop your portfolio over time in a way that protects your present career and brings you closer to achieving your career dreams.

Many people have concerns about the stability of their present employment situation and most people have dreams about what they hope to be doing in the future. A portfolio can alleviate anxieties and help make dreams come true. In this chapter we'll show you how. Specifically, we will show you how developing three key portfolio habits will enable you to:

- Achieve greater security in your present career
- Position yourself to realize your career dreams

YOUR MASTER PORTFOLIO CAN MAKE YOUR PRESENT CAREER MORE SECURE

Much has been written about how lifetime employment and job security are a thing of the past in most organizations these days. It's true. Regardless of how well you perform and how well you are liked at your present job, all it takes is a downturn in the economy, a superior product or service suddenly being offered by a global competitor, or maybe being taken over by another company. And poof, through no fault of your own, you are suddenly "seeking other opportunities." It doesn't matter that your boss recently told you, "You'll always have a job here." She's been fired, too!

When working to achieve greater security in your career, here are some important things to keep in mind.

Your employability is your real source of security. An alternative to pinning all of your hopes for continuing employment on the "security" of your present job is to develop your "employability."

Your employability is the ability you have right now, given your present credentials, to find someone in the marketplace who would be willing to hire you. As many commentators have written, the quality of your employability is the best gauge these days of how strong your prospects are for continuing to be employed without prolonged involuntary disruptions.

Two key indicators of the quality of your current employability are (1) the *speed* with which you could be hired for a new job and (2) the *quality* of the job you could get.

Obviously, the current state of the economy and of the job market in your field set the general conditions for the quality of your employability at any given time. But your level of employability isn't something that just happens to you. There are steps you can take, particularly with a portfolio, to enhance your employability.

Your employability comes from having marketable P.E.A.K.S. It's quite simple: The more desirable your P.E.A.K.S. are to employers in a particular industry, the more employable you are in that field. And, of course, if you are versatile and have P.E.A.K.S. that would be considered valuable in more than one field, you are that much more employable. Having good contacts can bring you to the attention of prospective employers, but if you don't have the P.E.A.K.S. they are looking for, you are dead in the water.

Your Master Portfolio can be your "employability fund." If you suddenly found yourself unemployed and looking for a job, you would want to have some money in an account you could draw on to make up for your lost paycheck. The greater your savings, the more financial security you would have during periods of unemployment. But a "rainy day" fund won't get you a job!

Wouldn't it be nice if, in addition to having a savings account to deal with the financial issues associated with periods of unemployment, you could also have a "career account" that in times of emergency could be drawn on to help you get your career back on track?

This career account is, in fact, your Master Portfolio. Your deposits into this "account" are the documents you have added that demonstrate your P.E.A.K.S. If it is well stocked with the items that verify the P.E.A.K.S. that employers are currently seeking in candidates, it is, in effect, your "employability fund." If you find yourself suddenly needing a job, you can draw on this account to put together Can-Do Portfolios that give you your best chance of getting quickly employed again.

Later in this chapter we will go over the three key portfolio habits that will enable you to develop a Master Portfolio that becomes a very rich and well-diversified employability fund. Job security may be a thing of the past, but the confidence that comes from knowing you are very employable can definitely be part of your future.

MASTER PORTFOLIOS CAN ALSO HELP IF YOU HAVE A CAREER DREAM

So far we've talked about developing your Master Portfolio as protection against worst-case scenarios. A Master Portfolio is also an excellent vehicle for realizing career dreams. We will talk about the specifics of how this is done in a moment. But there's an important first step, and that is to have a career dream.

We are not talking here about your hoped-for next job, unless, of course, the next job you have in mind is *the* ideal job you were always hoping to someday have. We are talking about your dreams for the future, the career or job that you think would be ideal to have someday, but you are not so sure is very likely to happen. Your Master Portfolio can help you make it happen. But, again, a dream can only come true if you have one.

If you haven't done this already, you need to get some ideas as to what you might want to do in your future work life. The process of assembling your Master Portfolio is likely to have helped you identify the things you like to do and the situations that bring out the best in you. And this information in turn can suggest future jobs and careers that might appeal to you.

If you are still having trouble deciding what your ideal job or career might be in the future, we would recommend that you try some of the self-assessments provided in the best popular career development books, which include Richard Bolles' *What Color Is Your Parachute?* (Ten Speed Press, 2002), Mary Burton and Richard Wedemeyer's *In Transition* (HarperBusiness, 1992), and Edgar Schein's *Career Anchors: Discovering Your Real Values* (Pfeiffer, 1990).

Once you know what your career dream is, developing the *three key career portfolio habits* can make it become a reality.

THE THREE KEY CAREER PORTFOLIO HABITS

Once you have assembled your initial Master Portfolio, you can easily continue to develop it in ways that will prove extremely useful to you throughout your entire career. If you can make it a point to follow three simple portfolio rules for a while, the results will be so rewarding these portfolio "rules" are likely to become your "portfolio habits." The three key portfolio habits are:

1. Keep learning about the P.E.A.K.S. you need.
2. Always get documents for the P.E.A.K.S. you have developed.
3. Pursue activities that will develop your missing P.E.A.K.S.

Let's have a look at each of these useful habits.

Habit 1: Continuing to Learn about the P.E.A.K.S. You Need

To update and develop your Master Portfolio in a useful way, you need to know what kinds of documents to go after and collect. The basic guideline for identifying items to pursue is to determine whether or not these items verify one or more of the P.E.A.K.S. you might need to protect or advance your career. We suggest that you keep learning as much as you can about the P.E.A.K.S. required to achieve the following:

1. Getting the near-term things you have already targeted, such as a next job or raise,

2. Enhancing your employability, in case you suddenly need a new job, and

3. Positioning yourself to go after your long-term dream job or career.

Since the world of work is continually changing, you would do well to develop the habit of *continually* learning about the P.E.A.K.S. you will need to protect and advance your career. It would make good sense to do this, even if you weren't developing a portfolio. And so, we would encourage you to do the following things.

Keep on top of P.E.A.K.S. you will need to get the things you are going for right now. Whatever career opportunity is in your sights right now—a raise, a new work assignment, a next job—keep learning about the P.E.A.K.S. that the people who will be assessing you consider most desirable. To do this you can continue to use the techniques described earlier in this book in Chapters 3 and 4 for identifying the key P.E.A.K.S. associated with targeted opportunities.

Keep tracking the P.E.A.K.S. you would need to be hired for a job like yours. Yes, you already have this job, but if you were to lose it, what P.E.A.K.S. would you need to have to get another position like yours somewhere else at your present salary? It is easy to get so caught up in the demands of your current job you neglect the professional development activities that keep you up to date in your field. You may also find yourself becoming a "local expert" in areas that are useful to your current organization but have little value to other organizations. If people are turning to you because of your expertise in an arcane computer system that was customized for your company years ago, that's not necessarily a specialized knowledge that other employers would value.

To learn about the "employability P.E.A.K.S." you need in order to get a job similar to the one you have right now, do some of the following steps:

■ Review recent job postings and job descriptions for positions like yours.

■ Have conversations with knowledgeable insiders. Tell them you want to keep up and ask which P.E.A.K.S. are becoming most in demand for your kind of job.

- Read industry publications, paying particular attention to industry trends that may signal a shift in the P.E.A.K.S. needed for positions like yours.

- Attend professional conferences to learn about current issues in your field.

- Engage in shoptalk with your counterparts in other organizations to learn about the challenges they face and the P.E.A.K.S. they have demonstrated.

- Note the things you are told during a performance review that you are doing well and those things that you need to improve, as this could provide a succinct list of the key P.E.A.K.S. needed for your job.

- Seek feedback on your performance from work associates and customers, again to understand the P.E.A.K.S. needed for your job.

Learn as much as you can about the P.E.A.K.S. you need for your dream job. Once you know the kind of job you might want to have in the future, you will want to know what you should do to give yourself your best chance of being able to eventually get this job. Informational interviews can help you address both of these concerns, if you find the right people to interview and ask the right questions.

In Chapter 4, we explored the basic techniques for finding the best people to interview. These techniques still apply here, except that you now want to be on the lookout for people who, in addition to being knowledgeable insiders, also have a little bit of the visionary in them. Finding forward-thinking people to interview becomes particularly important if your ideal job or career is something you would like to do in the far-off future, since the desirable P.E.A.K.S. will likely have changed by then.

There's no perfect formula for finding visionary people to interview. But one way is to get the word out that you are particularly interested in talking to people who could offer insights into how the job and field that you are interested in learning more about may be changing in the future.

As for asking the right questions, we would suggest that, in addition to covering the topics recommended in Chapter 4, you also do the following:

- Try to get a "futuristic job preview." You should definitely still ask for a realistic job preview that describes the job as it is right now, since this is the known reality that, in fact, may not change very much in the future. But you should also ask for the interviewee's thoughts on what this job might be like in the future. Then ask yourself, Do these descriptions make you feel tingly with excitement? Or do they turn you off?

- Get your interviewee's thoughts on the P.E.A.K.S. that candidates for these jobs will need to have in the future. Can you develop these P.E.A.K.S.? More importantly, do you *want* to develop these P.E.A.K.S.?

- Make sure to get a thorough explanation of the interviewee's thoughts on the personal characteristics that incumbents of the job will need to have. If it sounds like the job would be a "natural" for you, great. But if it doesn't fit your natural style, that's a flashing yellow light, signaling, "Caution!"

- Ask your interviewee about the specific things you would need to do to eventually get the kind of job you have been discussing. Will you need further formal education? Are there particular kinds of work assignments or other projects you should be seeking? Are there certain kinds of job experience you will need before you can go after this job? Ask yourself if these are things you are willing to do in order to get this job. And if they are, find out about the specific P.E.A.K.S. that you should endeavor to develop at each stop along the way.

Since the P.E.A.K.S. associated with the jobs and careers you are considering for the future are likely to change over time, you would be wise to keep finding out as much as you can about latest developments in these areas. Articles in industry publications and conversations with informed insiders are particularly good sources for this kind of information.

Learning about the P.E.A.K.S. you will need to protect and advance your career will give you a good idea as to the kinds of documents you would like to have in your Master Portfolio. Developing the next two habits will enable you to *get* these documents.

Habit 2: Always Getting Documents for the P.E.A.K.S. You Have Developed

If you do nothing else with regard to developing your Master Portfolio, at least do this: Whenever you've done something that demonstrates one of the P.E.A.K.S. you might need, get something tangible you can put in your portfolio that verifies this.

The document may just come your way, like a letter of appreciation. Or it could be a natural by-product of something you've done, like an end-of-the-season group photo of a children's team you coached.

If something useful falls in your lap, that's easy, just save it in your Master Portfolio collection. But sometimes you have to be more proactive and go after items that will document what you have done.

As we mentioned in Chapter 2, if there are no items readily available to give tangible evidence of something important you have done, you should create such a document. To remind yourself how to do this, you might want to take another look at Chapter 2, under the section entitled "Strategies for Creating New Documents for Your Collection."

Habit 3: Pursuing Activities That Will Develop Your Missing P.E.A.K.S.

Your missing P.E.A.K.S. are the ones you haven't developed yet. It's no good looking for a document to verify one of these P.E.A.K.S., since you haven't done anything yet to merit such a document.

The way to rectify this situation, of course, is to pursue activities that will both develop your missing P.E.A.K.S. and at the same time give you the opportunity to prove you have done so. For example, if you need a certain computer skill that you don't have right now, you could sign up for a course or workshop that teaches this skill and also gives certificates upon successful completion. A student who needs evidence of real-world marketing experience to get a desired job upon graduation could volunteer to do a marketing plan for a struggling charity that would write a letter of appreciation at the end of the project.

The following are ways to go about pursuing activities that will develop your missing P.E.A.K.S.

Establish priorities for developing your missing P.E.A.K.S. Because you are unlikely to develop all of your missing P.E.A.K.S. simultaneously, it is a good idea to set some priorities. To help you do this, here are some questions you might ask yourself:

■ How secure is your current job right now?

■ Is there something very important you need to remain employable that you are missing?

■ Is there something that is glaringly missing from your portfolio that you will need in order to achieve your next career goal?

■ What are the most important P.E.A.K.S. you are lacking that you will need to achieve your long-term career plans?

Identify activities that will develop your high-priority missing P.E.A.K.S. Choosing the right activities to develop your missing P.E.A.K.S. is very important. To help you do this we have included a worksheet in the appendix, "The Career P.E.A.K.S. Aspiration Worksheet," which takes you step by step through the process of identifying the development activities that are right for you. Whether or not you choose to actually use this worksheet, you might want to at least take a look at the step-by-step process for filling it in, as doing so may inspire you to come up with some good ideas. We also encourage you to consider the following questions before deciding which activities to pursue:

■ What professional development activities have you been meaning to get around to doing for some time now? You probably already know what you should be doing to develop your P.E.A.K.S.

■ What sort of development activities were you told in informational interviews would be helpful?

■ How long would it take to do each activity you are considering? You can pick up a workshop quickly, but getting a further professional degree is going to take a lot of advance planning.

■ What will these activities cost you in both financial and personal terms? And how great is their anticipated yield?

■ Will you enjoy doing the activities you are considering? The bigger the project the more difficulty you will have sticking with it, if it's not something that grabs your interest. And if you are not going to enjoy this activity, will you really enjoy the job or career that requires it?

Consider creating a Will-Do Portfolio. Your Will-Do Portfolio is your Can-Do Portfolio of the future. This is the targeted portfolio you hope to be able to assemble when it comes time to apply for whatever it is you are seeking in the future. A Will-Do Portfolio is, in effect, your P.E.A.K.S. vision statement. It states the P.E.A.K.S. you intend to have at a specific time in the future and it lists the specific documents that you intend to have to verify these P.E.A.K.S.

The following are steps you need to create a Will-Do Portfolio:

1. List all of the P.E.A.K.S. you need to be able to achieve a future career goal.
2. List the documents you presently have, or could get, that demonstrate one or more of the above P.E.A.K.S. you have already developed.
3. List your missing P.E.A.K.S. These are the underdeveloped P.E.A.K.S. for which you do not have documents.
4. List the activities you intend to pursue to develop your missing P.E.A.K.S. and the documents you intend to earn to demonstrate these P.E.A.K.S. The protocol for filling out the aspiration worksheet that is included in the appendix will help you define these future activities and documents.

It takes extra effort to actually create these lists, but consider the benefits. A Will-Do Portfolio can help you maintain a proper focus on the things you must do to get where you want to go. And it can also help you identify the things you must *not* do—like pursuing superficially appealing career "opportunities" that sound nice but won't actually help you develop the P.E.A.K.S. you need to achieve your future career goal.

You don't need to write a fancy essay to create a Will-Do Portfolio. Just make a few lists you can look at every now and then.

Make sure it's fun. If developing your missing P.E.A.K.S. sounds like too much work, then you could very well be in the wrong field right now or targeting the wrong future for your career. If that is the case, doing further self-assessments and informational interviews could help you identify what's right for you.

Make it happen. All this planning is great, but it doesn't mean a thing if you don't actually go out and do it. Once you have identified a step you know you should take, today's probably a good day to start.

FINAL THOUGHTS

There's a danger here that we've made so many suggestions of ways you can continue to develop your Master Portfolio that you will say, "Sounds good, but I can't possibly do all this stuff!" Fair enough. Neither of the authors does *all* of these things *all* the time. And we don't expect you to, either.

We are not trying to organize your lives with all these helpful hints. We've made a lot of suggestions so that you can pick and choose the ones you think might work for you. And we hope you will give at least some of them a try. You will, after all, get out of your portfolio exactly what you put into it.

If you do nothing else as a result of reading this chapter, we do hope that you will develop Portfolio Habit 2:

Always get documents for the P.E.A.K.S. you have developed.

Make it a personal rule that whenever you have done something that demonstrates one of the P.E.A.K.S. you might need, you will find a way to get a document that verifies this. Do this one thing and your Master Portfolio "career account" will continue to grow in very useful ways. And here's a nice bonus: This is an account you can draw on as much as you like, without ever depleting it!

In the next chapter, we will explore some ways you can use a computer, if you are so inclined, as a tool for developing and using your portfolio.

9

Digital Options for Your Portfolio and Resume

In this chapter we will discuss ways in which you can use the computer and the Internet to facilitate and enhance both the creation and the presentation of your resume and portfolio.

Specifically, we will discuss the following:

- Creating and using digital resumes
- Getting digital help when creating your portfolio
- Presenting off-line digital portfolios
- Evaluating the pros and cons of having a Web-based portfolio
- The technical capabilities and constraints associated with different digital formats

We believe that in most career situations presenting hard copy portfolios in face-to-face meetings is the best way to achieve your career objectives. Nevertheless, we believe that you should use the computer and Internet to help with this process and to extend your reach. In this chapter we will show you the ways in which a digital portfolio can help you.

Let's begin with your resume.

We strongly encourage you to create your resume in a digital format, which will allow you to quickly target your resume by electronically "cutting and pasting." And, having your resume in a digital file means you will be able to rapidly transmit your resume to as many people as you like, provided that they have access to e-mail. Being able to quickly create the right resume gives you a clear advantage in most situations that require a resume.

In Chapter 5, where we discussed techniques for creating resumes that work particularly well with portfolios, we mentioned some advantages that come from using a digital format for your resume and some things to avoid, if you do so. The following is a review of what we said with regard to digital options for your resume.

Begin by having your master resume in a computer file. It is extremely helpful to have an updated master resume on file in a digital format so that you can put together a targeted resume on short notice. This digital format would include everything you might want to consider when creating a targeted resume and becomes a resource from which you can select particular items for inclusion in a resume that is targeted at obtaining a particular job or work assignment. If you save this master resume in your computer as a template, you will have the ability to quickly create a shorter targeted resume without danger of losing the original. To create a targeted resume, you would simply make a copy of your master resume, delete the items you don't want to include, and then edit the rest.

Use a digital format that cannot be altered when printed. When you e-mail a resume that is in a word processing format, such as Microsoft Word, the document may not print exactly as you sent it. For example, a one-page resume that is forwarded in a word processing format may come out as more than one page when the recipient prints it. For this reason, you may decide to e-mail your resume as an attachment in an Adobe Portable Document Format (PDF). If you do so, you will want to make sure that your recipient has the ability to read PDFs. For more details on the pros and cons of using Microsoft Word versus Adobe for transmitting documents, please see the section in this chapter entitled "Technical Considerations."

Use fonts and terms that computer programs will favorably identify. As mentioned in Chapter 5, keep in mind that resumes are often scanned for key words and phrases by computers that act as gatekeepers. Therefore, you will want to make sure that you use fonts that computers can recognize. Also, try to use words and phrases that computers are likely to have been programmed to pick up, both when describing the kind of job you are applying for and when describing your P.E.A.K.S.

Once you post your resume, you should not retarget it at that site very often. If you post your resume on a Web site, you can't keep changing it at that site or you will lose credibility. However, if you have the ability to post your resume at different Web sites that are meant for different audiences, you probably can post different resumes at each of these sites without undermining your credibility.

GETTING DIGITAL HELP WHEN CREATING YOUR PORTFOLIO

In addition to using the computer for word processing, there are other ways of getting digital help when creating your portfolio.

Use the Web to get images and information you want. You can use Internet search engines to get all sorts of useful information and images for your portfolio. For example, if you are applying for a raise and want to show your boss a printout that gives average salaries for your kind of job in your part of the country, you can probably get the information you need via the Web.

In Chapter 2, we mentioned that one of the authors of this book used an Internet search engine to find the Web site for a school in Brazil where he once was an instructor. He was able to download pictures of this school in Rio de Janeiro, which he then combined with other pictures he found of Rio, to create a visually appealing prop for discussing his international experience.

The same author also downloaded a full-color picture of the British flag from a Web site that sells flags, which he then attached to the first page of a consulting contract he had with a British company. The intent of including the flag was to visually reinforce the fact that he has significant international experience.

Use CDs to store extra copies of Master Portfolio documents. If you have access to the right computer equipment and software, you can scan all of your portfolio documents into your computer and then burn CDs to create backup copies of all of your documents. Obviously, you don't want to have everything only on the hard drive of your computer, since, alas, computers do crash. To be extra safe, it's a good idea to make several CD copies of your portfolio documents and then store these in separate locations.

PRESENTING OFF-LINE DIGITAL PORTFOLIOS

An off-line digital portfolio is one that is not posted at a Web site. In most face-to-face interviewing situations you will want to hand people documents that they can touch. They are more likely to trust an item they can hold than something they see on a screen. Nevertheless, in some situations presentation of your Can-Do Portfolio in a digital format can be quite effective.

You might *show your portfolio via computer to demonstrate your computer literacy.* If you are interviewing for a job in the computer field, consider bringing a laptop computer and showing items from your portfolio to establish that you are someone who really likes to work with computers. Having a digital portfolio on your laptop is not a dazzling technical feat, but it does show that you have computer sensibilities and might give you an opening to discuss your computer credentials.

Even in an intensely technical environment, it's still probably a bad idea to present your portfolio via computer. You run the risk of disrupting the flow of the interview. You might be perceived as trying to take control of the interview away from the interviewer by plopping your laptop down in front of him or her. And there's the danger that your portfolio will become the focus of the interview, not you.

You might e-mail copies of digitized documents to your interviewer after an interview. If you want to provide your interviewer with copies of documents from your portfolio, e-mailing these documents as an attachment might be an option, if they are digital files. Here are some technical issues to bear in mind, if you are considering e-mailing a document:

- Be sure the document is in a format that does not get changed with transmission.
- Be sure that the recipient has the appropriate software to open the file.
- Be sure that it won't take a long time for your recipient to open the file.
- If you compress the file so that it will not take a long time to transmit and open, be sure that the images don't become blurry as a result of compression.

For a more detailed discussion of the above technical issues, please see the section in this chapter entitled "Technical Considerations."

Whether you send your documents by e-mail or conventional "snail mail," it's important that you only send documents that have already been thoroughly explained, so that your interviewer understands the context for the documents and knows why they are important.

SHOULD YOU CREATE A WEB-BASED PORTFOLIO?

A digital alternative to e-mailing all or part of your portfolio as an attachment is posting your portfolio at a Web site. As we will see in the section below, "Technical Considerations," the Hypertext Markup Language (HTML) approach to transmitting your portfolio offers a number of technical advantages over e-mail with regard to speed of transmission and ease of display. If you create a Web-based portfolio, you can make your portfolio quickly available to as many people as you wish, without imposing the burden of downloading a multimegabyte attachment on anyone.

In addition to facilitating ease of transmission and display, a Web-based portfolio can include buttons for learning more, as well as all of the latest multimedia "bells and whistles," including animations, film clips of you in action, and voice-overs.

If a Web-based portfolio is done well, having one certainly conveys the impression that you are technologically savvy.

Scenarios in Which Having a Web-Based Portfolio Might Work for You

Use of Web-based portfolios presents certain problems, which we will discuss in a moment, but first note that in certain scenarios having a Web-based portfolio might make sense. Here are two.

You want to impress someone you happen to meet. Let's say that on an airplane or at a social function you happen to strike up a conversation with someone for whom you might like to work. To get this person more interested in you, rather than just give her a business card and probably never get a call, you could also give her a Web site address for your portfolio. The Web site address can be included on your business card. The person might find your portfolio intriguing and give you a call to set up an appointment to discuss a job opportunity.

You can't meet face to face. Perhaps you are granted a telephone interview with a prospective employer with only a few hours' notice. In this instance, having a Web-based portfolio might give you the option of being able to show items from your portfolio even though you can't meet face to face. If your interviewer has access to the Internet while talking with you, and you feel comfortable proceeding in this fashion, you can give him your portfolio's Web address and refer him to items in your portfolio that he would be able to quickly access.

Before you decide to create a Web-based portfolio, we would encourage you to consider the possibility that having to deal with one or more of the following issues might limit the effectiveness of your online portfolio.

Inclusion Issues

Certain items can't be included because of the public nature of a web site. Even if your Web site requires a password that restricts its audience, a Web site has a very public feel to it and is, in effect, a form of publishing. Anything of an intimate nature that was not originally intended for a public audience should be cleared with the people involved before making it available on the Internet. You may believe that you can include personal notes and e-mails you have received that give evidence of your admirable personal qualities. But the senders of these notes, who would not object to your showing these personal communications to someone privately, might feel their privacy is being invaded if you include these on your Web site. Unfortunately, items you have to drop from your Web site portfolio because of their personal nature might, in fact, be some of the most powerful documents you have because they verify personal characteristics that add value.

With a Web-based portfolio, you also have to make an extra effort to be sure you are not violating any copyright laws by posting, without written permission, things like newspaper articles in which you are featured. And you must be very sure that you are not unwittingly publishing proprietary information. For example, if you post a favorable performance evaluation you have received, even though you delete proprietary information included therein, you may still be on the wrong side of the law because you have distributed an organization's proprietary format for doing written performance evaluations.

Documents that are not self-explanatory are not likely to be very effective on a Web site. Any portfolio item that needs context and explanation to be understood is not likely to be a very powerful document in a Web-based portfolio. You can insert little text boxes that attempt to explain the relevance of the documents, and you can even try using voice-overs to explain how the documents demonstrate your important P.E.A.K.S., but it's not the same as being there yourself and responding to questions that the viewer might have.

Having to leave out documents that must be explained to be effective is likely to significantly dilute the impact of a Web-based portfolio.

Targeting Issues

The more precisely a portfolio is targeted, the more useful it is likely to be in helping you get the career opportunity you are pursuing. As explained in Chapter 3, you want to have documents in your targeted portfolio that demonstrate the particular P.E.A.K.S. that the people who can help you consider most important.

If you intend to target your online portfolio, here are some things to think about.

Creating a Web-based career portfolio that is open to all limits your options. If you create a single Web-based career portfolio that anyone can access, you lose the ability to offer different portfolios to different audiences. If, like Popeye, you decide "I yam what I yam," and you want to post just one portfolio and let the chips fall where they may, that's a worthy sentiment. But you are losing the ability to make subtle adjustments in how you present yourself to different people in different situations.

Web-based portfolios can be targeted. An alternative to the one-size-fits-all Web-based portfolio is to make different online portfolios available to different people by having different addresses for each portfolio. These addresses would be handed out selectively. Or, you can have one Web address for all of your portfolios, but have different passwords to access different versions of the portfolio.

People may notice when you retarget your Web-based portfolio. Be aware that once you have handed out an address and/or password for a Web-based portfolio, this information can be passed along to others to whom you might wish you could show a somewhat different version of your portfolio. This pass-along might become an issue if you are going through a series of interviews for a job. For the second and third job interviews in an organization, you might want to use a portfolio that has been retargeted because of things you learned in an earlier interview. You can, of course, change the content of your online portfolio along the way, but your interviewers might notice that you have done so and not feel comfortable with "someone who keeps changing his story." This issue is not so prevalent with a hard copy portfolio that you carry around in a briefcase. Since you don't show the whole portfolio at any given meeting, only you will know that you have changed its contents from one meeting to the next.

Presentation Issues

When you create a Web-based portfolio, you can specify the general look and layout of your Web site, as well as what's included, what goes where, the "tell me more" buttons, and the multimedia enhancements. In these ways you have a considerable amount of initial control over the presentation of your online portfolio. But, unfortunately, there are two very significant ways you do *not* have control over the presentation of items from your portfolio.

You can't selectively show the items within a Web-based portfolio. You can select what items to include in your online portfolio, but once these are posted, the viewer of a Web-based portfolio can choose to look at everything or nothing. Giving your interviewer the freedom to roam through your entire targeted portfolio significantly reduces your ability to control how it is used in an interview.

As we explained in Chapters 6 and 7, your targeted portfolio is *not* something you will typically want to show in its entirety in most interview situations. Your targeted portfolio is best thought of as an arsenal of different kinds of weapons that you might want to use to hit the mark, if the moment is right. You want to have many different weapons on hand, because, until you find out exactly what kind of a situation you are in, you can't know which weapon you will need. You don't know for certain going into an interview which items will prove to be most appropriate to show. The nature of the questions you get and the points you want to make in response to something that is said will largely determine which of the items in your portfolio you will want to bring to the interviewer's attention. It is unlikely that you would want to show all of the items in your portfolio, as doing so would be overkill. When you show everything, you are selling too much, and you run the risk of putting the emphasis on the portfolio rather than on you. If there is one rule we have emphasized for showing a portfolio, it's the oft-quoted architectural adage that applies to many successful strategies in life: Less is more.

Once you have posted a Web-based portfolio, those who have access to this Web site decide what they will look at. It is true that during a phone interview, if your interviewer has access to your online portfolio, you can refer her to particular items that she can view. But once your portfolio is onscreen in front of your interviewer, there's no telling what she will be looking at during the rest of the interview. For all you know, your interviewers will be idly scrolling through your entire portfolio while you babble on about a particular item they are no longer looking at. Or your interviewers might start grilling you about other items they happen to find that, given the direction that the interview has taken, you would rather not bring to their attention.

In sum, once your portfolio goes online and people have access to it, you've lost control not only over which items they will look at but also over how the portfolio will be used in an interview.

You can't explain the items in a Web-based portfolio the way you could in person. In general, portfolio items are best explained in the context of an ongoing conversation. A single document can reveal many different facets of your skills and experience. Which of these things you should emphasize is best determined by the nature of the person you are talking to and the kind of conversation you are having.

We mentioned earlier that you can use voice-overs and insert text boxes to give the context for items in your Web-based portfolio and to explain their relevance. But these explanations are necessarily generic, as opposed to being tailored to appeal to the particular mind-set of the viewer who happens to be looking at the item.

If you are on the phone with someone who is looking at your online portfolio, you can tailor your explanations up to a point. But you are limited by the fact that you can't see the other person's facial expressions in response to what he is looking at and what you are saying.

When you are in a face-to-face meeting, on the other hand, you can read your interviewer's facial expressions to help you decide how much explanation is needed to convince him that an item in your portfolio demonstrates one of your important P.E.A.K.S.

Professional Images

As noted earlier, having a Web-based portfolio does help you project the image of being up to date and computer literate, which can be quite useful—particularly if you are hoping to get a job that requires significant computer skills.

Having an "all-about-me" Web site, however, *may* also give the impression to some people that you are a person who is too focused on himself. An "I_am_it.com" Web site could turn some people off as being too boastful.

When presenting a portfolio during job interviews, you will want to demonstrate to potential employers that you can help them with *their* problems. As we noted in Chapter 6, you will want to engage an interviewer's interest in you, in part, by listening with empathy to the interviewer's description of the issues and problems associated with the job under consideration. Once you have determined what the key concerns are, you can present several documents from your portfolio as a way of demonstrating that you can help the interviewer with her problems. You position yourself not as an all-purpose fantastic person, but as someone who has P.E.A.K.S. that will be helpful to the interviewer.

If you create a Web-based portfolio, you should make a special effort to feature the kinds of problems you can help solve, as opposed to having your Web site look like a digital "Ain't I Great" brag sheet.

Computer Skill Issues

Creating a user-friendly, visually effective Web-based portfolio requires some computer knowledge. You can get programs that will enable you to create a Web site, but if this is the first time you have created a Web site, you will probably need help. For an overview of the technical issues associated with creating a Web-based portfolio, please see the section later in this chapter entitled "Hypertext Markup Language (HTML)."

TECHNICAL CONSIDERATIONS[1]

While most people can create an electronic portfolio of some kind, there are many technical requirements and limitations associated with this process that must be taken into consideration to create a valuable product. Considerable thought, technical aptitude, and time are required to reap the potential benefits of an electronic portfolio.

Technical Considerations When Selecting a Digital Format

Computer Literacy

Use formats that you have mastered. Ultimately, whatever electronic portfolio you present is a de facto piece of the portfolio itself. Presenting a mediocre HTML portfolio says that you produce mediocre work and are comfortable presenting it. On the other hand, a powerful, multifaceted Internet presentation of your portfolio could be a strong piece of documentary evidence about your technological capabilities.

Effective Format

It is important that your intended recipients be able to access your portfolio easily. Therefore, you must select a format that can be easily downloaded. After all, you want to talk with others about the content of your portfolio, not its problems with transmission.

Size

Bandwidth and storage limitations still play a large role in electronic communication. Many recipients will find it cumbersome to download and store a 5-megabyte mail message, even if they are anticipating your correspondence. An overly long transmission would certainly discourage people from passing it on to other parties who might be interested in seeing your portfolio. Even when using the latest technologies, keep it short and sweet.

Transmission Time

Select a format that can be transmitted quickly enough to add value to your portfolio. For instance, it would be very effective if you could say in a phone interview, "For an example of my work in restructuring, look at www.myname.com/portfolio/restructuring," and because this material is in HTML format, your interviewer could access it quickly.

Expense

Some formats require software and services that cost considerable amounts of money. These formats should be avoided, as your recipient may not have the appropriate software to work with them.

---

[1]This section was contributed by Ames Brown, with the reminder that the technical capabilities of the various digital formats described here will no doubt improve with the introduction of new versions.

Pros and Cons of Potential Digital Formats for a Portfolio

Electronic portfolios can be created in many different ways. Pros and cons associated with three of the most common formats are outlined below.

Microsoft Word

Summary: With this format, it's easy to create, modify, and store portfolios locally, but difficult to transmit portfolios to others.

Requirements:

1. If you have a computer, you probably have Microsoft Word, because it is the most popular word processing software in the world. Microsoft Word is available on nearly every university and commercial workstation, because it is the preferred software for editing documents. The creator of a Word document must have this software and the recipient must have Word or the Word Viewer to be able to view the transmission (see disadvantages below).

Advantages:

1. Since Word does not compress image content noticeably, it is an ideal place to store and edit portfolios. Word documents store the complete detail and clarity of the original digital image that is inserted. Consequently, the Word document's file size is large, but this size does not matter for your Master Portfolio because you will probably not need to transmit it frequently. From Word you can create a targeted portfolio and export it to a PDF or HTML format that is smaller in size.

2. Word makes it easy to position graphics and text and create attractive portfolios.

Disadvantages:

1. Word documents containing images are usually very large, making transmission by e-mail nearly impossible. This is because Word does not compress image content to preserve clarity. Alternatively, you can burn a CD with a large Word document on it and mail it, but that would eliminate the speed to be gained by using an electronic portfolio.

2. Documents opened and printed by the recipient closely resemble what is initially created, but significant discrepancies can exist. For example, if you create a one-page resume on a PC using Arial font and e-mail it to a Macintosh user, the document may print on two pages. This result occurs because many Macintosh computers do not have the Arial font and thus substitute the slightly larger Helvetica font. In Helvetica, a resume that was designed to fit on one page may get spread onto two pages. Other slight discrepancies arise with spacing and formatting between the various versions of Word. Therefore, no guarantee exists that what you save and transmit as a Word document will look the same once it has been transmitted.

3. You must be certain that all of your recipients are equipped with Word. Since Word costs nearly $200, it is unlikely that someone will purchase it just to view your portfolio. There is a free Word document viewer available from Microsoft, but unfortunately few people know about it.

4. Word documents can be changed (unless they are specially coded). This means that once your resume is circulated, someone could modify it to his or her liking before passing it on.

Adobe Portable Document Format (PDF)

Summary: This format is excellent for quickly transmitting portfolio documents to others, though documents may become distorted if the data is highly compressed to facilitate transmission.

Requirements:

1. PDF creation software, such as Adobe Acrobat or In Design, is required to read any document in this format. Recipients must have a PDF viewer, which can be downloaded from the Internet at no expense.

Advantages:

1. Creating PDF documents is easy, because you are usually converting from another format to PDF. PDF creation software such as Adobe Acrobat is essentially a converter that packages any printable file format (for example, Word, Excel, PhotoShop, HTML) into a PDF-formatted document.

2. PDF-reading software is ubiquitous. It is integrated into all the popular Internet browsers and comes with most new computers. The software is free. In fact, it is a required piece of software for many workplaces and universities. It is so common that most people are not aware they have PDF software on their computers, since it is integrated into the applications they use every day.

3. The output of PDF creation software is considered "portable" because it can be easily and reliably transmitted.

4. PDFs allow you to specify the quality of the image transmitted. When creating a PDF, you specify the level of detail you want for your portfolio's images. The more detail, the greater the file size.

5. PDF file size is generally very small. PDFs are known for preserving image quality at a small size.

6. PDFs are guaranteed to appear on-screen and print exactly the same on everyone's computer, including yours and your recipients'.

7. PDF files are unchangeable once they are created (unless you specify otherwise).

Disadvantages:

1. The compression of data that reduces the size of the file being sent, and thereby facilitates transmission, may also cause blurry images and even distorted text. As a general rule, the greater the compression of the data, the greater the distortion. There are, however, tools

you can use when publishing a portable PDF to determine the level of compression and consequent level of detail in your PDF file.

Hypertext Markup Language (HTML)

Summary: This format enables you to post your portfolio at an easily accessible Web site; results are impressive on-screen but usually not on print output; usage requires a higher level of computer knowledge.

Requirements:

1. You will need a host. Free hosts usually put advertisements on your page, which creates an unprofessional impression. To avoid having advertisements on your HTML, you will probably need to pay a monthly fee, unless you are affiliated with a university, in which case free hosting is usually provided. You may wish to secure a domain such as www.yourname.net so that the location of your portfolio will be easy for others to remember.

2. Unless you are a real techie, you will need HTML coding software. There are many user-friendly, inexpensive packages available.

Advantages:

1. There is no need to transmit your portfolio to others; they simply need to know the address. This setup saves you from imposing a multimegabyte attachment on someone's mailbox, which the recipient might find cumbersome. Others can easily share your portfolio, since they need only pass the address along.

2. An HTML format is universally accessible. Only Internet browsing software is required, and this software is built into every major operating system.

3. Access is much faster because images on the Web appear as soon as they are downloaded. A portfolio transmitted as an attachment, however, must be transmitted completely before viewing by the recipient can begin. So, if you are in the middle of a phone interview and decide to share your portfolio electronically, it is much more convenient to suggest "Go to [your e-mail address]" than to say "Wait for this 5-megabyte download and then open it up."

4. Only you can modify your Web site. Better yet, you can update your portfolio at your leisure and when people look back at it or pass it on, they will see your updated version. With other print or electronic formats, once your portfolio is in someone else's hands or e-mail box, you cannot change it. A Web-based portfolio gives you added control.

5. A Web portfolio is, itself, portfolio material; it is a demonstration of computer and Internet literacy.

6. You can distribute different targeted portfolios to different people. For example, you could give a prospective employer one address and then provide someone else with a different version of your portfolio at a different address.

7. Value can be added to your portfolio with the Internet in many different ways, including interactivity, links, and access to real-time data.

8. You can limit access to your portfolio by adding a simple password. A guest book can be included and, using a standard or hidden counter, you can also monitor how frequently people view your portfolio.

9. A Web site can easily capitalize on the benefits of the other document formats. For example, your page could display your portfolio as HTML and also offer a link to download your portfolio as a printable PDF or Word document.

10. An HTML format offers the ability to produce multimedia portfolio content such as audio, video, animated graphs, live formulas, and queries.

Disadvantages:

1. Unfortunately, Web content still tends to print poorly. Even the finest Web pages cannot compare to a well-crafted Word or PDF document. However, if printing is not important, then Web content can be impressive.

FINAL THOUGHT

The computer can be a wonderful tool. Let it be your servant, not your master.

10

Portfolios on the Fly: Creating a Portfolio in a Few Hours

OVERVIEW

This is the short course. In this chapter we show how you can put together a career portfolio in a few hours that will help you to be successful in whatever career opportunity you are pursuing. We assume that you are starting from scratch and haven't previously read any other sections of this book. And you haven't started collecting any documents yet. You may not even have much of a clue as to what a career portfolio is and how it can help you achieve your next career goal. But you are hoping that a career portfolio can help you get what you are going for. And you are in a *big* hurry.

We can help you. If you have an important interview coming up in a few days or less, and you would like to have a portfolio that will give you a competitive edge, we'll show you how you can do this in the amount of time you have available.

To put together your very best portfolio, you would want to read through this book in its entirety and follow the suggestions contained herein, but you may not have that luxury.

Then again, maybe you're not in such a hurry. You may be curious about career portfolios and what they can do for you, but you are not prepared to commit to reading through an entire book on the subject, just yet. We can help you, too. We'll give you the short course, so you don't have to wait for this book to come out as an "executive digest."

Specifically, the key topics in this chapter will be:

- A brief overview of what career portfolios are and how they can help you
- How to create *in ten quick steps* a career portfolio that will help you achieve your next career goal

At the conclusion of this chapter, we will refer you to specific sections of the book that will quickly explain how you can use your portfolio to good effect in a face-to-face meeting.

Throughout this chapter, we will include cross-references to other sections and chapters of the book so that, if you wish to do so, you can learn about specific topics in greater depth elsewhere.

We do hope that you will be inspired to learn about portfolios in greater depth. But for now, if you are reading this chapter to learn how to quickly assemble a portfolio, you've got a job to do. So let's go for it!

CAREER PORTFOLIOS DEFINED

In the next section we provide ten steps for putting together a *targeted* career portfolio that is designed to help you achieve your career goals. Before proceeding to these ten steps, let's review a few important terms and definitions that we have plucked from other chapters to explain what career portfolios are and the kind of portfolio that you will be assembling to suit your specific needs.

A *career portfolio* is a collection of documents and other easily portable artifacts that people use to validate claims they make about themselves.

A career portfolio is not a resume, which simply lists things about you. Nor is it a cover letter in which you write about yourself and your qualifications for a particular job. Instead, a career portfolio is a collection of documents that support and make tangible the things you want to say about yourself in a cover letter, a resume, or a face-to-face interview. Letters of commendation, performance evaluations, certificates, papers, images of things created or of activities led, are all examples of items that might be included in a career portfolio.

A *Master Portfolio* is compiled over time and is meant to be an up-to-date, complete collection of every item that you feel you *might* be able use at some future date in a career portfolio. These documents come not just from your work life but also from volunteer activities, from courses taken, from extracurricular activities you were involved in at school, and, in some cases, from hobbies and leisure activities. Any document that gives evidence of a skill, accomplishment, or other dimension to you that might make you an attractive candidate for a future career opportunity can be included in your Master Portfolio. A more accurate term for this compilation might be "master collection of potentially useful portfolio documents." For simplicity, we call it your Master Portfolio.

Your Master Portfolio is *not* meant to be the portfolio you would show to someone in an interview. It is likely to be too bulky to lug around and many of the items might not be of particular interest to the person to whom you would be showing your portfolio. The proper function of a Master Portfolio is to provide you with a broad selection of readily available documents to choose from when it comes time to put together a portfolio to take to a particular interview.

Because you are probably in a hurry, we are going to skip the step of creating a Master Portfolio. But, if you would like to learn more about Master Portfolios, take a look at Chapter 2.

A *targeted* career portfolio, which is what we will be focusing on in this chapter, is a collection of career-relevant documents that have been chosen because of their intended appeal to a particular audience. Simply put, these are the dozen or so items that you would bring to a meeting, hoping to impress the person or people with whom you are meeting.

We call a targeted career portfolio that is designed to appeal to a particular audience a *Can-Do Portfolio*. We use the term *Can-Do* because it gives evidence that you can do whatever is considered most important in the job under consideration, whether it's a full-time job, a consulting assignment, or the "job" of being a successful student in college or graduate school. A good Can-Do Portfolio enables you to make a convincing case that you are ready, willing, and able to get the job done. It helps you differentiate yourself from other candidates along important, job-relevant dimensions.

To get a quick idea of how a Can-Do Portfolio can be used in a job interview, see the section entitled "How Do You Actually Use a Career Portfolio—and When?" in Chapter 1.

A Can-Do Portfolio can be a great self-marketing tool when it is well targeted and properly used. If you follow the ten steps below, you can quickly create a Can-Do Portfolio that is designed to suit your specific needs. Later in this chapter we'll refer you to sections of the book that will tell you how to use your Can-Do Portfolio as an effective self-marketing tool in interviews.

TEN STEPS FOR QUICKLY CREATING A CAN-DO PORTFOLIO

Our plan is to explain each step as succinctly as possible and, where appropriate, give the locations in the book where these steps are explained more thoroughly, should you want further explanations and details on how to proceed.

Before beginning to do the first step, we suggest you quickly read through all ten steps to get a general understanding of how doing these steps, in the order presented, will enable you to create a portfolio that suits your present needs.

To get the best results, you would be wise not to try and skip any steps. As you will see, each step builds on the preceding steps.

Step 1: Specify the Type of Career Opportunity You Are Pursuing

In order to create a portfolio that is targeted for a specific purpose, you first need to know the particular *type* of career situation in which you intend to use it. Applying for a new job or for a promotion are two typical reasons for creating a Can-Do Portfolio. But there are other reasons as well, which include the following:

1. Having a successful annual performance review
2. Getting a raise
3. Getting a new work assignment or responsibilities (within the company)
4. Getting a different kind of job within your organization
5. Making a career transition
6. Getting consulting assignments
7. Getting into college or graduate school

For further ideas and a more detailed discussion of the types of career situations in which having a targeted portfolio can prove useful, see "Why Should You Use a Career Portfolio?" in Chapter 1. Also refer to all of Chapter 7.

If you still do not have a specific use in mind for your career portfolio, there is really no point in trying to create a targeted portfolio, since there is nothing to aim at. If this is the case, we recommend that you skim the rest of this chapter to get a general idea of how targeted portfolios are assembled. And if you think being able to create a first-rate Can-Do Portfolio could prove useful to your career, we suggest that you learn how to create and develop a Master Portfolio that will give you a broad selection of readily available documents to choose from in the future. Chapter 2 and Chapter 8 are particularly useful in this regard.

Step 2: Review Examples of Portfolios Targeted for Specific Uses

To get a feel for what a targeted Can-Do Portfolio looks like, look at the sample portfolios provided in Part 2. Each of these portfolios has been labeled according to the type of situation for which it has been targeted. Do not be concerned if the use you have in mind for your Can-Do Portfolio is not included in this collection of examples. In the next eight steps we will show you how to create a portfolio that is suited to *your* particular needs.

And do not worry if you do not happen to have many (or, in fact, *any*) of the kinds of documents included in these sample portfolios. All sorts of documents can be used effectively in a portfolio. We will tell you how to identify and get the documents that will work for you.

Again, the goal in Step 2 is to give you a general idea as to what Can-Do Portfolios look like. We will explain the actual process of creating a Can-Do Portfolio in the next eight steps.

Step 3: Obtain an Understanding of the Importance of Your "P.E.A.K.S."

As you reviewed the sample Can-Do Portfolios in Part 2, you probably noticed that frequent reference is made to "P.E.A.K.S." This is an acronym for the following five categories that are used to describe an individual:

- **P**ersonal Characteristics
- **E**xperience
- **A**ccomplishments
- **K**nowledge
- **S**kills

The fundamental strategy when creating a Can-Do Portfolio is to try to feature the P.E.A.K.S. that are likely to be considered desirable by the people who will be evaluating you. The particular P.E.A.K.S. that are considered most important will depend upon the kind of opportunity you are pursuing and the preferences of the people who will be assessing you. In Step 5, we will show you how, even when you are in a rush, you can at least make an "educated guess" as to which P.E.A.K.S. will be considered most desirable.

Our research has revealed that the most important category of P.E.A.K.S. in the minds of the majority of people who evaluate candidates for jobs is *personal characteristics*. By personal characteristics we mean personality traits or characteristic behavior patterns, such as being gregarious or highly detail-oriented. Which particular personal characteristics are considered most desirable in a candidate will depend upon *who* is doing the evaluating and the nature of the job and organization.

One of the great advantages of having a portfolio is that it enables you to present documents that give evidence of your highly valued personal characteristics. Being able to hand an interviewer a copy of a letter of appreciation from a client who thanks you for "always understanding what I need and being so responsive to my concerns" is far more powerful than just saying in an interview, "People find me responsive." A portfolio document can make the intangibles tangible.

For more information on the research we've done on P.E.A.K.S. and the kinds of items that might be included under each of the P.E.A.K.S. categories, you can refer to "The P.E.A.K.S. Categories" in Chapter 1.

Step 4: Describe the *Specific* Opportunity You Are Pursuing, Accurately

In Step 1, we asked you to specify the situation in which you hope to use a career portfolio—to get a new job, to build a consulting practice, to gain admission to college or graduate school, or whatever. The point was to make sure you have a specific use in mind, so that it makes sense to proceed with creating a targeted portfolio. In Step 4, we are asking you to get much more *specific* about the particular career opportunity you are pursuing.

The more accurately you are able to describe the real responsibilities, activities, and goals associated with the career opportunity you are pursuing, the easier it will be for you to identify the particular P.E.A.K.S. that are considered most desirable in candidates seeking this opportunity. The goal is to be able to describe the opportunity you are seeking with enough details so that in Step 5, you will be able to identify the key P.E.A.K.S. associated with this specific opportunity.

If you are applying for a promotion within your organization or a new job on the outside, what are the specific responsibilities, activities, and goals associated with the job? If a job description has not been posted, you can call ahead and ask for one. And if one doesn't exist, it is perfectly appropriate to ask to speak to someone who can give you a quick description of what the job entails. (If you intend to call the office of the person who will be interviewing you, please see Step 5 before doing so, since there are some P.E.A.K.S. questions you can ask as well.)

If you are going for a raise, you should be able to describe in specific terms the performance criteria associated with your present job, along with whatever additional responsibilities you may have taken on that justify the raise.

If you are a consultant seeking to strengthen or expand your practice, you should know specifically what kinds of clients and consulting assignments you are seeking.

If you are a student applying for college or graduate school, you should know which schools and programs you are targeting.

You will know that you have completed this step successfully when you can describe the career opportunity you are targeting to someone who is knowledgeable about the kind of opportunity you are seeking, and this person knows exactly what you are talking about. For example, you should be able to describe a job you are interested in with enough precision for an industry insider to know exactly what position you are seeking. It's not enough to say, "I'm looking for a well-paying, interesting job in marketing." If that is all you can come up with in terms of level of specificity, you need to do some *informational interviews* to learn about specific jobs in your field of interest. To learn how to do informational interviewing, refer to Chapter 4.

For further ideas on how to generate accurate descriptions of the opportunity you are seeking, refer to "Describing the Opportunity You Are Pursuing in Realistic Terms" in Chapter 3 and have a look at Chapter 7.

Step 5: Identify the Key "P.E.A.K.S." Associated with This Opportunity

Once you are able to describe with precision the career opportunity you are targeting, your next step is to identify the particular P.E.A.K.S. that are considered most desirable in candidates seeking that opportunity.

The most important point to remember is that you should be trying to determine the P.E.A.K.S. that will be important to the person or people who will be interviewing you and to whom you will be showing items from your portfolio.

If you are in a huge rush, you may only have time to guess at what these P.E.A.K.S. might be. But you can, at least, make an *educated* guess that is informed by what you already know about the opportunity you are pursuing. To do this, put yourself in the place of the interviewer and ask yourself what would be the most important P.E.A.K.S. given what you know about the activities, responsibilities, and goals associated with this opportunity.

If you can find the time, we strongly encourage you to talk to a few people who know enough about the kind of opportunity you are seeking to be able to give you some ideas as to what the key P.E.A.K.S. might be in the minds of your interviewers. Even if you only have a short phone conversation, if you talk to the right person you are likely to get some very useful advice.

When pursuing a specific job, a particularly good person to talk to is someone who works with the person who will be interviewing you. It is not unreasonable to call the office of the person who will be interviewing you and ask if you can have a quick phone conversation with one of his or her assistants "to learn more about the job for which I'll be interviewing." If you are able to get a hold of a person who works with your interviewer, in addition to finding out about the particulars of the job, you can ask about the particular P.E.A.K.S. that are important to the person with whom you will be meeting. The person who answers the phone, regardless of his or her level in the organization, may be able to give you some useful information.

If you can't hook up with someone who works with the person who will be interviewing you, try to at least talk to an industry "insider"—someone who is in a position to know about the kind of opportunity you are seeking and may even know something about the person who will be interviewing you. Suppliers of the organization and former employees, customers, and competitors all have their biases, but they also have a lot of inside information that doesn't show up anywhere else. You might also try to talk to someone who has worked at an equivalent job in a different organization.

Ask the people you talk with to specify the particular P.E.A.K.S. that are considered desirable. And be sure to find out about the personal characteristics that are valued, as these characteristics are likely to be particularly important to the interviewer. It is especially helpful if you can get the people with whom you speak to specify which of the particular P.E.A.K.S. they have mentioned are of the highest priority.

If you are seeking a raise, speak with someone who has been successful at getting a raise from your boss. Find out about the particular P.E.A.K.S. that most impressed your boss in this situation.

If you are applying to a school, try to talk to someone closely associated with the school about the P.E.A.K.S. that are most valued in candidates for admission. Ideally, you'd like to talk to someone in the admissions department prior to your interview. But you can also learn a lot about valued P.E.A.K.S. by talking to successful students, professors, and recent graduates.

Given your time constraints, you will probably only be able to do abbreviated informational interviews with the people with whom you talk. But if you would like to learn more about how to conduct an informational interview, refer to Chapter 4. And if the career opportunity you are pursuing is something other than a job, you might also have a look at Chapter 7.

To complete Step 5, *make a list of the particular P.E.A.K.S.* the person you will be showing your portfolio to is likely to consider most desirable. And again, be sure to include key personal characteristics. If possible, indicate which of the P.E.A.K.S. on your list are of the highest priority. This list is your best guess at this point in time, based on all of the information you have gathered.

Step 6: Find Documents That Demonstrate Your Desired P.E.A.K.S.

In this step, your mission is to gather all of the documents you can quickly get your hands on that give evidence of P.E.A.K.S. you have that would *appeal to the particular people* to whom you will be showing your portfolio. From Step 5, you have a list of the P.E.A.K.S. that are likely to be considered most desirable by the person or people who will be evaluating you. Your job now is to do the best you can, in the time you have, to find documents that demonstrate you have these desired P.E.A.K.S.

Letters of commendation, performance evaluations, certificates, papers, images of things created or of activities led are just a few examples of the kinds of items that might be included in your Can-Do Portfolio.

As we noted earlier, it is important to remember that portfolio documents can come not just from your work life, but also from volunteer activities, from courses taken, from extracurricular activities you were involved in at school, and, in some cases, from hobbies and leisure activities. *Any* document that gives evidence of one or more of the desired P.E.A.K.S. on your list should be collected.

To get an idea of the range of items that might be included in a portfolio, and to get you thinking about useful items you might have, read "What You Should Be Looking For," in Chapter 2. The table entitled "Examples of Portfolio Documents" might be particularly useful for giving you some ideas.

We should point out that Chapter 2 focuses on casting a wide net to collect items for a Master Portfolio. But right now, you are looking for items that give evidence of the specific P.E.A.K.S. on your list from Step 5. To get a clear understanding of how to identify items that support particular P.E.A.K.S., refer to "Selecting Items That Best Demonstrate How You Have the Desired P.E.A.K.S." in Chapter 3.

Remember that your portfolio documents do *not* have to be self-explanatory. You will be explaining whatever items you show during an interview. Portfolio items should be used in the context of a conversation, not as stand-alone items that tell their own story. For a quick synopsis of how portfolio items should be used in an interview, see "How Do You Actually Use a Career Portfolio—and When?" in Chapter 1.

It's nice if you can find enough documents to cover all five P.E.A.K.S. categories. But you should put particular emphasis on finding items that demonstrate the P.E.A.K.S. that are likely to be considered of top priority by the people to whom you will be showing your portfolio. Items that give evidence of desired personal characteristics are likely to fall into this category.

To save time, we are focusing on gathering pre-existing documents that you can put your hands on without too much trouble. In Step 9, we will discuss some ways to get and create documents you feel you should have but don't. Honest ways, that is!

Step 7: Use a P.E.A.K.S. Format to Organize Your Documents

Your goal in this step is to put together a rough draft of your Can-Do Portfolio that is organized according to the five P.E.A.K.S. categories. To do so, we recommend that you get five manila folders and print the following headings on the tabs:

- Personal Characteristics
- Experience
- Accomplishments
- Knowledge
- Skills

Once you have created folders that have these tabs, do a rough sort of the documents you have collected, filing each document according to which of the above P.E.A.K.S. that document demonstrates.

Clearly, some of your items could be filed under more than one of the above categories. In these cases you can put photocopies of the same document in two or more different sections.

If you are thinking of using a loose-leaf notebook instead of manila folders to hold the documents for your draft, that's fine, but do *not* punch holes in original documents, since this can make them less appealing visually. Either place the documents in translucent sheet protectors with holes or make photocopies of your original documents and then punch holes in the copies.

Don't spend a lot of time agonizing over what should go where. This is a rough draft that you can refine and hone in the next two steps.

Step 8: Assess the Draft of Your Portfolio, Strategically

Now that you have a rough draft of your Can-Do Portfolio, your task is to assess your draft from a *strategic* point of view in order to select the best documents to include in your final draft and identify the holes that you should try to fill.

It is important to understand that your portfolio is meant to be a tool you can use to enhance the presentation of your qualifications for the opportunity you are pursuing. In most situations, your portfolio should *not* be the central feature of the interview. You will want the emphasis to be on you, not on your portfolio.

You do not have to have a perfect portfolio that you would show from cover to cover. What you do want to have is a collection of items that you can strategically draw on to support claims you wish to make about yourself.

If you have not done so yet, you might want to take a look at "How Do You Actually Use a Career Portfolio—and When?" in Chapter 1, to get an idea of how a portfolio can be used strategically.

If you are intending to use your portfolio for something other than getting a new job outside your current organization, you can consult Chapter 7 to learn more about the specific strategy your portfolio should support.

To assess the strategic value of the items in your draft portfolio, we recommend that you keep the list of desired P.E.A.K.S. that you developed in Step 5 readily visible and ask yourself which of the items in your draft will enable you to achieve one or more of the following four strategic objectives:

1. *Covering the high-priority P.E.A.K.S.* If there is a particular personal characteristic or a specific kind of experience, accomplishment, knowledge, or skill that is likely to be considered *highly* desirable in a candidate, you should try to include several different documents that give evidence that you have this special something.

2. *Demonstrating key personal characteristics.* You may not be able to include entries in all of the P.E.A.K.S. categories, but you should give a high priority to identifying documents that indicate that you have the particular personal characteristics that the interviewer is likely to consider desirable. Remember, your portfolio gives you the opportunity to make these intangibles tangible.

3. *Leading from strength.* Any of the desired P.E.A.K.S. that are particular strengths of yours should be documented, if possible.

4. *Addressing important concerns.* Is there something about your candidacy that makes you vulnerable? An example of a vulnerability that can be effectively addressed with a good portfolio item is the gender issue that the male OB/GYN physician featured in Part 2 faced. Roughly 80 percent of the doctors he would be competing against for a position in the women's health field are female physicians. The burden was on him to overcome the presumption that female patients find female doctors far more sensitive to their needs and concerns than he, as a male, could ever be. For this reason he included in his portfolio a letter from a female patient that thanked him for his caring manner and sensitivity to her concerns and needs.

Items that allay any concerns that might arise about your qualifications are strong candidates for inclusion in your final draft.

To complete Step 8, *pick the eight to twelve items* that you believe will best help you *achieve the above strategic objectives*. (Okay, you can go higher, but, please, no more than twenty!)

Identify the "holes" in your targeted portfolio. Are there strategic objectives that your current collection of documents will not help you achieve? If so, what are the particular P.E.A.K.S. that you would need to demonstrate to be able to achieve these objectives? *Make a list of these still-needed P.E.A.K.S.*

Step 9: Fill the Holes

Your mission in this step is to do the best you can, in the time you have, to fill the holes you have identified in your targeted portfolio. Take a look at your still-needed P.E.A.K.S. list from Step 8. Which of these still-needed P.E.A.K.S. represent the most serious shortcomings in your targeted portfolio? And of these "gaping hole" P.E.A.K.S., which represent ones you have already developed but don't have documents for? These are the areas you should be focusing on.

You simply don't have time right now to develop new P.E.A.K.S. But you can go after and create, if need be, documents that demonstrate P.E.A.K.S. you have *already* developed. In Chapter 8, we discuss activities you can pursue in the future to develop your not-yet-developed P.E.A.K.S. But, again, there's little time for that now.

Use your time wisely in this step. Go after the documents you really need that you can get or create in the time you have available to you.

To get the things you need may take a bit of extra effort on your part. You have to be willing to contact people who can help you *and* be willing to do most of the work associated with your request.

If someone, for example, has sent you a letter of appreciation that gives evidence of one of your important P.E.A.K.S. and you've thrown it out or can't find it, you may need to obtain a replacement. In most cases, it is perfectly appropriate for you to ask the person who sent the letter for help—particularly if this person still feels kindly disposed toward you. You can explain why you need the letter and ask if the person can send you another copy. Actually, this is a great opportunity to get an even better letter of appreciation than the one you originally received, if you are willing to do the work of drafting it the way you want it. Simply explain to the person which of your P.E.A.K.S. you are trying to verify with the letter and offer to write a draft for her review and signature.

If someone once complimented you for something you did that demonstrated one of your still-needed P.E.A.K.S., even though he never sent you a letter, you could explain why you need a letter now and offer to draft it. Even if you didn't receive any compliments at the time, you can still ask a person who can verify what you did to "write" a letter that you would draft for them.

If you are willing to make these requests and to do most of the work yourself, you are likely to be pleasantly surprised by how quickly you can get the testimonials you need. To make sure that you get these documents in time to use them, it is helpful if you can make arrangements to personally pick them up.

One word of caution: You must never, ever ask for and/or create a document that is less than truthful. You won't feel good about items in your portfolio that are dishonest. And, if you ever get caught using something that is not authentic, your credibility will be totally destroyed—the very opposite of what you are trying to achieve with your portfolio.

In addition to going after needed testimonials, you can also use images as visual props for discussing important accomplishments. For a few tips on how to do this and some further thoughts on how to create documents that are based on P.E.A.K.S. you have already developed, refer to "Strategies for Creating New Documents for Your Collection," in Chapter 2.

At the conclusion of Step 9, you should have between eight and twenty documents filed in your manila folders for inclusion in the Can-Do Portfolio.

Step 10: Assemble Your Can-Do Portfolio

In this final step, your task is to take what you've decided to go with and put it into a presentable format. You will need an appropriate carrying case for the documents you have selected, and you will want to have an attractive way of presenting each of these documents. Consider the following ideas for putting the final touches on your portfolio.

Carrying Case

Consider using some form of standard-size, three-ring binder for your Can-Do Portfolio. Loose items that are stuffed into a briefcase can get damaged and are hard to find when you are in the middle of an important conversation. Alternatively, these same items can be readily retrieved if they have been filed under headings in a three-ring binder. Furthermore, a person who is calmly flipping through the pages of a binder appears to be a lot better organized than someone who is fishing about with head stuck in briefcase.

The style of the binder that you use should support the image that you are trying to project. A binder that can be zippered shut and looks like a briefcase can be quite effective because you can also use it as a briefcase, bringing along a notepad and extra copies of documents you might want to leave behind. If your portfolio looks like a briefcase, it will not draw attention at the start of the interview, which means you can use your portfolio at your discretion.

Tabs

The items you bring with you need to be easily retrievable under pressure. We suggest that you use dividers with tabs that have the same five P.E.A.K.S. headings that you have used in the steps above. If a document could be filed under more than one heading, make extra copies of this document and file it under as many headings as you like, if that makes it easier for you to retrieve it when you are distracted and under pressure.

In addition to the five P.E.A.K.S. headings, you might also want to have a heading labeled "Resume," since it is a good idea to bring extra copies of your resume to an interview.

We strongly encourage you *not* to include original documents in your Can-Do Portfolio. Since portfolios can get lost and even stolen, we suggest that you make high-quality photocopies of your original documents and then store your originals in a safe place.

Photocopying documents will enable you to reduce or enlarge the originals so that they can fit comfortably in a binder that will hold 8½-by 11-inch sheets.

Photocopying allows you to create "collages" of documents, when appropriate. For example, you can create a collage of several favorable customer service comments on one page.

Although it does cost more, photocopying your documents in their original colors is probably worth the extra expense, since when the photocopying is done well, the copies look like the real thing.

Be very careful to delete any information that should not be shared from the documents you place in your portfolio. The photocopies that you present should certainly not be "doctored" in a way that creates any misrepresentations of what the original documents contained. But when you make copies, you should make whatever deletions are necessary to protect the rights of the authors of the documents you use. Deleting proprietary information from company documents is especially important if you will be showing these documents to a competitor.

Rather than punch holes in the documents you present, we suggest that you place these documents in standard-sized sheet protectors that are clear on both sides and are equipped with holes. Documents usually look better without holes in them. And, typically when you are showing documents from your portfolio, you will take them out of the binder and hand them to your interviewer. Having your documents in sheet protectors keeps them from becoming damaged and worn.

Using sheet protectors that are clear on both sides also gives you the option of displaying two items that are linked in some way in one plastic sleeve.

The above suggestions for assembling your portfolio are all discussed in greater depth in "Getting the Right Look for Your Can-Do Portfolio," in Chapter 3.

You will know you have completed this final step when you have a Can-Do Portfolio that you are looking forward to showing to other people. In the next section we will refer you to parts of the book that will tell you how to make the best use of your portfolio.

HOW TO GET READY TO SHOW YOUR PORTFOLIO

You are now eligible to add "Portfolio available upon request" to the bottom of your resume. But don't think that once your portfolio is ready to show, you can just hand it over when you get to an interview. If that's what you are planning on doing, you'd be better off leaving your portfolio at home!

During the course of a meeting, your portfolio should typically be used very selectively to support important claims you wish to make about yourself at the right moments. To be able to do this effectively, we suggest that you do the following.

Know your portfolio. Be thoroughly acquainted with what's in your Can-Do Portfolio, and know why each item is there. In Step 8, we reviewed the four key strategic criteria for including items in a targeted portfolio: (1) to verify high-priority P.E.A.K.S. (2) to demonstrate key personal characteristics, (3) to lead from strength, and (4) to address important concerns. Your portfolio will be useless if you can't remember what's in it, why these items are there, and how to find each item quickly. Flipping through the pages of your Can-Do Portfolio, while mumbling to yourself why each item is there, is a good way to become fluent with its contents.

Learn how to effectively show items from your portfolio. If there is one rule to follow when showing items from your portfolio in a job interview, it is to do so *selectively*. As stated earlier, your portfolio should *not* be the central feature of the interview. You want the emphasis to be on you, not on your portfolio. Your portfolio can be a wonderful tool for enhancing the presentation of your credentials, if used properly.

If you are intending to use your portfolio in a job interview, we suggest that you have a look at Chapter 6. For a quick review of the key things to keep in mind, be sure to see the "Portfolio Dos and Don'ts."

If you will be using your portfolio in pursuit of something other than a job, in addition to the above "Dos and Don'ts" section in Chapter 6, you would do well to consult Chapter 7, since the above "show it selectively" rule does not apply to all situations.

Practice, practice, practice. Once you know what's in your portfolio and how you should show items from it, it is very helpful to practice presenting your portfolio. Do so with someone who can give you good feedback, or if that's not possible, practice by yourself, saying out loud the kinds of things you would like to say about each item. When practicing, you should go through your *entire* portfolio, since you can't know in advance which items you will actually have the opportunity to show.

A P.E.A.K.S. resume is useful in conjunction with your portfolio. You should give top priority to practicing using your portfolio. But if you have some time left over, you might also consider creating a P.E.A.K.S. resume that sets you up to show key items from your portfolio during an interview. If you want to learn how to create one of these resumes, have a look at Chapter 5.

FINAL THOUGHTS

If you have worked very quickly, you may be wondering if your portfolio is good enough to use. A portfolio, we should point out, is always a work in progress. No matter how hard you work at it, there will always be something that could be improved.

The real issue is not, "How good is my portfolio?" The question to ask yourself is: "Am I better off having this portfolio than not having it?" The odds are that, even if you have put your portfolio together hastily, there will be one or two documents that you can use during your upcoming meeting that will give you a significant advantage that you would not otherwise have.

When you do have the time, we hope that you will explore other sections of this book so that in the future you can get the many benefits that will come from continuing to develop your Career Portfolio.

Part II

EXAMPLES OF TARGETED PORTFOLIOS

INTRODUCTION

In this part of the book we present five examples of targeted Can-Do Portfolios. Each portfolio is targeted at a particular job for a person who is in a particular career situation.

We have tried to provide enough details about each person's "case" for you to be able to understand why each document was included in a given portfolio.

Although it is true that your portfolio may have as many as twenty documents in it, for reasons of space, no more than a dozen documents are included in each portfolio here. Do not be concerned if you do not happen to have any of the documents that we have included here or if the documents you have in mind for your portfolio are quite different. You should use whatever works for you. Nevertheless, looking at these examples should spark some ideas. Consult Chapters 2 and 3 for further ideas about the kinds of documents you might want to include in your targeted portfolio. Hopefully, you will be able to come up with some color documents, which, for reasons of cost, we could not include here.

In addition to presenting examples of the kinds of documents that might be used in a portfolio, we also wanted to give you an opportunity here to follow the strategic process associated with targeting an effective portfolio. As explained in Chapter 7, different career situations require different strategies. And so we recommend that in addition to looking at the portfolio documents in Part 2, you also take note of the fact that different strategies are associated with each case.

Part 2 illustrates *what* might go into a particular portfolio and tells you *why*. We do not, however, discuss in any depth *how* these documents should be presented during a meeting. Nor do we discuss here *how many* documents should be presented. To review the specific techniques that should be used for presenting portfolios in each of the career situations described in Part 2, see Chapters 6 and 7.

The documents in this section are based on real documents but have been changed to protect the privacy of the individuals who have sent and received them.

The people in these cases are composites of people we have coached. All names have been changed to protect these people's coaches! Any resemblance to a real person bearing these names is purely coincidental.

The documents and people have been made up. But the cases, we hope you will agree, are based on very real situations!

CASES

Zachary Schwartz:	**Getting a Job in a Highly Competitive Field**
Gwen Johnson:	**From Homemaker to Paid Job**
Peter Evans:	**Getting That First Job After Graduating from School**
Karen Cresson:	**Changing Careers**
Amanda Ferraro:	**Getting That Promotion**

Zachary Schwartz: Getting a Job in a Highly Competitive Field

Zachary Schwartz, M.D., who is completing his residency, targets his portfolio to get an edge in a highly competitive job market.

CAREER SITUATION

Zachary Schwartz, M.D. is a fourth-year resident in an OB/GYN (obstetrics and gynecology) residency program at City Medical Center in Boston. His residency training is coming to an end, and he is now applying for a job in private practice.

Zachary has done very well in his residency program, but he is concerned about his job prospects. Not only is he in a very competitive field but he is also a male in a specialty that is rapidly becoming a predominantly female occupation. Of the residents completing their OB/GYN training at City Medical Center this year, Zachary is the only male. There is also a general trend in the OB/GYN field of women patients preferring female physicians. This is a point of vulnerability in Zachary's candidacy that must be overcome.

On the positive side, Zachary has performed exceedingly well during his residency, receiving many kudos from both patients and supervisors. He was selected to be the administrative chief in the final year of his residency, has learned advanced surgical techniques not normally offered in residency programs, has published articles in prestigious journals, and has taken a series of supplementary workshops on the business aspects of the practice of medicine.

Though he did not grow up in Boston, Zachary has fallen in love with the area. He doesn't want to leave Boston, but is afraid that unless he can make a particularly strong presentation of his credentials to job interviewers and find a way to allay concerns about his being a male in a predominantly female specialty, he will have to move to find a job. He decides to create a portfolio to help him make his case in job interviews.

TARGETED JOB

Zachary responded to the following ad that ran in a professional journal, and is offered a job interview.

Obstetrician/Gynecologist

OB/GYN position in North End of Boston. Position available to join a group of nine board certified OB/GYN's with excellent training. The group currently does 400 deliveries per year and each physician has a substantial surgery schedule. Expect about 40% of the practice to be OB and 60% GYN. The group has a favorable payer mix, shares calls equally, and has been in existence for 35 years. The group is looking for a new, well-trained physician with a commitment to the Boston area and a quality background. The physicians in the practice all come from top-notch programs. We are offering a base salary, productivity incentives, partnership potential, and benefits including 4 weeks of vacation, and 2 weeks of CME.

DESIRED P.E.A.K.S.

Prior to assembling a portfolio to take to this job interview, Zachary did an informational interview with a friend who is a partner in a successful Boston OB/GYN practice. He learned that the following P.E.A.K.S. are considered highly desirable in physicians seeking the kind of job advertised.

Personal Characteristics

Compassionate, sensitive, responsive, professional, ethical, intuitive, flexible, energetic, honest

Experience

Worked in a busy OB/GYN setting

Extensive surgical and obstetric experience

Accomplishments

Proven leader

Published

Knowledge

Advanced specialties within OB/GYN

Understanding of management and business aspects of practice of medicine

Skills

Obstetric and surgical skills

PORTFOLIO STRATEGY

Given the fact that residents have similar experiences during their training, Zachary needs a portfolio that would help him differentiate himself from his peers in favorable way. And he needs to allay concerns that OB/GYN patients might not be as comfortable with him as they would be with a female physician.

He will want to be able to demonstrate that he has developed the very P.E.A.K.S. that he knows from his research are considered highly valuable in candidates for the position he is seeking. And, in particular, he will want to be able to give evidence that:

- His patients are evidently not put off by the fact that he is a male physician and, in fact, find him a very caring and compassionate doctor who is sensitive to the emotions associated with their health concerns.

- He has very strong medical credentials that include an excellent knowledge of the latest findings in his field and training in surgical techniques that are not typically covered in residency programs.

- He has exceptionally good training in the business of medicine. He has taken a series of workshops on how to handle the management and business issues that come up in private practice. And he has been very successful as the administrative chief during the fourth year of his residency.

Finally, he would like to be able to give some evidence of the commitment he has to staying in the Boston area, as this would reassure his interviewers that if they hire him, he won't quit after a couple of years because he wants to live somewhere else.

CONTENTS OF THIS SAMPLE PORTFOLIO

Resume: This is a P.E.A.K.S. resume that is targeted at the job for which Zachary will be interviewing. It sets him up to discuss and verify P.E.A.K.S. he has that are likely to be considered desirable in candidates for this position.

P: Personal Characteristics

Letter from female attending physician. This letter, from a doctor who supervised Zachary during a segment of his training, praises Zachary for his ability to establish rapport with his patients.

Letter from a patient. This letter thanks Zachary for the sensitive and caring way that he attended to her concerns.

Picture of his new house. This picture of a house that he and his wife recently bought in a Boston suburb can be used as a prop to discuss his commitment to the Boston area, and to mention that his wife, who has joined a local architecture practice, feels the same way.

E: Experience

Residency review. This verifies his excellent all-around experience and performance as a resident in a very busy OB/GYN setting.

A: Accomplishments

Administrative chief recognition letter. This letter verifies his excellent leadership skills in a very challenging and busy setting.

Collage of logos from medical journals. This can be used as a prop to discuss research he did that was published in prestigious journals. If the interviewer seems particularly interested in one or more of the topics, copies of actual articles can be sent to the interviewer after the interview. Zachary might also store copies of article abstracts inside the plastic sheet protector, between the front and back display documents. He could pull these out if the interviewer seemed interested in his research. He could also store actual copies of these articles elsewhere in his portfolio carrying case. By doing so, he could leave one behind after the interview, if appropriate.

K: Knowledge

Letter on grand rounds presentation. This demonstrates his knowledge of the latest findings in his field.

Med-BiZ curriculum. This shows the breadth of his training in the business and management aspects of private practice.

S: Skills

Certificate for laser cosmetics course. This certificate also gives evidence of an advanced surgical skill not usually received during an OB/GYN residency.

Certificate for laparoscopy course. This certificate also gives evidence of an advanced surgical skill.

Zachary Schwartz, MD

1234 Shaw Ave, Boston Suburb, MA 02111
Telephone: (555) 555-5555 Pager: (555) 555-5555 #1234 Email: Zschwartz@hospital.org

Overview: OB/GYN physician with exceptional medical credentials who is responsive to patients in a way that will strengthen and build a practice's reputation. Caring, understanding, and compassionate. Willing to work the hours necessary in order to be successful.

Objective: Work in a busy group practice in the Boston area specializing in women's health. Utilize and continue to develop my surgical and obstetric skills. Add value to a practice.

Education:	**OB/GYN Residency** City Medical Center Boston, MA June 1998–June 2002
	Medical School State University School of Medicine 1994–1998
	Undergraduate State University, 1990-1994 Magna cum laude
Work Experience:	City Hospital Women's Clinic Resident-In-Training
Experience:	275 normal deliveries; 225 c-sections; surgical case list with more than 500 procedures.
Accomplishments:	Administrative Chief 5 published journal articles
Knowledge:	*Med-BiZ* Participant (Business Training)
Skills:	Laparoscopy, Cosmetic Laser, Obgyn Proclog, and Coding,
Certifications:	ACLS
Licensure:	Massachusetts State License
Languages:	Fluent: English & Spanish
Memberships:	CREOG Fellow
Honors:	Golden Key National Honor Society
Interests:	Cooking, Boston sports, golf, reading, history
Personal Information:	**Citizenship:** United States

References and Portfolio Available upon Request

CITY MEDICAL CENTER

Dr. Zachary Schwartz
Resident
City Medical Center
Boston, MA 02111

April 13, 2001

Dr. Schwartz,

As this block comes to a close, I wanted to recognize you for your compassion and sensitivity with our patients. As an attending physician it is always rewarding and encouraging seeing new physicians who are able to establish a true rapport with their patients. I received many positive comments from patients about the caring way that you interacted with them and their families.

The population we serve is deserving of the respect and compassion you show on a daily basis and you should be commended.

Keep up the good work and good luck with the remainder of your training.

Maria Zuelinski

Maria Zuelinski, MD
Reproductive Endocrinology

From the desk of Jane Smith

Dr. Zachary Schwartz
City Medical Center
Boston, MA. 02111

October 15, 2001

Dear Dr. Schwartz,

I am sending you this note to say thank you for all your concern, caring and compassion over the past few months.

I am aware that our situation is one you probably deal with on a regular basis, but for us it was extremely trying. You not only helped to reassure us, but also thoroughly explained the situation in a way that was easy for us to understand. I know we were fortunate that we had a positive outcome, as we were aware of what could have happened.

You are an extremely caring physician; we wish you all the success in your future when you enter into private practice. Your future patients will be fortunate to have such a skilled and compassionate physician.

Sincerely,

Jane Smith

Jane Smith

PS: We named our new son Zachary, enclosed is his photo from the hospital.

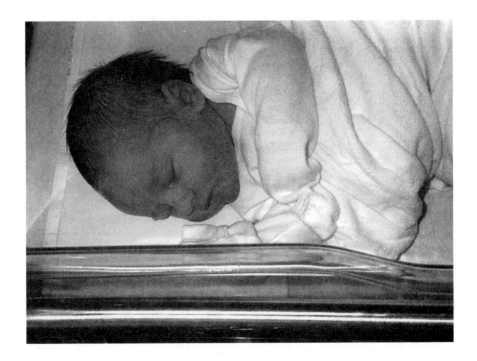

We have just purchased this home in a suburb of Boston

RESIDENCY REVIEW

Final Review

Resident: Zachary Schwartz, MD

Date: June 5, 2002

PGY Level: 1__ 2__ 3__ 4_**X**_   **Date of Evaluation:** June 1, 2002

Rating:
  5 = Excellent, 4 = Above Average, 3 = Average, 2 = Below Average, 1 = Unsatisfactory, 0 = Cannot Evaluate

Knowledge Base for PGY Level   5   4   3   2   1   0

Clinical Care

	5	4	3	2	1	0
History/Physical/Social Assessment	X					
Management Plans/Orders	X					
Progress Management of Patients	X					
Discharge Planning	X					

Comments: Excellent job in this area. Mastered level

Technical Dexterity Skills for Diagnostic/Therapeutic Procedures

	5	4	3	2	1	0
Operating Room	X					
Labor and Delivery	X					
Emergency Room	X					
Other	X					

Comments: Outstanding skills and procedures

Record Keeping/Chart Performance/Medical Record Dictation

	5	4	3	2	1	0
	X					

Comments: Consistently on time and complete records

Outpatient Clinics and Patient Care

	5	4	3	2	1	0
		X				

Comments:

Personal Attributes

Judgment	X					
Reliability	X					
Setting of Priorities	X					
Stress Management	X					
Accepting of Instruction		X				
Flexibility	X					
Compassion	X					

Comments: Well-rounded, ethical, energetic and responsible physician

Administrative Skills

Department Policy Compliance	X					
Dictation of Medical Records	X					
Submission of Statistics	X					
Other						

Comments: Compliant, on time and complete

Teaching Skills

Patients	X					
Students	X					

Comments: Excellent teacher. Responsive to individual needs

Interpersonal Relationships

Patients	X					
Nurses/Staff	X					
Peers	X					
Students		X				
Faculty	X					

Comments: Caring, compassionate and understanding

Areas of Excellence/Strengths: You continue to look out for the interest of others and insist on accuracy.

Areas of Needed Improvement: Try to learn to "compartmentalize" so that you do not take your patients' problems home with you, during the time you should be recharging your batteries.

Evaluation reviewed with the Resident: __X__ yes ____no

Residents Signature: *Zachary Schwartz, MD*   **Date:** *June 2002*

Evaluator's Signature: *Martin Carbone, MD*   **Date:** *June 2002*

CITY MEDICAL CENTER

Dr. Zachary Schwartz
Chief Resident
City Medical Center
Boston, MA 02111

June 21, 2002

Dr. Schwartz,

Administrative Chief duties are never easy, particularly in a busy hospital like ours. But somehow you made the job seem quite manageable and I have never seen our residency program run as smoothly as it has this year. Your organization of the schedule and the leadership skills you demonstrated with the whole residency program earned you the respect of everyone connected with this program. For this, we would not only like to offer our congratulations but also extend our heartfelt thanks.

Influential leaders can wield a tremendous amount of influence in the practice of medicine. Under your capable leadership, administrative issues did not get in the way of the smooth delivery of services and the training of our residents.

Thank you for an exceptional job as administrative chief!

Best of luck in the future,

Martin Carbone

Martin Carbone, MD
Program Director

THE REGIONAL JOURNAL OF MEDICINE

Annals of Reproduction

IJMR
THE INTERNATIONAL JOURNAL OF MEDICAL RESEARCH

Journal of OBGYN Research

NSI Journal of the
National Society of Internists

CITY MEDICAL CENTER

Dr. Zachary Schwartz
Chief Resident
City Medical Center
Boston, MA 02111

March 15, 2002

Dr. Schwartz,

Congratulations on your successful Grand Rounds Presentation. Your topic, "Recent Research Findings on Complications of Pregnancy," was well received and very informative. You have a special talent, teaching and explaining complex topics. I am confident that everyone in attendance learned something new and will use this information as they manage their patients.

You were very well organized and your presentation skills are excellent. The result was a Grand Rounds Presentation that was really brought to life.

Keep up the good work,

Martin Carbone

Martin Carbone, MD
Program Director

Med-BiZ Curriculum

Attended Regularly During Four-Year Residency

The *Med-BiZ* program was created by two physicians with MBAs who believe that residents can learn to apply business and management principles in a way that is beneficial to both their patients and the development of their practices. Through a series of workshops that include hands-on training exercises, the *Med-BiZ* program provides residents with the opportunity to acquire management skills and knowledge in the following areas:

Workshop topics:

- Communication Styles
- Communication
- Financial Management
- Effective Presentations
- Leadership/Managing Change
- Office Coding
- Activity-Based Costing
- Running an Effective Meeting
- Financial Planning
- Practice Management
- Team Building
- Teamwork
- Practice Marketing
- Practice Efficiency
- Patient Satisfaction
- Avoiding Burnout
- Negotiations
- Ethics
- Malpractice Issues

CERTIFICATE OF COURSE COMPLETION

This certificate is awarded to

Zachary Schwartz, MD

In recognition of completion of a course in Laser Cosmetics

AMERICAN LASER INSTITUTE

Sandra O'Brien   4/2/02

Instructor   Date

CERTIFICATE OF COURSE COMPLETION

This certificate is awarded to

Zachary Schwartz, MD

In recognition of completion of a course in Laparoscopy

American Endoscopy, Inc.

Kenneth P. Fontes
_____
Instructor

4/5/01
_____
Date

Gwen Johnson:
From Homemaker to Paid Job

Gwen Johnson creates a portfolio to demonstrate that many of the things that she has done in her role as an energetic, actively engaged mother make her a strong candidate for the paid job she is now seeking.

CAREER SITUATION

Gwen Johnson has been a homemaker for the past fourteen years. She got married just before her senior year of college, and shortly after graduating had a baby girl and then, a year later, a little boy. Instead of pursuing a career, she became a very dedicated, full-time mother. In this role, she coordinated her children's participation in numerous extracurricular activities, led some of the programs they've been involved with (such as Scouting), and did a lot of volunteer work for her children's schools. She also did a considerable amount of volunteer work for a local foundation, Wishes and Dreams, that finds ways to grant wishes to children with life-threatening illnesses who would not otherwise be able to realize their dreams.

Since her children are now older and less dependent upon her, Gwen finds she has much more free time and would really like to get going on her own professional career with a full-time, paid job. She wants to get into an active, multitasking work environment that can absorb her abundance of energy and she wants to continue to be actively involved in things that are meaningful to her. She knows that she very much enjoyed the two times she participated in volunteer fund-raising activities and would like to be paid to do that for an organization that has a cause to which she can relate.

Gwen is afraid that that she will have difficulty getting a "paid" job at a professional level, since she hasn't been paid for anything since her part-time jobs in college. Yet she knows she has talents and has been able to achieve a lot in her volunteer work. She feels she could excel as a professional fund-raiser and decides to assemble a Can-Do Portfolio to demonstrate this capability.

Through a friend, she has gotten an interview for a fund-raising job with For the Kids, a small, nonprofit organization that provides free books, science kits, and other learning materials for needy children.

TARGETED JOB

Prior to her job interview, Gwen contacted For the Kids to get a job description and learned that this fund-raising position includes the following responsibilities:

- Organize and plan fund-raising programs for the organization, and make contact with individuals or establishments to solicit funds or in-kind gifts.
- Gather and evaluate information about potential contributors to develop a mailing or contact list and to plan sales approaches.
- Prepare fund-raising brochures for mail-solicitation programs.
- Contact potential contributors and persuade them to contribute funds or in-kind gifts by explaining the purpose and benefits of the fund-raising program.
- Receive pledges or funds from contributors. Record expenses incurred and contributions received.
- Write letters of appreciation for donations.
- Act as an ambassador for the organization.
- Design and implement fund-raising events. Oversee event details from inception to completion. Coordinate public relations for the events.
- Coordinate the sale of emblems or other tokens of the organization represented.
- Organize and train volunteers and plan social functions to raise funds.

DESIRED P.E.A.K.S.

Before assembling a targeted portfolio to bring to her job interview, Gwen showed the above list of responsibilities to a professional fund-raiser she knew at Wishes and Dreams, where she has been a volunteer. She learned that the following P.E.A.K.S. would be considered highly desirable in a candidate for this position:

Personal Characteristics
  Leader
  Well organized
  Enjoys multitasking
  Outgoing
  Strong determination/perseverance
  Shows initiative
  Enterprising

Experience
  In nonprofit organizations

Accomplishments
  Proven ability as a fund-raiser in nonprofit settings

Knowledge
  Knowledge of fund-raising techniques

Skills
  Writes persuasively
  Makes an effective group presentation
  Trains others effectively

PORTFOLIO STRATEGY

Gwen wants to be able to use portfolio documents to overcome possible concerns about the fact that she has never had a full-time, paid job. And, most importantly, she wants to be able to demonstrate that during her career as a homemaker she has developed P.E.A.K.S. that make her a strong candidate for this fund-raising position. To do so, she particularly wants to be able to do the following:

- Demonstrate the relevance of her volunteer experience for being a professional fund raiser.
- Feature and make the most of her fund-raising experience, even though she has only done this twice.

CONTENTS OF THIS SAMPLE PORTFOLIO

Resume: This is a P.E.A.K.S. resume that is targeted at the For the Kids fund-raising job for which Gwen will be interviewing. The headings set her up to discuss and verify the P.E.A.K.S. she has that are likely to be considered desirable in candidates for this position.

P: Personal Characteristics

Collage of homemaker's multitasking life. Gwen can use this as a prop to discuss the fact that, as an actively engaged mother, she has had to become quite expert at *multitasking*. She can make the point that given all of the homemaker's activities she's been involved in, many of them simultaneously, she will have no trouble keeping up with the pace of the work world. And she can talk about how her natural inclination was to be the parent who was the *leader* of many of the programs her children have been involved in, such as Scouting.

Letter from parent thanking her for creating the "Granny Corps" crossing guards. This letter gives evidence of Gwen's *initiative, strong determination*, and *perseverance*. Although many of the moms had thrown up their hands and said it couldn't be done, Gwen found a creative way to provide free crossing guards for her kids' school. She can talk about all the red tape she had to cut through to get her Granny Corps idea approved. And as a way of underscoring her *organizational* and *training* skills, she can talk about the techniques she used for recruiting, organizing, and training grandmothers to be crossing guards.

Thank-you letter from fifth-grade class teacher. This letter shows she is *enterprising* and *well organized*, and knows how to create and coordinate special events that are both enjoyable and have a message.

Congratulations letter for making a very sick kid's dream come true. This letter gives evidence of Gwen's strong personal commitment to helping needy children, which is the fundamental mission of the For the Kids organization, where she is hoping to get a job. The fact that she has been a champion for making the dreams of many kids come true is also a testament to her *perseverance*.

E: Experience

Letter welcoming her to the board of Wishes and Dreams Foundation. This letter verifies that she has had significant *experience at a nonprofit* organization whose mission, like that of For the Kids, is to help needy children.

A: Accomplishments

Certificate of appreciation for being top fund-raiser at Wishes and Dreams. This certificate verifies that during a recent fund-raising campaign at this foundation, Gwen was the top fund-raiser on the board. She can use this as a prop to discuss some of the techniques she used to make successful solicitations from corporations.

K: Knowledge

Certificate for completing fund-raising course. Soon after being appointed to the board of the Wishes and Dreams Foundation, Gwen signed up for this series of workshops on fund-raising. She can use this document to talk about how she used her knowledge of fund-raising techniques that she gained in this course to become the top fund-raiser on the board of Wishes and Dreams.

After showing her certificate for this course, she might also mention that she has an undergraduate degree in educational psychology and talk about how her training in education, along with being a parent, enables her to have a good understanding of the educational service that For the Kids provides for needy children. There's no need to show her undergraduate degree to make this point.

S: Skills

Letter from school thanking her for chairing fund-raising drive. This document is particularly useful because it identifies some of the key qualities and skills that Gwen has that enabled her to reach her fund-raising goal four months early. Specifically, it lauds her for being a *well-organized leader* who did a superb job of *training* others.

Since it praises the effectiveness of the fund-raising letter she created, this document can also be used as giving evidence of her *ability to write persuasively*. Ideally, Gwen should have a copy of that fund-raising letter in her portfolio, but since she has misplaced it, using this document to show praise for the letter she wrote is the next best thing.

Gwen Johnson

45 Trail Lane • Corpus Christi, TX 02920   (555) 555-5555   email: Gjohnson@web.com

Overview

Objective:

Seeking full-time fund-raising position in a nonprofit institution.

Personal Characteristics That Add Value:

A well-prepared professional with an academic background in educational psychology and experience in successful fund-raising. Strong leader who is well-organized, creative, outgoing, and determined to succeed. Enterprising, strong initiative and innate ability to multitask.

Experience:

Fund-Raising Experience
Volunteer Fund-Raising
Wishes and Dreams Foundation; Wish Grantor
Board of Directors

Accomplishments:

Fund-Raising

Successfully headed fund-raising campaign to raise $1.5 million for school addition 3 months ahead of schedule.

Recognized as Top Fund-Raiser for Wishes and Dreams Foundation.

Special Knowledge:

Participated in two workshops on fund-raising techniques.

Skills:

Fund-raising letter writer

Ability to write persuasively

Training

Education

Texas State College   **Dallas, Texas**
B.S. Educational Psychology   1988

Community Service

St. Peter's School, Wishes and Dreams Foundation

References and Career Portfolio Available upon Request

Gymnastics

Little League

CUB SCOUT
LEADER

P

PTA
LEADER

Girl Scout Leader

Karate

SCHOOL

Dance

Golf
Lessons

Swim Lessons

Family

House Management
House Management
House Management

Wishes and Dreams

From the Desk of Joan Hennessey

Gwen Johnson
45 Trail Lane
Corpus Christi, TX 02920

September 19, 2001

Dear Mrs. Johnson,

Just a quick note to thank you for finding a way to get a crossing guard for our children. We've brought this problem up many times in the past, and each time were told that it would be too expensive to do. Your idea of forming a "Granny Corps" was brilliant, and you made it happen.

Thanks to you, now we know our kids will come home safely! You got it done, when others said it couldn't happen.

Sincerely,

Joan Hennessey

Joan Hennessey

St. Peter's School
Corpus Christi, TX 02920

Gwen Johnson
45 Trail Lane
Corpus Christi, TX 02920

May 5, 2000

Dear Gwen,

The 5th grade class would like to thank you for all your help this year as our room mom. Your coordination of all the special events, including class parties, field trips, cultural fairs and other extra-curricular events was very special.

As a teacher, I particularly liked the way each of the events you suggested and organized was not only fun but also educational. The trip to the Port of Texas to see the tall ships and learn about maritime navigation and the importance of protecting our seas is just one example of your creativity.

Never before have I seen such excitement from the children. And the fact that you did all of this keeping well within budget is a testament to your excellent business skills.

Thank you again for all your help.

Sincerely,

Miss Kathy Day

5th Grade Teacher

cc: Bro. John Pricine

WISHES & DREAMS FOUNDATION

Mike O'Neill
Executive Director

John Milluck
President

Joan Lutz
Vice President

Paul Quintz
Treasurer

Ellen Webber
Secretary

Mrs. Gwen Johnson
45 Trail Lane
Corpus Christi, TX 02921

October 12, 1998

Dear Gwen,

Congratulations on fulfilling your twenty-third dream. Michael B. and his family had a great time at the resort and have lots of pictures to share. Granting wishes is never easy but as you know it is very rewarding.

Your organizational skills and dedication have been a welcome addition to our organization. Your commitment to the children is obvious and is recognized by everyone you come in contact with.

Letters of appreciation from all the families you have worked with continue to show that your commitment is sincere and your dedication absolute.

Keep up the good work and thank you for your quality time.

Sincerely,

Mike O'Neill

Mike O'Neill
Executive Director

WISHES & DREAMS FOUNDATION

Mike O'Neill
Executive Director

John Milluck
President

Joan Lutz
Vice President

Paul Quintz
Treasurer

Ellen Webber
Secretary

Mrs. Gwen Johnson
45 Trail Lane
Corpus Christi, TX 02921

January 3, 1997

Dear Gwen,

Your request to be placed on the Board of Directors for the Wishes and Dreams Foundation has been reviewed by the external committee. We are honored by your request and would like to welcome you to our Board effective January 15th.

Your sincere commitment and community service experience make you a welcome addition to our board.

We would like to grow in the area of fund-raising and corporate sponsorship. We are confident that you are the right person for this board position. You have demonstrated strong fund-raising skills and will no doubt work well with Corporate America.

Keep up the good work and thank you for your time.

Sincerely,

Mike O'Neill

Mike O'Neill
Executive Director

CERTIFICATE OF APPRECIATION

WISHES AND DREAMS

This certificate is awarded to

GWEN JOHNSON

For her valuable contributions as Top Fund-Raiser

Mike O'Neill
Executive Director

9/22/97
Date

Certificate of Completion

Fund-Raising Consultants, Inc.

This certificate is awarded to

Gwen Johnson

In recognition of completion of Workshop I and II in Fund-Raising Techniques

Mark Nelson
Instructor

9/18/97
Date

St. Peter's School
Corpus Christi, TX 02920

Gwen Johnson
45 Trail Lane
Corpus Christi, TX 02920

January 24, 2002

Dear Gwen,

Fund-raising is no easy task. Companies and individuals are solicited regularly to help out with everything from school events to public television, and from church events to personal tragedy. When everyone is asking for support, funds become more difficult to receive. We were fortunate when you agreed to chair our fund-raising campaign.

Our goal was to raise 1.5 million dollars to build a much-needed addition of four classrooms to our existing school building. In fact, although there were many who thought this goal was too ambitious, your leadership and fund-raising skills made it happen.

Drawing on your leadership and training skills you did a superb job of converting a group of volunteers into a team that worked as a cohesive unit. The fund-raising letter you wrote was particularly effective in raising the funds we needed for our addition. We are truly fortunate to have had your volunteer services for our now successful campaign.

Our goal was to raise the necessary funds in twelve months. We reached our goal in only eight months. You are a gifted fund-raiser. We thank you for your efforts and the children thank you for the new addition, which is scheduled to begin in March.

Gratitude and heartfelt thanks,

Bro. John Pricine

Bro. John Pricine
Principal
S. Peter's School

Peter Evans:
Getting That First Job After
Graduating from School

Peter Evans targets his portfolio to demonstrate that although his G.P.A. has been average, he can be an exceptional performer in the job he is hoping to get.

CAREER SITUATION

Peter Evans is about to graduate from a community college with an associate's degree in marketing and is hoping to get a job as an assistant marketing manager for a fitness club. He's had an up-and-down academic record, doing very well in the courses that interested him and not so well in courses that didn't hold his attention. Now that he's competing for his first job, he wishes he'd worked a little harder in the courses that bored him, since his overall grade point average, or G.P.A., puts him pretty much in the middle of the pack.

Peter is applying for a marketing job in a fitness center because he's passionate about fitness and he loves promoting. He's not a great athlete, but he is a real fitness buff who tries to work out every day, and runs as many marathons as he can fit into his schedule. His passion for promoting was very much in evidence this past year when, as promotions coordinator for his school's Future Marketers' Club, he pumped new life into the organization. As promotions coordinator, he used his own creative ideas to recruit new members. He also did exceptionally well in the segments of the marketing courses he took that focused on the creative aspects of doing marketing strategy and promotions.

About a year ago, Peter decided that he'd like to get into the business of promoting fitness. With this in mind, just before the start of this academic year, he conducted an informational interview with the marketing director of a health club where he is a member in order to learn about the qualifications he'd need to get a marketing job in this field.

He learned that while real-world marketing experience is preferred in candidates, if he could demonstrate that he has done some promotional work while at school, and been successful at it, that would make a positive impression on interviewers. And so Peter, who's never had anything other than cut-the-lawn type summer jobs, decided to make an extra effort in his role as the Future Marketers' Club promotions coordinator, which he thoroughly enjoyed doing. He also learned that presentation skills and the ability to use the computer to create marketing materials would be particularly valued in candidates for entry-level marketing positions. To develop his skills in these areas, Peter took some workshops for which he received certificates.

There are some soft spots in his academic record, but Peter has also been industrious in important ways during his school career. He now needs a way to get potential employers to see the things he can do for them. Peter is confident that he will succeed in a marketing job if given the opportunity. He decides to create a Can-Do Portfolio to get that opportunity.

TARGETED JOB

Peter responded to the following ad in the newspaper and was offered a job interview.

Assistant Marketing Manager for Fitness Club

The role of the assistant marketing manager is to support the development and distribution of marketing and sales materials and to assist in the production of advertisements, marketing brochures, sales kits, and other promotional materials. Responsibilities also include designing layouts, assisting with the creation and implementation of strategic marketing plans, making presentations to institutional customers, staging promotional events, creating customer surveys, and writing articles. The position requires at least a two-year degree and relevant experience in the field or academic equivalent.

DESIRED P.E.A.K.S.

As noted earlier, before the start of his final year at a community college, Peter conducted an informational interview with the marketing manager of a local health club to find out what the key qualifications would be for an entry-level marketing job in the fitness field. He learned that the following P.E.A.K.S. are highly desirable for this type of work:

Personal Characteristics
   Creative
   Enthusiastic
   Strong follow-through
   Team player

Experience
   Marketing/promotional experience in work world or at school
   Fitness background

Accomplishments
   Proven ability to get things done, preferably in marketing

Knowledge
   Fundamentals of marketing

Skills
   Developing marketing plans
   Creating marketing tools
   Using computers to develop marketing materials
   Presentation skills
   Writing skills

PORTFOLIO STRATEGY

Being a new graduate who has never had a full-time job, Peter is concerned that he may be viewed as lacking the experience and other qualifications needed to be successful at this marketing job. And he knows he may be asked about his G.P.A., which has been less than distinguished. His goal, therefore, is to be able to demonstrate that he, in fact, has the very P.E.A.K.S. that are being sought in candidates for this position. In particular, he wants to be able to impress the following points upon his interviewer:

- The courses and activities he excelled at during his school career are relevant for this job.
- He has pursued special training in computers and in oral presentation techniques that will make him immediately productive at this job.
- He has already demonstrated creativity in developing a fitness marketing tool.
- He knows from the inside the whys and hows of physical fitness, because of his own regimen of personal training.
- He has had considerable success marketing a student organization.

In sum, he wants to be able to use his portfolio not only to remove any reservations about his academic record but also to demonstrate that he is uniquely qualified to excel at this job.

CONTENTS OF THIS SAMPLE PORTFOLIO

Resume: This is a P.E.A.K.S. resume that is targeted at the fitness club marketing job for which Peter will be interviewing. The headings set him up to discuss and verify the P.E.A.K.S. he has that are likely to be considered desirable in candidates for this position. Note that he does not list his G.P.A. He does list marketing courses he took that are relevant to this job, and that he can discuss with confidence because he has in his portfolio examples of two projects he did in these courses that received high grades.

P: Personal Characteristics

Letter of recommendation from a marketing professor. After doing very well in two courses that he took with this professor, he asked her to write a letter of recommendation. He knew her well enough to ask her to mention his *creativity, follow-through,* and the fact that he is a *team player.* She agreed that he has these qualities and included them in her letter. He can now use this letter as evidence that he has these important personal characteristics.

E: Experience

Medals for completing four marathons. These are medals he received for completing four big city marathons in the past year. He can use this as a prop to discuss his background in fitness. He can make the point that because of his personal experience in this area, he will be able to create marketing messages that explain the pleasures and benefits of fitness. The fact that he completed these marathons can also be used as evidence of his follow-through. He finishes what he starts.

A: Accomplishments

Congratulatory letter from the faculty advisor to the Future Marketers' Club. This letter demonstrates his success at staging a promotional event for a student organization. He can use it as proof that he not only has *experience in marketing,* he *can get things done.* He can discuss how he *followed through* on an idea he had and *got great results.* Once he uses this document to establish that he's had a notable success as a promotions person, he can also use this as a springboard to discuss other things he accomplished as the promotions coordinator for this student organization.

K: Knowledge

Synopsis of marketing concentration courses. This document is basically a rewrite of the descriptions of applicable courses in the school's course catalog. Since the write-ups are brief enough to be taken in at a glance, Peter can hand this document to his interviewer to quickly establish that he has a solid foundation in the *fundamentals of marketing.* He can use these descriptions to segue into a discussion of the outstanding projects he did in these courses.

S: Skills

Picture of a marketing tool with professor's note. Peter developed this marketing tool for the promotions segment of one of his marketing courses. His assignment was to pick an industry and then come up with a memorable message for a pin that a company could use to promote its product or service. Peter picked the fitness industry and came up with the "Do you want a pill or the sure cure" message. Although not required to do so, he took the assignment further and actually designed and produced a set of pins with this message on it. His teacher was thrilled. For his portfolio, Peter has included a picture of the pin he created with his professor's note. Alternatively, he might have stuck an actual pin onto the professor's note. Either way, this is a very effective way of illustrating his *skill at creating marketing tools*.

Certificate for Computer-Aided Design for Marketing course. Peter knows from his informational interview that *using computers for creating marketing materials* is considered an important skill to have. He can make the point that he took this series of workshops on top of his regular course work because he wanted to have the skills to be immediately productive in a marketing job.

Certificate for Oral Presentation Skills course. Peter also learned in the informational interview he did that *presentation skills* are considered particularly important in the marketing field. He can make the point that because he really enjoys making presentations he took this extra workshop to learn how to excel at doing this. His keenness to develop himself, now that he's found what he wants to do, will help deflect attention from his mediocre G.P.A.

Title page and first page from a marketing plan he did for a course. This paper that Peter did for his strategic marketing course demonstrates that he knows how to *develop a marketing plan*. He can also use this as a sample of his *writing skills*. He can display the title page and the abstract for this paper on the front and back sides, respectively, of a sheet protector, and then stuff a copy of the entire paper in between, if it's not too bulky. Or he can store a full copy of this paper elsewhere in the carrying case for his portfolio. However he decides to present this paper, he should make sure that the excellent comments and grade he received are clearly visible!

Peter Evans

45 North Street • Bradford, Iowa 50041 • (555) 555-5555   email: Pevans@scc.edu

Overview

A well-prepared individual with solid academic background and experience in marketing, seeking a marketing management position where he can make a difference. A team player who is creative, enthusiastic, and likes to get things done. Strong background in fitness.

Education

State Community College   **Bradford, Iowa**
AS Marketing   2002

Highlights of Educational Career

Experience:

> *Fitness*—completed four marathons this past year

Accomplishments:

> As *promotions coordinator* increased membership of student organization by 43%

Special Knowledge:

> Marketing concentration included excellent courses in:
>
> - *Marketing Promotions and Communications*
> - *Consumer Behavior*
> - *Marketing Research*
> - *Strategic Marketing Management*

Skills Developed:

> - *Making oral presentations*—certificate earned for completion of special course.
> - *Using computers to develop marketing materials*—certificate earned for special course.
> - *Creating effective marketing tools*—received high grade and praise for skill in this area.
> - *Developing strategic marketing plans*—received high grade and praise for skill in this area.

References and Career Portfolio

Available upon request

From the Desk of Dr. Cynthia Clarke
Professor of Marketing
State Community College

Letter of Recommendation for Peter Evans

June 3, 2002

To Whom It May Concern:

I had the pleasant opportunity of having Peter in my class over the past two semesters at State Community College. The two courses he took with me were "Marketing Promotions and Communications" and "Strategic Marketing Management." In each of these courses we do major hands-on projects that prepare our students to be immediately productive as marketers in the workplace. I was very pleased with both the marketing tools and the strategic marketing plan that Peter created in the two courses he took with me.

Not only were his projects both creative and practical, his manner of interacting with other students during the collaborative projects we did in class was most commendable. He is able to not only come up with a lot of good ideas but also clearly be an enthusiastic "team player."

Peter always did more than his fair share of the work needed to be done on the projects we did in class. He took the initiative to get things started and, demonstrating great follow-through, picked up the slack when things were going slowly. His teammates all seemed to respond favorably to Peter both as a team member and as a person, and the output of his groups was always excellent.

I was glad to have Peter Evans as a student in my marketing courses. I highly recommend Peter as an excellent person to hire for a marketing position. He will be the type of employee anyone would be pleased to have on board.

Sincerely,

Cynthia Clarke

Dr. Cynthia Clarke
Professor
Marketing Concentration

Part II: Examples of Targeted Portfolios

FUTURE MARKETERS' CLUB

STATE COMMUNITY COLLEGE

8/17/2001

Peter Evans
Future Marketers' Club
Promotions Coordinator
Street Address
City, State 02222

Dear Peter,

The enrollment for the *Future Marketers' Club* is up 43% year to date. Congratulations on this fantastic achievement. Growth like this is a testament to your hard work and dedication to the success of the *Future Marketers' Club*.

All those in attendance enjoyed the event you coordinated during orientation. Your creative idea of having every member serve as a greeter to those who came worked out brilliantly. Everyone felt as though they were part of our club. I am confident that this is why our membership is up so significantly.

Again, congratulations, and thank you for your leadership.

Sincerely,

Francine Spencer

Dr. Francine Spencer
Faculty Advisor

K

Marketing Promotions and Communications

In this course I learned how to choose and create the basic promotional tools that are available to the marketing manager, including advertising, sales promotion, personal selling, and publicity. We were given assignments where we actually created marketing tools.

Consumer Behavior

In this course I studied consumer behavior in the context of the overall marketing environment and market segmentation. There was a tremendous emphasis on understanding the turbulent environment surrounding the marketing decision-maker.

Market Research

Here we learned how marketing information can be used as the basis for decision making. Topics included the cost and value of information, research design and instrumentation, data analysis, and forecasting.

Strategic Marketing Management

This was the capstone course in marketing that integrated the marketing functions of product, price, channels, and promotion with the concepts of strategic planning. Emphasis was on the importance of this integration for carrying out effective marketing. This course essentially summed up the entire core curriculum for the AS in Marketing. Each of us was assigned a company for which we were required to develop a strategic marketing plan that we had to present and defend in an oral presentation. And we participated in many group problem-solving exercises.

Peter,

The marketing tool you developed for your fitness industry project is a winner!

I showed it to some marketers at a conference I attended last weekend, and they loved it. To quote a marketing director I showed it to, as an example of the kind of work one of my students is capable of:

"Tell the kid, if he doesn't trademark it, I will!"

Maybe you should.

You've got a real knack for coming up with creative ideas for marketing tools.

I hope you pursue a career in this field!

Professor Clarke

Project Grade A+

P.S. Needless to say, I was very impressed that you took your idea to the next step and actually created a real pin. The graphics look great.

CAD-Zukes, Inc. Specializing in CAD Training and Certification

Certified CAD Specialist

Peter Evans

Computer-Aided Design for Marketing

11/14/2001

Date

Chester P. Little

Instructor

Certificate of Completion

Presentation professional
development services

This certificate is presented to

Peter Evans

In recognition of having successfully completed a course in
Making Effective Oral Presentations

Linda D. Stewart

Instructor

5/9/2002
Date

S

201

State Community College
Bradford, Iowa

Associate Degree Program in Marketing

Marketing Plan for *I.Java Café*

A Marketing Plan Submitted
in Partial Fulfillment
of the Requirements for the
Degree of
Associate in Marketing

Peter Evans

April 5, 2002

Peter, this is an excellent example of a well-thought-out marketing plan. Your company will succeed with this plan.

Marketing Plan Grade A+
Presentation to Class A+

First page of a marketing plan I did for my Strategic Marketing Course

Marketing Plan: *I.Java café, an Internet café*

1.0 Executive Summary

The goal of the *I.Java café* marketing plan is to outline the strategies, tactics, and programs that will make the sales goals outlined in the *I.Java café* business plan a reality in the year 2002.

I.Java café, unlike a classic café, provides a distinctive forum for communication and entertainment through the use of the Internet. *I.Java café* is the answer to a growing demand. The public wants: **1.** access to the Internet, and **2.** a place to socialize with friends and colleagues.

Marketing will play an essential role in the success of *I.Java café*. *I.Java café* must build a brand around the services it offers by heavily promoting itself through local radio and print advertising. Although our marketing programs are just beginning, a strong emphasis will be put on keeping customers and building brand loyalty through various programs focusing on customers, staff, and experience.

Our targeted markets include:

1. Students from nearby colleges.
2. Businesspeople from the downtown business centers and professional buildings.
3. Senior Centers

2.0 Situation Analysis

I.Java café opened its doors a little over two months ago. Business is steady, and customers have been impressed with our setup and uniqueness, however, we need to focus our attention on implementing the strategies and tactics outlined in our original business plan.

Differentiating ourselves from the more traditional café has given us the ability to successfully compete with the doughnut and coffee side of the business. Sales are in line with projections.

The target markets are rapidly accepting the Internet services side of the business. Club memberships are exceeding the projections outlined in the business plan. College students tend to gather for late-night sessions, nearby seniors from the center are getting a glimpse of what the Internet has to offer, and local businesspeople continuously stop by for a quick lunch and an email check....

Karen Cresson: Changing Careers

After ten years as an elementary school teacher, Karen Cresson prepares her portfolio to get a job as an account executive with a computer company.

CAREER SITUATION

Karen Cresson wants to change careers. She's been a sixth-grade teacher for the past ten years, has enjoyed many aspects of her job, and has done well at it. But she's ready to move on. She enjoys teaching and believes in education, but she feels constrained by the classroom and by the limits of her duties as a sixth-grade teacher.

Not sure what direction she wanted to go in next, Karen started assembling a Master Portfolio. She hoped that gathering together documents that demonstrate important things about her might give her some ideas. And it did. The note she got from a colleague thanking her for restoring his computer when it crashed in the middle of class reminded Karen that people were always turning to her for help with computers. The certificate she received for completing a course on educational software brought back memories of how much fun she had taking a course that many of her colleagues found intimidating. And the letter from the principal of her school thanking her for persuading a local company to donate computers to her classroom made her feel all tingly. Why tingly, she asked herself? Was it the praise? Not really. There were many notes of praise she'd received from the principal that she was pleased to get, but that didn't excite her *that* much.

What made her heart dance, she realized, was remembering the thrill of the chase. And all for a good cause. She had loved being in the role of sitting down with decision makers and pitching computers for kids. She truly believed that getting the right educational software into the classroom should be at the top of every school's agenda. Persuading, even educating, decision makers to buy into this idea would be something worth getting up in the morning for, she told herself.

Her pulse quickened again when she saw an ad in the paper for a sales position with an educational software company she admired. Knowledge of educational software, teaching experience, and advanced courses in education were required. She had all of the above.

But she also realized that coming from the world of education, with no experience in business or sales, might be an obstacle. Maybe she should try to get a preview of what this job would really be like for a person like herself. She called the alumni office of her alma mater and discovered that one of her classmates had made the switch several years ago from elementary school teacher to working for a software company. She was able to do an informational interview over the phone with this person, and decided she really did want to proceed with her application.

Karen decided to create a Can-Do Portfolio to demonstrate that she can make the transition from elementary school teacher to high-performing account executive.

TARGETED JOB

The advertisement for the job that caught Karen's eye read as follows:

Account Executive for Educational Software Company

Edu-Soft Inc. provides state-of-the-art educational software, including both courseware and network solutions for the educational community. Account Executive will sell the full breadth of our educational software product line to elementary school systems. Job requires a balanced sales effort involving sales/account management skills and product knowledge/problem-solving/solution skills. Account Executive must be an experienced and fully capable individual who has the professional presence to independently call on and lead the sales process at present and potential accounts. Applicants must have knowledge of educational software, teaching experience, and advanced courses in education.

DESIRED P.E.A.K.S.

Since Karen is not from this industry, the above job advertisement did not provide her with enough information to fully understand what P.E.A.K.S. would be considered most desirable in candidates for this job. The job lists minimum requirements at the end, but that doesn't tell her which of her P.E.A.K.S. she should be featuring to be considered an exceptional candidate. In order to target both her resume and her portfolio, she needed to rely on the information she gathered from the informational interview she did with her former classmate who is now in the computer industry. Here are the desired P.E.A.K.S. she learned about in this informational interview:

Personal Characteristics
> Quick and dedicated learner

Professional presence
> Enthusiastic
> Well organized
> Good planner
> Creative
> Persuasive

Experience
> Teaching experience at elementary level

Accomplishments
> Initiative taken *outside* of classroom

Knowledge
> Elementary school curricula
> Role of educational software in curriculum
> Master's degree in education

Skills
> Selling skills
> Presentation skills
> Writing skills

Using the above information, Karen was able to create a P.E.A.K.S. resume that got her a job interview with Edu-Soft.

PORTFOLIO STRATEGY

Karen's goal is to be able to present her qualifications in a way that establishes her ability to make a quick and successful transition to this new career. She wants the interviewer to know that not only would she be productive shortly after taking this job, she would also be an exceptional performer in the future.

To do this she will want to be able to demonstrate that she has strengths in the advertised formal requirements, and that she would bring other very valuable P.E.A.K.S. to this job, as well.

Through the informational interview she did with her former classmate, Karen was able to learn not only what the desired P.E.A.K.S. are but also *why* these P.E.A.K.S. are considered important. The following P.E.A.K.S. she learned were considered particularly important for a "career switcher," like Karen, to be able to demonstrate:

■ *Quick and dedicated learner.* This is an important trait for everyone to have in the computer industry, but particularly important for a newcomer to the software business, because there is a huge amount to learn about the company and product line just to get up to speed.

- *Professional presence.* This was mentioned in the job advertisement. The reason it is considered important is because an account executive has to make presentations to senior executives. The interviewer will want to know whether someone who has spent her professional career so far in a sixth-grade classroom can do so and would not be overwhelmed in such a situation.

- *Initiative demonstrated* outside *of classroom.* The interviewer will want to know if Karen is able to take action and be creative outside of the four walls of her sixth-grade classroom, where she has spent most of her work life these past ten years.

The key will be to have documents available in her portfolio that will enable Karen to demonstrate that she has these and other important P.E.A.K.S. The documents do not have to be self-explanatory. Karen can interpret the meaning of these documents for the interviewers. And she probably will have to do a fair amount of explaining, since her P.E.A.K.S. were developed and demonstrated in a different field from the computer industry.

CONTENTS OF THIS SAMPLE PORTFOLIO

Resume: This is a P.E.A.K.S. resume that is targeted at the job for which Karen will be interviewing. The P.E.A.K.S. headings set her up to discuss and verify P.E.A.K.S. she has that are likely to be considered desirable in candidates for this position.

P: Personal Characteristics

Teacher Evaluation. The comments at the bottom of this document praise Karen's *creativity*. This form also indicates that Karen's *organization* and *planning* are rated "excellent."

Handwritten note from colleague thanking her for fixing computer glitch. Karen can use this note to discuss the fact that she is the person at the school to whom people are continually turning for help with their computers. She can then segue into making the point that she is handy with computers because she is a *quick and dedicated learner*, particularly when it comes to computers. As noted earlier, being able to pick things up quickly is particularly valued in career switchers.

E: Experience

Teacher of the Year certificate. This certificate would help her make the point that not only does she have the *teaching experience* required for the job, she, in fact, has been recognized as being an outstanding teacher.

A: Accomplishments

Letter from principal congratulating her for getting extra computers. This is a nice example of Karen showing *initiative outside of her class-*

room. When she learned that her school did not have the money to buy more computers, she persuaded a local bank to donate used computers to her school. She can talk about how she truly enjoyed meeting with senior decision makers at this organization to sell them on the idea of the importance of computers in the classroom. This document also demonstrates that she has a *professional presence* outside the classroom.

Thank-you letter from family she helped in an emergency. This is another example of Karen *showing initiative outside the classroom*. She can talk about how, when she learned that this family in her neighborhood was in a tight financial bind because of a fire, she organized a fund-raiser to help them out. Showing this document might seem a bit off the topic of selling educational software. But if she explains it properly, she can make the point that she feels she's been cooped up in a classroom for too long now and that she finds she really likes to get out and make things happen in the world.

K: Knowledge

Master's degree in education. This certificate demonstrates that not only does she have the "advanced courses in education," called for in the ad for the job, she also has a *master's degree in education*. She can also use this degree as a prop to discuss the fact that she is *dedicated to learning*.

Elementary School Teaching Certificate. This document helps her make the point that, as a fully certified elementary school teacher, she has an in-depth *knowledge of elementary school curricula*.

Certificate for course on educational software. This certificate demonstrates that she has an up-to-date understanding of the *role of educational software in the curriculum*. Since this was an extensive course that yielded far more credits than she was required to get to maintain her teacher certification, she can also use this certificate as an example of the fact that she is *dedicated to continuous learning*.

S: Skills

Proposal for curricular change. This letter can be used as an example of her *writing skills*. She knows from her informational interview that proposal writing is an important part of the account executive's job, and that she is likely to be asked for a writing sample. She should have an extra copy of this letter available, which she can offer as a writing sample. This letter also gives evidence of her *selling skills*, particularly if it is shown along with the next item.

Letter from principal. This letter verifies that the above proposal for a curricular change was accepted and worked. Admittedly, no money exchanged hands, but if she presents this item properly, she can make the point that she has the ability to sell a curricular idea to a key decision maker in a school system.

Certificate for course on presentation skills. Since Karen knows from her informational interview that the job interviewer is likely to be seeking evidence of a candidate's presentation skills, this document could prove to be good to have in her portfolio.

Karen P. Cresson

1234 Washington Street • Palisades, California 90272 • phone: (310) 555-1234 • email Kcresson@teacher.com

Overview

Objective:

To obtain a sales and marketing position with a leading educational software company.

Personal Characteristics That Add Value:

Quick and dedicated learner, resourceful, and innovative instructor who strives to help others learn and grow; exceptional communicator who is well organized, creative and persuasive. Regarded as a key resource and problem solver by colleagues and administrators in the area of computers.

Professional Experience

State Public Schools   Palisades, California
Elementary School Teacher
6th Grade School Teacher

- **Experience:**

    Ten years' teaching experience at the elementary school level
    Outstanding Teacher of the Year

- **Accomplishments:**

    Persuaded local company to donate used computers to our classrooms.

    Recognized for organizing an event to help a local family that was displaced from their home due to fire.

- **Knowledge:**

    Master's degree in education
    Elementary School Teaching Certificate
    Certification for educational software

- **Skills:**

    Outstanding writing skills
    Strong selling skills
    Trained in presenting

Education

State University   Phoenix, Arizona
M. Ed. (Master's of Education), 1997
B.S., Education, 1992

Elementary School Certification

Professional Associations
National Education Association
Educational Technologists of America

References
Available upon request; Career Portfolio

Teaching Evaluation
State Public Schools

P

Teacher: Karen P. Cresson   **Grade 6**   **Date** June 31, 2002

Rating:
  5 = Excellent, **4** = Above Average, **3** = Average, **2** = Below Average, **1** = Unsatisfactory, **0** = Cannot Evaluate

Knowledge Base for PGY Level   5   4   3   2   1   0

Classroom Management

	5	4	3	2	1	0
Organization	X					
Curriculum Planning	X					
Management of Student Activities	X					
Creativity	X					

Comments: Excellent job in this area.

Student Management

	5	4	3	2	1	0
Standardized Testing		X				
Extracurricular	X					
Advisory	X					
Compassion	X					

Comments: Outstanding management of students

Record Keeping/Administrative

	5	4	3	2	1	0
	X					

Comments: Consistently on time and complete records

Presentation Skills

	5	4	3	2	1	0
Clear, concise, articulate	X					

Comments: Karen, your creativity in the classroom is inspirational to your students. You continue to keep your students involved and interested in learning. Proof of this is the fact that you had 100% participation in the regional science fair and 100% participation in the cultural fair. Overall you demonstrate good judgment in the classroom and are reliable and patient with your students. They look to you as a role model.

Congratulations on having this year's student yearbook dedicated to you.

Evaluator's Signature *Joseph Alcazino*   **Date** *6/31/02*

Dear Karen,

Once again, you saved me from a near disaster. I don't know what I would do without you. When I turned on my computer last Friday and saw nothing but gibberish on the screen, I panicked. I am so fortunate to have a colleague like you. You went to work and in no time at all figured out what the problem was and got me up and running. It was very kind of you to interrupt your own busy schedule to do so. Then again, you never hesitate to help any member of the faculty. You certainly have become our school's resident "computer whiz."

Thanks again for your help. I know you saved me hours of work, and I let Mr. Alcazino know that once again you saved the school money as well. Because of you we didn't have to call in a computer technician to fix my computer. I hope he appreciates you as much as we all do.

Sincerely,

Lucy James

Teacher of the Year

Brown Avenue Elementary School

Selects

Karen P. Cresson

as the teacher of the academic year 2000

WHOSE EXCELLENCE IN TEACHING AND
MENTORING MAKE HER TEACHER OF THE YEAR

Joseph Alcazino
Principal

5/28/00
Date

E

From the desk of Joseph Alcazino
Principal
Brown Avenue Elementary School

October 21, 2002

Dear Karen,

What an accomplishment. Our school had a need to enhance our technology resources and you had the vision to get it done. Because of your efforts and friendly persuasion, our school is now fully equipped to handle all our technological needs.

Regional Bank was upgrading its IT department and your idea and initiative to solicit the bank for a donation of their old computers could not have worked out better. Because of your efforts our children now have a computer in every classroom and a fully equipped computer lab.
Karen, you have always led the way with technology in your own classroom and now you have helped the entire school be leaders in technology, as well.

Thank you for your continued hard work and initiative.

Sincerely,

Joseph Alcazino

Joseph Alcazino
Principal

THE NELSON FAMILY

Ms. Karen Cresson
Brown Avenue Elementary School
Palmdale, CA 11111

October 21, 2000

Dear Ms. Cresson,

Our family cannot thank you enough for all that you have done for us. The fire in our home on October 3rd was obviously a traumatic experience for my family. At least nobody was hurt.

The biggest question we had was, what do we do now? How do we get back on our feet? Well thanks to you we had less to worry about. You had everything under control. A fund raiser was just what was needed to help our family. You are a true leader. You took control of the event and organized and planned the car wash that raised enough money to help settle the family until our insurance kicked in. We are forever grateful. I do not know how anyone could get things done as quickly as you did, but you did it!

Thank you, Thank you, Thank you; you made our lives a little easier during an extremely difficult time.

Warmest regards,

The Nelsons

The Nelson Family

State University

Be it known that

Karen P. Cresson

having successfully completed all necessary requirements in the prescribed course of study is hereby awarded the degree of

Master of Education

with all the honors, privileges and responsibilities pertaining thereto. In witness whereof we have affixed our signatures on May 21, 1997

Dr. Paul Long   5/21/97
President   Date

Dr. Jeffery Pleason   5/21/97
Chancellor   Date

Department of Education

School Certificate

This Certifies That

Karen P. Cresson

Having satisfactorily met certification requirements of the Board of Regents for elementary education, has been granted a certificate and is authorized to serve in the public schools of our state as an

Elementary School Teacher

Certificate Number 0355098883

6/19/92
_____
Date

James Dugan
_____
Commissioner of Education

CERTIFICATE OF CONTINUING EDUCATION

Computer Certified Professional

This certificate is awarded to

KAREN P. CRESSON

Course Completion and Certified Educational Technologist

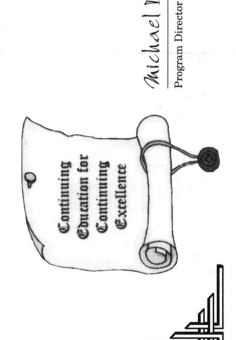

Continuing Education for Continuing Excellence

Michael Daulton

Program Director

5/8/01

Date

From the Desk of Karen Cresson
Brown Avenue Elementary School

September 3, 2000

Dear Mr. Alcazino,

This letter is a re-cap to our discussion of my proposal for the implementation of an advisory period for all students. As you know, research has shown that it is crucial that each student is known well by at least one adult during his years in school. This is easy during the early years of elementary school when self-contained classrooms allow for a teacher-student bond. It is not so convenient during the later years.

I recommend an advisory period twice a week. Each professional in our school would have an advisory consisting of between 10 and 15 students. The advisor serves as a mentor and an advocate for each of his/her advisorees. During the advisory period, the advisor will:
- Assess any problems, academic or personal, for each advisoree.
- Focus on interpersonal skills, such as peer relationships and bullying, and any obstacles to success, such as drugs, alcohol, and gangs.
- Help each advisoree become a better student by working on study skills, test-taking strategies and organizational skills.

A successful advisory incorporated into the curriculum will improve morale, performance, motivation, trust and overall school climate.

An advisory is an extremely important aspect of the school experience. I hope that you will consider including specified advisory time in next year's curriculum. If you need further information in order to make your decision, please do not hesitate to ask.

Sincerely,

Karen

Desk of Joseph Alcazino
Principal
Brown Avenue Elementary School

May 25, 2002

Dear Karen,

This letter is long overdue. I want to thank you for encouraging me to consider adding an advisory period to the curriculum. It has been a fantastic success. I have documented evidence that discipline referrals are less than last year, test scores have improved and absenteeism has dropped. The school climate is much more relaxed and our students have a strong motivation to perform well.

Most importantly, because of the advisory period, we were able to intercede in a near disaster in our school. It was during an advisory that we learned of the drug dealers trying to find a willing student to infiltrate our school. I am certain that the group that came forward did so because of the relationships we have developed with our students because of advisory.

Keep up the good work, Karen.

Sincerely,

Joe

CERTIFICATE OF COMPLETION

THIS CERTIFICATE IS AWARDED TO

KAREN P. CRESSON

IN RECOGNITION OF COMPLETION OF WORKSHOP ON EFFECTIVE PRESENTATION SKILLS

EDUCATIONAL PROFESSIONAL DEVELOPMENT SERVICES

Mitchell Reading   11/5/99

PROGRAM DIRECTOR   DATE

Amanda Ferraro: Getting That Promotion

Amanda Ferraro, whose goal is to get a promotion, assemble this portfolio in order to win out over her competitors, who have all been with the company longer than her.

CAREER SITUATION

Amanda Ferraro, who has been a sales representative at Rx Pharmaceutical Company for the past three and a half years, is applying for a promotion. Her present job involves calling on the physicians who are in private practice and the community (nonteaching) hospitals in her territory. She has done an excellent job of developing existing accounts and opening new ones, and she feels she is ready to take on a bigger challenge. The job she has in her sights is that of institutional manager, which recently became available in her territory and would involve handling the large teaching hospitals in her district, known as institutional accounts.

Institutional managers at Rx Pharmaceutical are more than just sales representatives. They are also goodwill ambassadors for the company who, among other things, sponsor, and often present, continuing education programs for the medical personnel at these hospitals. Amanda feels that her teaching experience as an adjunct professor in a local M.B.A. program has prepared her to do an excellent job of developing workshops on the business of medicine for medical residents. In fact, soon after learning that the institutional manager's position was becoming available in her district, Amanda interviewed the director for medical education at one of the large teaching hospitals that she would be responsible for, if promoted, to discuss the kind of management education that would be desirable for this hospital's residents. Together, she and the director created an outline of the topics that should be covered in a series of workshops on the business of medicine.

Amanda has good ideas, but she is up against very stiff competition. She knows of at least six other sales representatives who have applied for this highly coveted position. All of these sales reps have been with the company seven or more years. They have more pharmaceutical experience, more company knowledge, and because of their greater longevity, more long-standing friendships with decision makers within the company. All of these factors are working against Amanda.

Amanda wants to find a way to impress upon the district sales manager who will interview her that she has great ideas and is a performer who catches on quickly and gets the job done. Prior to coming to Rx Pharmaceutical, she had many successes in her two previous marketing and sales jobs and she has been an outstanding performer in her present job. Her experience is that of being successful when given new opportunities in the general area of marketing and sales.

And so, she decides to create a portfolio to demonstrate that she can do whatever is needed to be successful in this new job.

JOB DESCRIPTION FOR DESIRED PROMOTION

The institutional manager position that Amanda is applying for was posted as follows:

> *Reporting to the District Sales Manager, the Institutional Manager is responsible for achieving sales forecasts, promoting products, and selling these products to assigned institutions, key accounts and key customers. This is accomplished by establishing mutually beneficial, long-term business relationships with influential residents, fellows, attending physicians, pharmacists, and health care providers who are key to the sales success of promoted products. The Institutional Manager is also responsible for coordinating hospital sales strategies with appropriate teammates to maximize sales in the district and in assigned institutions. Additionally, the Institutional Manager is responsible for conducting large-scale educational workshops and facilitating national and regional meetings.*

DESIRED P.E.A.K.S.

Amanda already reports to the district sales manager, Frank DePeters, who will be interviewing candidates for the institutional manager position. Because she has a solid professional relationship with DePeters, Amanda already has some thoughts about the P.E.A.K.S. that DePeters most values in sales representatives at her level. But, since this would be a promotion to a new job at a higher level, Amanda does an informational interview with an institutional manager who has won several company awards and who also reports to DePeters. She learns during this conversation that, because this job involves focusing on teaching hospitals, DePeters believes that his institutional managers will be most successful in developing accounts if they can present educational workshops that these accounts feel are useful.

Based on this informational interview, Amanda is confident that DePeters is seeking the following P.E.A.K.S. in candidates for the institutional manger position:

Personal Characteristics

    Dedicated and persistent

    Reliable

    Well-organized planner

    Ability to build lasting relationships

    Leader who is a team player

    Enthusiastic

Experience

    In pharmaceutical industry

Accomplishments

    In sales

Knowledge

    Of curriculum

    Of training concepts

    Of products and the market

Skills

    Teach in a way that motivates participants

    Presentation skills

    Selling skills

    Ability to organize and carry out large-scale workshops

PORTFOLIO STRATEGY

Amanda's goal is to present herself as a reliable performer who is ready for this new challenge. To emphasize her reliability, she will need enough documents in her portfolio to be able to remind the interviewer (who is also her current boss) that she has consistently met, and often exceeded, past expectations in her present job. But her primary focus, of course, must be on the future and what she would bring to this new job.

Since her boss knows her in her present job, the burden is on Amanda to demonstrate that there are important dimensions to her that he may have overlooked that would make her very successful in the new job. Since she knows what the key P.E.A.K.S. are for this new job, Amanda will want to highlight the ones she has that her boss may not yet know about. The fact that she is a highly regarded adjunct professor in an M.B.A. program should be brought to her boss's attention, as this responsibility bears on her ability to develop and deliver the high-quality educational programs for her future customers that De-Peters believes are important. Verifying her success as a professor would also give evidence of group presentation skills her boss may not have known she had. She should also have available a copy of the "business of medicine" outline she developed with a potential customer. This demonstrates not only her educational expertise but also her enthusiasm and her ability to quickly build relationships with key customers.

Because she has less company experience than the other candidates for this position, she will want to highlight the sales and marketing experience she gained in her two previous jobs outside the company. A Can-Do Portfolio that enables her to accomplish all of these things would indeed help Amanda make the case that she is ready, willing, and able to move up to this new job.

CONTENTS OF THIS SAMPLE PORTFOLIO

Resume: This is a chronological P.E.A.K.S. resume that is targeted at the job for which Amanda will be interviewing. The P.E.A.K.S. sub-headings set her up to discuss and verify P.E.A.K.S. she has that are likely to be considered desirable in candidates for this position. Because the P.E.A.K.S. format is easy to read, this resume can be more than one page.

P: Personal Characteristics

Letter from boss commending Amanda for achieving a difficult market-share goal. She can use this letter to remind her boss that she has the personal qualities of being *dedicated* and *persistent* that he admires, and that she is a *reliable performer* who meets goals. He may have forgotten that he sent her this congratulatory note, since he has fifteen other people who report to him as well.

Congratulatory letter for a Visiting Faculty Lecture Series that Amanda organized. This letter demonstrates her boss's belief that Amanda can *build lasting relationships* with her customers, because her customers turned out in such high numbers for this event that she organized. She can also use this letter to talk about the fact that she had to be a *well-organized planner* to create and coordinate this event. In fact, she can present this letter in the course of discussing her organizational skills and let her boss read that he had praised her ability to build lasting relationships.

E: Experience

Coach Plan—New Drug Post Launch. This can be used to make the point that, while she may not have been at the company as long as the other candidates for the institutional manager position, she has already done an excellent job of mastering the company's prescribed techniques for making sales calls. She has sufficient company and pharmaceutical experience to move up to a higher job.

A: Accomplishments

Regional Representative of the Year letter. This is a reminder that she has already had exceptional sales accomplishments at the Rx Pharmaceutical Company. A copy of this letter can also be filed in her portfolio under "Skills" to verify her selling expertise.

Because this letter also commends her for her "commitment to teamwork," a copy of this letter might also be filed in her portfolio under "Personal Characteristics."

The Copiers' Copy newsletter. This is a newsletter put out by her former employer, Copiers Are Us, where Amanda was an account executive. The headline for the lead article announces that she has been the top salesperson for three years in a row. This fact demonstrates that she has a history of being an exceptional salesperson. She can make the point that, if promoted, she will find a way to be exceptional in her new position.

A copy of this newsletter could also be filed in her portfolio under "Skills" to verify her selling skills.

Certificate for developing a new initiative in company. This is an award for developing a new way of tracking the effectiveness of the Rx Pharmaceutical Company's educational programs in terms of the sales they generate. Because DePeters believes that institutional managers are most successful when they come up with strong educational programs, this document is a particularly useful one for Amanda to include in her portfolio. She can use it to demonstrate her ability to identify the most profitable educational programs.

K: Knowledge

Hospital Training Program Sample Curriculum for Management Education. This is the curriculum that Amanda designed in consultation with the director of medical education at a major hospital in the territory she would get, if promoted. It is meant to be an example of the kind of curriculum she could develop for institutional customers, if she were promoted to the position of institutional manager. Developing and presenting these supplementary management education workshops would give her an "in" at key accounts.

Because the fact that she put this together can also be used to demonstrate her *enthusiasm* for the new job, a copy of this might also be filed under "Personal Characteristics" in her portfolio.

S: Skills

E-mail from Dean of Admissions at Johnston Fischer University. This e-mail demonstrates that Amanda has the ability to teach in a way that immediately captivates her audience. Since Amanda's boss may not know much about the fact that she teaches during the evening as an adjunct in a local M.B.A. program, this document can be a good prop for discussing how her M.B.A. teaching skills could be useful for putting on workshops at teaching hospitals.

Letter of recognition for gaining formulary positions for two key drugs. Amanda received this letter of congratulations after getting an account that is known for never adopting new drugs to add two recently introduced drugs to their list of drugs that their physicians can prescribe. This achievement demonstrates Amanda's exceptional sales skills in the pharmaceutical field.

Copy of invitation for Visiting Faculty Lecture Series. Amanda created this event for the customers in her territory. This achievement demonstrates her ability to organize and carry out large-scale workshops, which is an important skill for institutional mangers to have.

Amanda Ferraro, MBA

23 Carpleton Rd, Raritan, NJ 07066   phone: (555) 555-5555; email: Aferraro@rxrep.net

Overview

Objective:
Professional sales representative with a diverse range of successful sales experience seeking Institutional Manager position within the pharmaceutical industry.

Personal Characteristics That Add Value:
Enthusiastic, dedicated, persistent, able to build lasting relationships. A leader who is also a team player.

Professional Experience

Rx Pharmaceutical Company
Raritan, NJ
June 1999–Present

Professional Pharmaceutical Representative
Promote the company's products to a variety of private practice health care professionals in the New Jersey and New York markets. Train and facilitate educational programs for health care professionals in the assigned territory. Deliver oral and written presentations for medical meetings, district meetings and day-to-day business operations. Attend and organize local and national medical conferences as a representative of the company. Regional trainer of new hires/Regional Product Manager/Fleet Safety Coordinator.

- **Experience:**
  Coordinating educational programs to meet the needs of customers
  Personal and group training
  Creating supplementary marketing tools to use in field.
- **Accomplishments:**
  Outstanding Regional Sales Representative of the Year
  Great Idea Award
  Consistently met or exceeded sales plan
- **Knowledge:**
  Keen understanding of the educational and training needs of pharmaceutical customers
  MS Office, PowerPoint, Excel, Outlook, Navigator, Lotus Notes
- **Skills:**
  Selling
  Convincing customers that having Rx Co. deliver educational workshops would be beneficial
  Adapting and delivering courses and training to target audiences
  Developing innovative teaching materials and approaches

Oscar Hammer Food Products Corporation
New Brunswick, NJ
1993–1999

Account Manager
Responsible for marketing and sales of Oscar Hammer's food products at retail level in major chains and independent markets.

- **Experience:**
  Placing advertisements
  Merchandising

Copiers Are Us, Inc.

Somerville, NJ
1989–1993

Account Representative
Responsible for selling and maintaining copiers in a large and diverse geographical area.

- **Accomplishments:**
  Top performer three consecutive years

Johnston Fischer University

Newark, NJ
1996–Present

Adjunct Faculty, Graduate School of Business
Teach both foundation and advanced management courses for evening sessions of MBA program.

- **Experience:**
  Teaching MBA courses to a diverse group of students
  Managing and presenting to large, graduate-level classes
- **Accomplishments:**
  Developed the curriculum and materials for two new courses
- **Knowledge:**
  Principles of business management
  Principles of marketing
- **Skills:**
  Teaching in a motivating way
  Creating a learning environment

Education

MBA in Organizational Leadership   1996
Johnston Fischer University Newark, New Jersey

BA in Liberal Arts   1989
New Jersey State College   New Brunswick, New Jersey

Volunteer
Red Cross, Scouting

References & Portfolio Available upon Request

Rx Pharmaceutical Company
Raritan, New Jersey 08867

Amanda Ferraro
23 Carpleton Rd.
Raritan, NJ 07066

December 21, 2001

Dear Amanda,

CONGRATULATIONS! Your dedication and persistence have paid off. Your goal of increasing your market share to 24% this year has been achieved.

Amanda, this is a tremendous accomplishment and one you should be extremely proud of. You were given a difficult objective and succeeded in accomplishing it. Our company has truly benefited from your hard work.

I look forward to continuing to work with you.

Good Selling,

Frank DePeters

Frank DePeters
District Manager

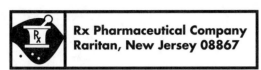
Rx Pharmaceutical Company
Raritan, New Jersey 08867

Amanda Ferraro
23 Carpleton Rd.
Raritan, NJ 07066

May 20, 2002

Dear Amanda,

CONGRATULATIONS! on conducting a successful Visiting Faculty Lecture Series. In all there were 125 health care providers in attendance, which by any standard would be considered outstanding. Given the turnout you got for this event, it is quite obvious that you have built and maintained productive, long-lasting business relationships with your customers. I am confident that you will reap the rewards of such a successful program.

As you are aware, the key here is to follow through with those in attendance and make sure they completely understood our message. The spreadsheet you developed for tracking purposes is ideal for this.

Again, congratulations! and keep up the outstanding work.

Good Selling,

Frank DePeters

Frank DePeters
District Manager

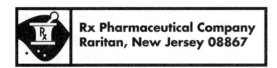 **Rx Pharmaceutical Company**
Raritan, New Jersey 08867

Coach Plan—New Drug Post Launch*

Associate: Amanda Ferraro   **Date of Session: May 15, 2001**
Manager: Frank DePeters

Current Market Data:

QTD	ABC Drug		Rx Sel.		O-P		Overall Rank	
Apr.	Share	Change	Share	Change	Share	Change		
Nation	24.1	0.1	3	3	3.3	−0.3		
Region	24.1	0.5	3.2	3.2	3.9	−0.1	5	
District	20.4	0.4	4.2	4.2	2.0	−0.2	7	
Territory	27.6	1.9	5	5	4	.5	1	

Comments: Thank you for a good and productive day in your territory. Today is the beginning of what should be a very fun and exciting year for us. The following is a review of our time together.

Field Trip Objectives

1. **Delivering Effective Core Message for Rx Sell on every call**
2. **Closing "EST" Engineering a Successful Trail with every customer**
3. **Multiple Product Presentations**
4. **Effective Planning & Routing**

Overall Scoring 9/10

*Note to reader: This is a very favorable evaluation Amanda received from her boss after he spent a day with her as she called on accounts in her territory. It continues on the next page.

Skill 1—Effective Rx Sell Core Message

You consistently delivered the full suggested presentation on every call. Nice job pushing HCPs for quality time. An example of this was seen at XYZ Hospital OB grand rounds when Dr. Ace gave you 10 minutes (15 MD's in attendance). You did a great job communicating that this is not a niche product and should be offered to all patients regardless of age and lifestyles (let them decide). Be sure to clearly explain (in a non-defensive way) the fact that 26% of patients had 7 or more days of nausea by keeping it simple (new definition that the FDA used). You need to routinely incorporate the Rx Sell name when bridging from one page in the visaid to another (especially during your summary). An example of this is when you say "the pill has excellent efficacy and it is well tolerated". Name recognition is critical to establishing this as a mainstream option.

Comments: 1. Continue to utilize the demo scripts on every call 2. Deliver a full Rx Sell message to all staff members, nurses & doctors - enlist them to prescribe it early and often! No Niche

Skill 2—"EST"

# of calls: 5
% Demonstrated: 100%
Comments: Overall, you were able to utilize the EST close on all of your calls throughout the day. Keep the order of the EST close simple and focused on a time commitment. Clarify and be very DIRECT with what you are asking them to do. (Ex: regardless of age and lifestyles will you offer...mainstream") Make sure your customers commit to "offering Rx Sell to all patients for 2-3 months" before you show the sample kit. This will help you summarize what you want them to do at the end of the call (dual close). Do not rush through the sample kit components—hand each piece to the provider and let them get familiar with the contents. (Ex: Rxed in program, extra script program). Stress the importance of sample management (1 per patient)—do not assume they know what you mean—explain the rationale

Skill 3—Multiple Product Presentations

# of calls: 5
% Demonstrated: 100%
Comments: Overall, you effectively delivered a solid ABC message on every call. It was amazing to see how much time you were able to get by leading off with ABC. Utilize your call continuum with ABC on your next call and target a competitive product by incorporating the CSS model. EX: "The last time I was in we discussed the performance & tolerability of ABC, today I would like to show you how that compares to .... (competitive product). This remains a critical part of our business.

Skill 4—Review Planning & Routing

Comments: We talked about the importance of REACH vs. Frequency for the launch of Rx Sell. Continue to set up grand rounds (Ex: Tuesday & Wed at City Hospital) in an effort to reach all of your customers.

Rx Pharmaceutical Company
Raritan, New Jersey 08867

Amanda Ferraro
23 Carpleton Rd.
Raritan, NJ 07066

December 15, 2001

CONGRATULATIONS! On being selected as the Regional Representative of the Year.

Amanda,

Throughout the year, you have executed excellent production and coverage reaching 89% of your MD coverage throughout the year. Such coverage is consistent with a PCA over 6.8 and a TCA over 8.0. Your sales numbers speak for themselves.

You also have been very diligent in your pharmacy work. In fact your training workshop at the last district meeting was well received by the entire district. The workshop clearly demonstrated your commitment to both teamwork and production—two very critical aspects of our business.

I am not alone in conveying this praise; the entire district feels very strongly about your performance and teamwork and is very excited to be able to reward these accomplishments. Congratulations on your being selected as this year's Representative of the Year!

Sincerely,

Frank DePeters

Frank DePeters
District Manager

A

The Copiers' Copy
A company newsletter

Copiers are US

Summer 19XX

Amanda Ferraro Ranks #1 Third Year in a Row

This is an article in the company news letter that is commending Amanda on her accomplishment. She has earned number one status for the third year in a row with her company. What a great way to get unsolicited recognition.

xxxxxxxxxxxxxxxxxxxxxxxxx
xxxxxxxxxxxxxxxxxxxxxxxxx
xxxxxxxxxxxxxxxxxxxxxxxxx
xxxxxxxxxxxxxxxxxxxxxxxxx
xxxxxxxxxxxxxxxXxxxxxx
xxxxxxxxxxxxxxxxxxxxxxxxx
xxxxxxxxxxxxxxxxxxxxxxxxx
xxxxxxxxxxxxxxxxxxxxxxxxx
xxxxxxxxxxxxxxxxxxxxxxxxx
xxxxxxxxxxxxxxxxxxxxxxxxx
xxxxxxxxxxxxxxxxxxxxxxxxx
xxxxxxxxxxxxxxxxxxxxxxxxx
xxxxxxxxxxxxxxxXxxxxxx
xxxxxxxxxxxxxxxxxxxxxxxxx
xxxxxxxxxxxxxxxxxxxxxxxxx

xxxxxxxxxxxxxxxxxxxxxxxxx
xxxxxxxxxxxxxxxxxxxxxxxxx
xxxxxxxxxxxxxxxxxxxxxxxxx
xxxxxxxxxxxxxxxxxxxxxxxxx
xxxxxxxxxxxxxxXxxxxxx
xxxxxxxxxxxxxxxxxxxxxxxxx
xxxxxxxxxxxxxxxxxxxxxxxxx
xxxxxxxxxxxxxxxxxxxxxxxxx
xxxxxxxxxxxxxxxxxxxxxxxxx
xxxxxxxxxxxxxxxxxxxxxxxxx
xxxxxxxxxxxxxxxxxxxxxxxxx
xxxxxxxxxxxxxxxxx

What a great accomplishment

Amanda says being #1 three consecutive years was not easy. Hard work and persistence!

Inside this issue:

Performance	2
Industry Standards	2
Copy Voice	2
Job Postings	3
Rankings	4
Competition	5
Personnel Feature	6

Special points of interest:
- XXXXX
- XXXXX
- XXXXX
- XXXXX
- XXXXX

Ferraro Shares Her Business Strategy

This is an article written by Amanda for her company newsletter. It is an easy way to demonstrate initiative, experience, knowledge and skill.

xxxxxxxxxxxxxxxxxxxxxxxxx

xxxxxxxxxxxxxxxxxxxxxxxxx
xxxxxxxxxxxxxxxxxxxxxxxxx
xxxxxxxxxxxxxxxxxxxxxxxxx
xxxxxxxxxxxxxxxxxxxxxxxxx
xxxxxxxxxxxxxxxxxxxxxxxxx
xxxxxxxxxxxxxxxxxxxxxxxxx
xxxxxxxxxxxxxxxxxxxxxxxxx

xxxxxxxxxxxxxxxxxxxxxxxxx
xxxxxxxxxxxxxxxxxxxxxxxxx
xxxxxxxxxxxxxxxxxxxxxxxxx
xxxxxxxxxxxxxxxxxxxxxxxxx
xxxxxxxxxxxxxxxxxxxxxxxxx
xxxxxxxxxxxxxxxxxxxxxxxxx

GREAT IDEA AWARD

THIS CERTIFICATE IS PRESENTED TO

Amanda Ferraro

FOR THE INITIATIVE AND
DEVELOPMENT OF THE VISITING
FACULTY TRACKING PROGRAM

RX PHARMACEUTICAL COMPANY

Stephen Phillips   10/5/02
Vice President Operations   Date

A

*Hospital Training Program**

Sample Curriculum for Management Education

Developed by Amanda Ferraro, MBA

Communication I II (February)

Understanding the Organization (March)

Selecting a Practice (April)

Specialist, Generalist or Primary Care (May)

Selecting a Practice Location (May)

Financial Planning I II (June)

Teamwork/Teambuilding (July)

Change/Future of OB/GYN and Medicine (August)

Interviewing (September)

Career Development/Portfolio Design (September)

Negotiation I II (October)

Negotiating a Contract I II (October)

Activity-Based Costing (November)

In-house Testing (December/January)

*Note to reader: This is the curriculum that Amanda designed in consultation with the director of medical education at a major hospital in the territory she would get, if promoted. It is meant to be an example of the kind of curriculum she could develop for institutional customers, if she were promoted to the position of institutional manager. Developing and presenting these supplementary management education workshops would give her an "in" at key accounts.

—— Original Message ——-
From: "Allan Frishman"
To: aferrraro@rxrep.com
Sent: Friday, November 03, 2000 4:32 PM
Subject: appreciation

Amanda,

I would like to thank you for allowing a very strong prospect to sit in on your class on Wednesday, Nov. 1, 2000. He was undecided until he attended your class. He was more impressed with your class and teaching style than the classes and professors he visited at other schools.

The best way to summarize: His application is in the mail.

Regards,
Allan G. Frishman, Ph.D.
Dean of Admissions
Graduate School
Johnston Fischer University

Rx Pharmaceutical Company
Raritan, New Jersey 08867

Amanda Ferraro
23 Carpleton Rd.
Raritan, NJ 07066

July 6, 2001

Dear Amanda,

Congratulations on getting the Township Community Hospital to adopt two of our company's recently introduced medications. You have proven the skeptics wrong and accomplished what most said was impossible.

There is no doubt that your recent achievements will be spoken of for some time and that the admiration for your accomplishments is felt by all of us within the company.

Please accept my heartiest congratulations for your success.

Best regards,

Joan Belmont

Joan Belmont
VP Therapeutics

 New RX Options:
A Focus on the Medical Options

Visiting Faculty Lecture Series

Educational Objectives

After participating in this educational activity, the clinician should be able to:

1. Discuss the differences between efficacy of available methods in perfect and actual use.
2. Evaluate factors that women consider when choosing a particular method.
3. Identify new options.
4. Compare new and current options in terms of efficacy, side effects, convenience of use, and patient adherence.
5. Review clinical trial data on the transdermal systems.
6. Discuss issues important to successful patient management.

Accreditation Information

Physicians: This activity has been planned and implemented in accordance with the Essential Areas and Policies of the Accreditation Council for Continuing Education Credit (ACCEC) through the joint sponsorship of the University of New Jersey and SnyerMed Communications. The University of New Jersey is accredited by the ACCEC to provide continuing medical education for physicians.

The University of New Jersey designates this educational activity for a maximum of 1.00 hour in category 1 credit toward the AMA Physician's Recognition Award. Each physician should claim only those hours of credit actually spent in the educational activity.

Credit is also available for **Nurse Practitioners, Physician Assistants, Pharmacists and Nurse-Midwives**.

Speaker: James P. Leyden, MD

Affiliation: Professor of Molecular Genetics Deputy Head
Dept. of Molecular Biology, Director
Division of Genetics
Daley University
Chicago, IL

Date/Time: Wednesday June 27, 2001
6:30pm–9:00pm

Location: **Ambrea**
16 Huntington Avenue
Newark, NJ 08878

Kindly confirm your attendance by calling: 800-555-5555 Ext. 5555

Jointly Sponsored by University of New Jersey and SnyerMed Communications
Supported by an educational grant from Rx Pharmaceutical, Inc.

APPENDIX: WORKSHEETS

Career P.E.A.K.S.

Measurement Form

Name of Document: _____

Description: _____

Code: _____

	SPECIFY	RATE: 1 TO 5 (5 = highest score)
Personal characteristics that add value		
Experience		
Accomplishment(s)		
Knowledge		
Skills		

Total:

Career P.E.A.K.S

Master Summary Sheet

For Portfolio Categories

On a scale of 1 to 5, rate each item for its P.E.A.K.S. (5 being most important)

Master Portfolio Category:	**P** Personal Characteristics That Add Value	**E** Experience	**A** Accomplishments	**K** Knowledge	**S** Skills	**Totals**

Job P.E.A.K.S. Worksheet

This worksheet should be completed after you have collected as much information as you can about the P.E.A.K.S. that employers are evidently seeking in candidates who are applying for a job that interests you. The P.E.A.K.S. you list below are meant to be your best guess, based on the research you have done.

1. **Job Title and Brief Description:**

2. **P.E.A.K.S. that employers are seeking in candidates applying for jobs in this area:**

   Personal Characteristics:

   Experience:

   Accomplishments:

   Knowledge:

   Skills:

3. **Sources for the above P.E.A.K.S.:**

   Interviewees   *Title & Organization*

Job P.E.A.K.S. Worksheet (Continued)

4. Assessment of the degree to which I have the desired P.E.A.K.S. for this job[1]:

The most desired job P.E.A.K.S. are: (From #2 above)	*My level of development for each is:* (10 = High; 1 = Low)
Personal Characteristics That Add Value:	
_____	1 2 3 4 5 6 7 8 9 10
_____	1 2 3 4 5 6 7 8 9 10
_____	1 2 3 4 5 6 7 8 9 10
_____	1 2 3 4 5 6 7 8 9 10
Experience:	
_____	1 2 3 4 5 6 7 8 9 10
_____	1 2 3 4 5 6 7 8 9 10
_____	1 2 3 4 5 6 7 8 9 10
_____	1 2 3 4 5 6 7 8 9 10
Accomplishments:	
_____	1 2 3 4 5 6 7 8 9 10
_____	1 2 3 4 5 6 7 8 9 10
_____	1 2 3 4 5 6 7 8 9 10
_____	1 2 3 4 5 6 7 8 9 10
Knowledge:	
_____	1 2 3 4 5 6 7 8 9 10
_____	1 2 3 4 5 6 7 8 9 10
_____	1 2 3 4 5 6 7 8 9 10
_____	1 2 3 4 5 6 7 8 9 10
Skills:	
_____	1 2 3 4 5 6 7 8 9 10
_____	1 2 3 4 5 6 7 8 9 10
_____	1 2 3 4 5 6 7 8 9 10
_____	1 2 3 4 5 6 7 8 9 10

5. Based on this self-evaluation my next steps should be:

[1]The issue here is the degree to which you have developed these P.E.A.K.S., *not* whether or not you have documents to demonstrate that you have done so.

Informational Interview Debriefing Form

The following worksheet should be reviewed in preparation for an *informational interview* and then completed after the *informational interview* has concluded.

Interviewee_____

Title _____

Company & address _____

_____

Name of Assistant/Secretary _____

Phone number _____

E-mail _____

Job title(s) discussed _____

_____

Contacts given:

    Name   *Title & Company*   *Telephone / E-mail*

Next, complete the following:

1. Unexpected information learned about the field/job/organization:

2. Areas where I could make a real contribution in the field/job/organization:

Informational Interview Debriefing Form (Continued)

3. P.E.A.K.S. that, according to this person, employers are seeking in candidates applying for jobs in this area:

Personal Characteristics:

Experience:

Accomplishments:

Knowledge:

Skills:

4. Other important things learned:

Next steps, based on this discussion:

Career P.E.A.K.S. Aspiration Worksheet

Aspiration Worksheet

This worksheet helps you identify the kinds of activities you will want to engage in to create an ideal portfolio for your future. There is an explanation of how to use this worksheet on the following page.

	SPECIFY	RATE: 1 TO 5 (5 = highest score)
Personal characteristics that add value		
Experience		
Accomplishment(s)		
Knowledge		
Skills		

*Proposed Activity:*_____

*Items that would document this activity:*_____

_____

_____

How to Use the Aspiration Worksheet

Step One:

Under "Specify," list in bullet form the P.E.A.K.S. you would like to develop. Do <u>not</u> fill in any of the ratings to the right of this list and leave blank the "Proposed Activity" section below.

Step Two:

Make several dozen photocopies of the above form that has your hoped-for P.E.A.K.S. filled in.

Step Three:

Take a P.E.A.K.S. category you would like to develop and then start thinking about activities you might like to pursue that would give evidence of the P.E.A.K.S. you are hoping to develop.

This effort is not as hard as it may at first seem. You will find that it is a lot easier to see opportunities once you know what you are looking for!

You might get some ideas by reviewing the items listed in the "Examples of Portfolio Documents" table in Chapter 2.

You might also consult with friends and colleagues for their ideas.

Step Four:

Once you have an idea of an activity you might like to pursue, ask yourself: "Is this something I'd really like to do?" If the answer is yes, you will probably stick with it.

If you answered yes, write a description of this activity under "Proposed Activity."

Step Five:

Think about things you would like to put in your portfolio about this activity and write these down under "Items that would document this activity."

Step Six:

Circle the P.E.A.K.S. associated with this proposed activity and, next to these, on the right, rate (1 to 5) how strong you feel the circled P.E.A.K.S. would be for this item.

If you follow these steps, over time you can develop a set of proposed activities you are motivated to pursue that will generate the P.E.A.K.S. you would like to have in your future portfolios.

You can file these worksheets under "Will-Do Portfolio." Each time you successfully complete one of these proposed activities and obtain a document associated with this, you will have a new item to add to your Master Portfolio for future use in your Can-Do Portfolios.

ABOUT THE AUTHORS

Frank Satterthwaite, Ph.D., received his A.B. in psychology from Princeton University and his Ph.D. in organizational behavior from Yale University. He is a former director of the M.B.A. program at Johnson & Wales University in Providence, Rhode Island, where he currently teaches courses he developed in career self-management and organizational leadership. Frank is also a principal in *Career P.E.A.K.S.*™, LLC, a career coaching and executive development firm based in Providence, Rhode Island. He has written numerous articles for major national magazines, including *Family Weekly* and *Esquire*, and has appeared on both network and public television programs in the United States and Canada.

Gary D. D'Orsi, Ed.D., M.B.A., is a career coach and corporate trainer who has earned numerous awards for his leadership and productivity. He has more than fifteen years of experience in sales, marketing, and training, in a variety of areas including academic, medical, pharmaceutical, and retail, most recently as an educational liaison for Johnson & Johnson. Additionally, Gary teaches graduate courses in career self-management and organizational behavior. As a principal in *Career* P.E.A.K.S.™, LLC, his work involves executive training along with career and outplacement consultation. He holds an M.B.A. in management and a doctorate in educational leadership. He has done extensive research on the use and content of Targeted Career Portfolios.

For workshops, career coaching, or to learn more about how to use the Career P.E.A.K.S. system to enhance the human resource activities of your organization, contact Frank Satterthwaite (fsatterthwaite@earthlink.net) or Gary D'Orsi (careerpeaks@cox.net).